The Reform of the Dutch Code of Criminal Procedure in Comparative Perspective

Nijhoff Law Specials

VOLUME 81

The titles published in this series are listed at brill.com/nlsp

The Reform of the Dutch Code of Criminal Procedure in Comparative Perspective

Edited by

Marc Groenhuijsen
Tijs Kooijmans

MARTINUS
NIJHOFF
PUBLISHERS

LEIDEN · BOSTON
2012

Library of Congress Cataloging-in-Publication Data

The reform of the Dutch Code of Criminal Procedure in comparative perspective / Edited by Marc Groenhuijsen, Tijs Kooijmans.
p. cm.
Includes bibliographical references and index.
ISBN 978-90-04-20493-5 (pbk. : alk. paper) 1. Criminal procedure--Netherlands. 2. Law reform--Netherlands. 3. Netherlands. Wetboek van Strafvordering. I. Groenhuijsen, M. S. II. Kooijmans, T.
KKM4604.31926.R44 2012
345.492'05--dc23

2012031722

This publication has been typeset in the multilingual "Brill" typeface. With over 5,100 characters covering Latin, IPA, Greek, and Cyrillic, this typeface is especially suitable for use in the humanities. For more information, please see www.brill.com/brill-typeface.

ISSN 0924-4549
ISBN 978-90-04-20493-5 (paperback)
ISBN 978-90-04-23259-4 (e-book)

This book is printed on acid-free paper.

The Reform of the Dutch Code of Criminal Procedure in Comparative Perspective

Edited by

Marc Groenhuijsen
Tijs Kooijmans

MARTINUS
NIJHOFF
PUBLISHERS

LEIDEN · BOSTON
2012

Library of Congress Cataloging-in-Publication Data

The reform of the Dutch Code of Criminal Procedure in comparative perspective / Edited by Marc Groenhuijsen, Tijs Kooijmans.
p. cm.
Includes bibliographical references and index.
ISBN 978-90-04-20493-5 (pbk. : alk. paper) 1. Criminal procedure--Netherlands. 2. Law reform--Netherlands. 3. Netherlands. Wetboek van Strafvordering. I. Groenhuijsen, M. S. II. Kooijmans, T.
KKM4604.31926.R44 2012
345.492'05--dc23

2012031722

This publication has been typeset in the multilingual "Brill" typeface. With over 5,100 characters covering Latin, IPA, Greek, and Cyrillic, this typeface is especially suitable for use in the humanities. For more information, please see www.brill.com/brill-typeface.

ISSN 0924-4549
ISBN 978-90-04-20493-5 (paperback)
ISBN 978-90-04-23259-4 (e-book)

This book is printed on acid-free paper.

CONTENTS

PREFACE

Marc Groenhuijsen and Tijs Kooijmans

In the autumn of 2008, the Department of Criminal Law of Tilburg University organized two conferences. The first conference dealt with the future of police and judicial cooperation in the European Union, the second conference dealt with recent developments in the law of criminal procedure. Both conferences were organized to mark the completion of the research programma carried out by the Department of Criminal Law on Dutch Criminal Justice in Europe.

The conference about police and judicial cooperation resulted in a book in which the various lectures given at this conference have been collected: Cyrille Fijnaut and Jannemieke Ouwerkerk (eds.), *The Future of Police and Judicial Cooperation in the European Union*, in 2010 also published by Martinus Nijhoff. That book about police and judicial cooperation is complemented by this book about the reform of the Dutch code of criminal procedure in comparative perspective.

We are very grateful to the various speakers for their kind agreement to adapt the text of their presentation as chapters of this book. In this book, the texts of the authors are presented in alphabetic order. By doing so, we deviate from the sequence in which their lectures were presented at the conference: in the plenary morning session mr. G.J.M. Corstens, prof.dr. T. Weigend and prof.dr. M.S. Groenhuijsen gave keynote presentations. In the afternoon sessions, the other authors gave workshop presentations. The keynote presentations aimed at providing a comparative perspective of Dutch criminal procedural law. In order to reach this aim, Corstens and Groenhuijsen presented an overview of recent significant developments in Dutch criminal procedure. In addition, Weigend commented several of the developments from a German legal point of view. Finally, Sir Robin Auld gave a keynote presentation at the plenary morning session. In this presentation, Auld – who had been appointed in 1999 to review how the criminal courts in England and Wales work at all levels – gave an insight into the 328 recommendations that he and his commission made. These recommendations however have hardly been adopted by the government of the United Kingdom. For this reason, as it finally turned out, the keynote presentation of Auld could not be adapted in this book. Although it took quite some time to collect the texts of the authors, we decided to publish their contributions in their original shape, notwithstanding the fact that several developments in the law of criminal procedure have taken place since the 2008 conferences. Those developments have not been elaborated upon in the authors' contributions.

We would like to take the opportunity to thank several people for their commitment to the organisation of the conference itself: our former colleague Remy Gaarthuis and the student-assistants Mark Tax and Iris Haenen (who is currently a PhD student at Tilburg University). They ensured that the conference ran smoothly and also provided assistance to speakers. Furthermore, we would like to thank Felipa Groenewoud Mealha who, as a student-assistant, took care of the layout of this volume.

Last but not least, we are also very grateful to the Board of Tilburg Law School for its financial support towards the costs of both conferences.

Tilburg, springtime 2012

25 YEARS OF CRIMINAL PROCEDURE IN THE NETHERLANDS

Geert Corstens[1]

1. INTRODUCTION

In the past quarter century, the Dutch law of criminal procedure has been radically amended. In this period, many interesting legislative and case-law developments can be pointed out. Examples are the emergence of confiscation legislation, the increasing influence of fundamental rights and the related case law of the ECHR, the introduction of new investigation methods (of internet, mobile telephony and DNA evidence existed hardly or not at all 25 years ago), the change in the position of witnesses, reorganisation of the preliminary investigation, the introduction of (new) obligations for the judge to provide grounds, the influence of Europe and – particularly after 11 September 2001 – the introduction of counterterrorism measures.

In this paper I shall explain four developments in more detail.[2] I shall discuss the emergence of consensus in the criminal procedure and the altered position of both the perpetrator and the victim in the trial, while, in addition, briefly touching on the expanding powers of the police and Public Prosecution Service and the increased flexibility of the criminal court judge's review of breaches of procedural rules. Fourthly, I focus more specifically on the role of the judge. I shall, however, start with a brief description of two projects which have had great influence in the past 25 years on the Dutch law of criminal procedure and have also had a major share in the above-mentioned four developments: the Moons Committee and the research project Criminal Procedure 2001 (*Strafvordering 2001*).

---

1 President of the Supreme Court (Hoge Raad) of the Netherlands.

2 I wish to thank *mr.* A. Dingemanse, former law clerk at the Dutch Supreme Court and now employed at the Ministry of Justice, who assisted me in editing the text.

2. MOONS COMMITTEE AND CRIMINAL PROCEDURE (STRAFVORDERING) 2001

During the development of the Dutch law of criminal procedure in the past 25 years, the Committee for Review of the Code of Criminal Procedure (Commissie Herijking Wetboek van Strafvordering), formed in 1998, which is named the Moons Committee after its chairman, played an important part. The Committee, which ended its work in 1993, made ten proposals in total. The main ones are those on the revision of the preliminary judicial inquiry[3] and on the breach of procedural rules.[4] The former proposal was incorporated in an Act,[5] which has resulted in a major amendment of, for example the provisions relating to the judicial inquiry, seizure and search. The report on breach of procedural rules includes proposals to abolish the tyrannical effect of the list of charges and for reserving procedural nullities for cases in which any breach of the relevant rule should result in nullity. For the rest, it is up to the judge to attach penalties to the breach of procedural rules. This report was also incorporated in the Act.[6]

Besides the Moons Committee, the research project under the name 'Criminal Procedure 2001' (*Strafvordering 2001*) is worthy of mention. In this project, under the direction of two professors from Tilburg and Groningen, research was done into the question whether – in the light of the legal amendments following each other in rapid succession – it was necessary to draft a new code. After all, owing to all those amendments, not much can still be recognised of the original starting points and system of the current code. The research resulted in a great many proposals.[7] One of the starting

---

[3] *Herziening van het gerechtelijk vooronderzoek*, Arnhem: Gouda Quint 1990.

[4] 'Recht in vorm', June 1993, included in *Rapporten herijking strafvordering 1993*, Arnhem: Gouda Quint 1993.

[5] Act of 27 May 1999, Bulletin of Acts and Decrees (*Staatsblad*) 1999, 243.

[6] Act of 14 November 1995, *Bulletin of Acts and Decrees* 1995, 441.

[7] See M.S. Groenhuijsen & G. Knigge (ed.), *Het onderzoek ter zitting. Eerste interimrapport onderzoeksproject Strafvordering 2001*, Deventer: Kluwer 2001; M.S. Groenhuijsen & G. Knigge (ed.), *Het vooronderzoek in strafzaken. Tweede interimrapport onderzoeksproject Strafvordering 2001*, Deventer: Gouda Quint 2002; M.S. Groenhuijsen & G. Knigge (ed.), *Dwangmiddelen en rechtsmiddelen. Derde interimrapport onderzoeksproject Strafvordering 2001*, Deventer: Kluwer 2002; and

points was "that the proceedings must have a focus and a course, determined first of all by what is at stake in the proceedings. This in turn may be largely dependent on the accused's attitude towards the offences of which he or she is accused".[8] In that context, the introduction of a three-track system was advocated: in cases where the most drastic penal sanctions are at issue, hearing by a three-judge division with specifically tailored procedural guarantees, hearing by a single judge for the medium category of offences and an extrajudicial procedure for the imposition of fines by the Public Prosecution Service. Some of the proposals have meanwhile resulted in laws and legislative proposals.[9] One of the main ones is the Public Prosecution Service (Settlement) Act (*Wet OM-afdoening*).[10]

3. *CONSENSUALITY IN CRIMINAL LAW*

About a hundred years ago, criminal law was still surveyable. Criminal law extended to a limited number of offences mainly included in the Criminal Code. After an investigation of the offence by the police or rural constable, the public prosecutor commenced prosecution and it was ultimately up to the court to decide on the sentencing. One could call this a classical model for classical offences. There was hardly any regulatory criminal law.

How differently criminal law has developed in the decades after the Second World War. Violations of regulatory legislation – environment, economy, finances, and traffic – take up increasingly more of the capacity of the criminal courts, even to such an extent that other ways must be sought to process the enormous influx of cases. Partly as a result of the increased workload on the judiciary, alternative possibilities for settlement are emerging. Some of these are: 'joinder *ad informandum*', settlement fine, out-of-court settlement, administrative fine and, as the last offshoot, the 'punishment

M.S. Groenhuijsen & G. Knigge (ed.) *Afronding en verantwoording. Eindrapport onderzoeksproject Strafvordering 2001*, Deventer, Kluwer 2004.

[8] See M.S. Groenhuijsen & G. Knigge, 'Algemeen deel', in: Groenhuijsen & Knigge 2001, p. 41.

[9] For example the Act of 10 November 2004, *Bulletin of Acts and Decrees* 2004, 580, regarding the confessing suspect.

[10] Act of 18 July 2006, *Bulletin of Acts and Decrees* 2006, 330.

order'.[11] A common feature of these types of sentencing is that they are based on consent, at any rate on not expressing disapproval,[12] thus a type of consensus for the purpose of not allowing the case to get to court. I have used the term consensuality in this context in previous publications.[13] This term means allowing consensus between the prosecuting authority and the accused to have legal consequences or decisive influence in the course of (criminal) proceedings or sentencing.

Consensual elements do not only exist in relation to settlement possibilities.[14] The consent of the accused also plays a part at other times in criminal procedure. In that case, usually shortening rather than avoiding the proceedings is concerned. Examples that can be cited are the times when the accused can make choices concerning a) the allowance of an application to amend the charges (Art. 314 CCP), b) whether or not to examine witnesses (further) (Art. 288 CCP), c) presenting documents (Art. 301 CCP) d) and the manner of resuming the examination after a suspension (art. 322 CCP). Case law on key roles can also be pointed out in which the consent of the accused played a part in the settlement or not of the case on appeal.[15]

---

[11] The punishment order is different in the sense that it is an act of prosecution in terms of positive law and it therefore does not prevent prosecution. The consensual element is a bit less emphatically present in it. See G.J.M. Corstens, *Het Nederlands strafprocesrecht*, sixth impression, Deventer: Kluwer 2008, pp. 827 and 828.

[12] This holds particularly for the administrative fine and the punishment order.

[13] G.J.M. Corstens, 'Consensualiteit', *Delikt en Delinkwent* 1994, pp. 4–8 and G.J.M. Corstens, 'Consensualiteit en strafsancties', *Ars Aequi* 1997, pp. 133–139. For an extensive treatment of consensuality, see also M. Hildebrandt, *Straf(begrip) en procesbeginsel* (diss. Rotterdam), Deventer: Kluwer 2002. Part of her research was aimed at answering the question of the effectiveness and legitimacy of consensual, punitive law enforcement. See further J.H. Crijns, 'De strafrechter buitenspel. Buitengerechtelijke afdoening van strafbare feiten in heden en toekomst', *Ars Aequi* 2002, pp. 513–521 and J.L. De Wijkerslooth & J. Simonis, 'Mag het strafrecht een beetje consensueel blijven?', *Trema* 2002, pp. 437–443.

[14] See also M. Hildebrandt, 'Het consensuele moment in het strafprocesrecht', *Delikt en Delinkwent* 1996, pp. 6–22. See further M. Hildebrandt, 'Consensualiteit in het strafprocesrecht', in: M. Hildebrandt, P.T.C. van Kampen & J.F. Nijboer (ed.), *Pleabargaining in Holland?*, Arnhem: Gouda Quint 1994, pp. 109–132.

[15] This case law concerns the situation in which the court should not have got round to the hearing on the merits at trial because one of the persons fulfilling a key role in the examination in court failed to appear, while the latter had not been notified in the manner prescribed by law of the date of the trial, nor had a circumstance occurred showing that he or she had known the date in advance.

Separate mention should be made of the so-called deals with criminals and the arrangement concerning crown witnesses. Here, too, consensus plays a special part in the prosecution. Lastly, I touch on the problems of the waiving of rights in the investigation stage.[16]

The consensual element has a basis in legislation as well as case law. For instance, joinder *ad informandum* is not regulated by law and the crown witness arrangement was not given a legal basis until 2006, while the settlement penalty does have older legal credentials. Consensual settlement of offences is here to stay. A very large number of the offences which were previously subjected to the judgment of the criminal court are now settled in a different way. This tendency is visible throughout Europe.[17] The European Commission also makes use of consensual settlement, for example in imposing sometimes very high fines (millions of euros).[18] In the Netherlands, administrative fines now run into millions as well. The future Fourth Tranche of the General Administrative Law Act (*Algemene wet bestuursrecht*) will provide for a further institutionalisation of the administrative fine.[19] The question sometimes arises whether the placement of a large part of socio-economic criminal law and environmental criminal law under administrative law originates partly in dissatisfaction among the administrative authorities with the length and severity of the sentencing in criminal law.

It is clear that in 25 years, a total reordering of criminal law has taken place. My speech on the occasion of my departure as professor at Radboud University in Nijmegen in 1995 included the following words: "No matter how the material is arranged, it is clear at any rate that a total reordering of what is now called criminal law will have taken place in the fist decade of the 21st century. One could call this a silent revolution in criminal law".[20] I still fully endorse those words. Even though the revolution was somewhat less silent; it has

---

[16] See J.M. Reijntjes, 'Het prijsgeven van rechten', *Strafblad*, 2008, pp. 547–559.

[17] See e.g. A.R. Hartmann, 'Buitengerechtelijke afdoening II', in: Groenhuijsen & Knigge 2002, pp. 119–134.

[18] Based on e.g. Art. 85 EC Treaty as well as Regulation 17/62.

[19] *Parliamentary Papers II* (*Kamerstukken II*) 2003/04, 29 702, no. 2, particularly Title 5.4.

[20] G.J.M. Corstens, *Een stille revolutie in het strafrecht*, Arnhem: Gouda Quint 1995, p. 38.

been abundantly written about and discussed. Certainly the latest developments concerning the punishment order have been followed very critically and closely by legal scholars. And rightly so. Because while the settlement figures may be the successful side of the story, objections can certainly be made against it.[21]

One must constantly ask oneself if voluntary consent has been sufficiently ensured and also whether the fundamental principles of the criminal justice system have indeed been sufficiently respected. Is consent voluntary if the offender receives a settlement proposal in a complicated environmental case but cannot estimate what his chances would be in a trial? And what about a Public Prosecution Service that tries to gain an advantage in a difficult and perhaps very weak case? In that case, at any rate, the establishment of the substantive truth as a goal of the trial comes off badly. And what about special and general prevention in this context as a goal of the criminal justice system? Are we creating calculating citizens in this way? The guilt principle is under pressure and external disclosure, in the sense of public accountability, is being forced out of the picture.[22]

The more uncertainty for the offender, the higher the fine and the more serious the offence or violation. In short the stronger the pressure on the fundamental principles of the criminal justice system, the more I question consensual elements. I therefore have reservations regarding the current tendency that more serious offences can also be punished by high sentences outside the criminal court. A recent, thorough cabinet memorandum about the weighing framework for the choice between an administrative fine, a punishment order or customary enforcement under criminal law cannot fully remove my concerns.[23]

---

[21] See Hildebrandt 2002, pp. 389–413.

[22] The latter has been somewhat compensated by guidelines prescribing that fines above a certain amount must be made public. See for example the *Aanwijzing hoge transactie en bijzondere transacties* (Instructions for Higher Settlement Penalties and Special Settlement Penalties), of 13 October 2008, *Government Gazette* (*Staatscourant*) 2008, 209.

[23] See *Parliamentary Papers II* 2008/09, 31 700 VI, no. 69. The leading principle in this is the effectiveness of enforcement.

The punishment order is more difficult to construe than the other alternative settlement possibilities. On the one hand, the arrangement is limited to the less serious offences and subject to more guarantees than the settlement penalty arrangement, which is to be abolished. On the other hand, the arrangement provides for the first time for extrajudicial imposition of penalties for classic violations and offences without the explicit consent of the accused. The accused's failure to take action will result in the order becoming final. Furthermore, a punishment order constitutes an act of prosecution and guilt has been established. The fact that the court is put at a distance partly for classical offences with a 'no-objection system' is cause to follow the new rules critically in the time to come.[24]

Regarding the interference of the criminal court, there seems to be a cyclical movement; we return more and more to the classical model; classical criminal procedure for classical offences. A lot can be said for this from the idea of the ultimate remedy. Minor offences can initially be disposed of outside the criminal court. I do not have any fundamental objections either to the decriminalisation of numerous offences, violations of traffic law or other regulatory legislation. But once again, under pressure of an alleged 'shortage of enforcement', the revolution, silent or not, threatens to get out of control.

I close this section with the recommendation that the imposition of penalties out of court can initially best remain reserved for simple, frequently occurring cases of little gravity in which a conviction is generally easily feasible and in which, by guidelines or otherwise, the amount of the penalty is determined at general level.[25] I add one more remark. Surprised, I ask myself why mediation in the context

---

[24] See also in this context the complaint of P.A.M. Mevis in his paper, 'Strafrecht, EVRM en Grondwet', in: A.H.E.C. Jordaans et al. (ed.), *Praktisch strafrecht* (Reijntjes collection), Nijmegen: Wolf Legal Publishers 2005, esp. p. 459, that major changes to criminal law are often poorly embedded and that one can wonder whether fundamental questions remain unaddressed.

[25] See Corstens 1997, p. 139. On this point as well, therefore, I have not changed my opinion.

of criminal law has not got a foot on the ground in the Netherlands up to now.[26]

4. *PROTECTION OF THE ACCUSED AND THE VICTIM*

4.1. The Accused

Developments in the past few years can arouse the impression that the position of the accused in the Dutch criminal justice system is in a bad way. A repressive wind blows. The adjustments to the Code of Criminal Procedure in connection with counterterrorism do not bode well for the (potential) accused. Many of these adjustments extend further than counterterrorism alone. The time of the so-called Utrecht School, in which the accent was on the person of the accused, seems to be over for good. And would all – justified – attention for the victim not distract attention for the accused? Concerns about, among other things, the position of the accused led in 2002 to an open letter from a large group of people employed at the criminal law departments of various universities in the Netherlands.[27] A heated debate was conducted over more recent 'terrorism measures' and I too expressed my concerns about this.[28]

Taking stock of the past 25 years, I am nevertheless of the opinion that, on balance, the protection of the accused has improved considerably. Strasbourg case law has contributed substantially to this. I specifically mention the rules laid down in the ECHR for testimony by witnesses (Kostovski, Van Mechelen, Bocos-Cuesta[29]), the case law on the right of the accused to be present (Lala and Pelladoah[30]),

---

[26] This has been dealt with regularly in the literature in the past years, but it seems mainly to be a matter for writers from the circle of the *Tijdschrift voor herstelrecht* (journal for restorative justice).

[27] *Netherlands Law Journal* (*Nederlands Juristenblad*) 2002, pp. 1609 and 1610. See further J. de Hullu, *Materieel Strafrecht*, third impression, Deventer: Kluwer 2006, pp. 15 and 16.

[28] G.J.M. Corstens, 'Dijkdoorbraken in de strafrechtspleging', *Netherlands Law Journal* 2005, p. 289.

[29] Respectively ECHR 20 November 1989, *Dutch Law Reports* (*Nederlandse Jurisprudentie*) 1990, 245 annot. EAA; ECHR 23 April 1997, *Dutch Law Reports* 1997, 635 annot. Kn and ECHR 10 November 2005, *Dutch Law Reports* 2006, 239.

[30] ECHR 22 September 1994, *Dutch Law Reports* 1994, 733, annot. Kn (Lala).

the case law on the *nemo tenetur* principle (Saunders and Jalloh[31]), and on trial within a reasonable time. This Strasbourg case law had a direct effect on Dutch practice. The law was sometimes adjusted with a view to the case law of the ECHR.[32] In short, a gain for the legal protection of the accused in many areas.

Finally, I mention the possibility of penalties for breach of procedural rules. Although the accused was generally still left empty-handed until far into the seventies if irregularities were committed during the investigation stage, it is now common practice that irregularities can be punished by the criminal court. The doctrine of the exclusion of evidence because it was obtained unlawfully has taken root, although now without the sharp edges. I will return to this briefly in section 6.

Numerous aspects of the legal protection of the accused in the Netherlands have undoubtedly improved in the past 25 years. Recent, minor deteriorations do not weigh up against that. All in all, I see no reason to take a glum view of the developments in legal protection of the accused. Such protection is on a high level. There are, however, certainly signs that the upward diagonal line is curving. Every reason thus to remain alert. One of the basic ideas of the CP 2001 research project still deserves attention in this context: the trial should be subject to more stringent guarantees as and when the stake is higher.[33] That idea may well have been worked out on the lower level of the system (extrajudicial settlement), but has hardly been worked out at the top by the legislature. Regarding the more serious cases as well, debates over legislative amendments are generally conducted from the angle of judicial efficiency rather than that of the guarantees for an accused person.

Once again, alertness is called for. Because the adage 'Better that ten or even a hundred guilty persons escape than that one innocent

---

[31] Respectively ECHR 17 December 1996, *Dutch Law Reports* 1997, 699 annot. Kn and ECHR 11 July 2006, *Dutch Law Reports* 2007, 226 annot. Sch.

[32] An example is the introduction of Art. 279 CCP, relating to the possibility of having a suspect who fails to appear defended at the trial by a lawyer who declares that he is explicitly authorised to do so.

[33] Groenhuijsen & Knigge 2001, pp. 27, 28 and 41. In this context, a differentiation is mentioned in a three-track trial.

suffer' still deserves strong support. Because if you yourself – innocent, of course – should ever be considered as a suspect, you would hope that you received proper legal protection and that in telling about how you were treated, you would not have to use the final words of Joseph K. in 'Der Prozeß' by Kafka "Wie ein Hund".

4.2. The Victim

The emergence of attention for the victim, partly within and partly outside the trial, stands out the most among all developments. Outside the trial, for example, one could think of the establishment of Victim Support in the eighties of the last century and its further professionalisation in the years afterwards. Within the trial there was a constantly farther-reaching legal protection of the victim, which ultimately resulted in the victim becoming an almost full party to the proceedings. Both national and international developments contributed to this. At national level, I mention as course-changing amendments: the Victim Support Act (*Wet Terwee*),[34] amendments to the 12 CCP procedure,[35] introduction of the right to speak[36] and, still pending at present as a kind of final element, a legislative proposal intended to strengthen the position of the victim.[37] The contribution to this made by the Groningen-Tilburg efforts cannot be underestimated. The victim now has a substantial role in criminal procedure. He or she can claim compensation with much fewer limitations than before can complain about failure to prosecute and has a right to speak during the trial. And the

[34] Stated concisely, this Act expands the victim's possibilities to join the trial as an injured party.

[35] Act of 1 November 2001, *Bulletin of Acts and Decrees* 2001, 531 (Amendment of the rules on guarantees relating to prosecution). In the Explanatory Memorandum to the legislative proposal, previous laws are pointed out which have strengthened the legal position of the victim and subsequently that the legislative proposal is for the purpose of further strengthening the victim's legal position. *Parliamentary Papers II* 1998/99, 26 436, no. 3, p. 5.

[36] Act of 21 July 2004, *Bulletin of Acts and Decrees* 2004, 382.

[37] Amendments to the Code of Criminal Procedure to strengthen the victim's position in the trial: *Parliamentary Papers II* 2004/05, 30 143, no. 2.

aforementioned legislative proposal strengthens the victim's position by way of a department bearing the inscription 'Victims' Rights'.

The international impulse comes from Europe. The independent position of the victim in the trial is recognised in various recommendations of the Council of Europe.[38] Even the European Court of Justice can now concern itself with the victim in the trial, as evidenced by the well-known Pupino case.[39] Who would have imagined this 25 years ago? The ECHR also helps to improve the victim's position. The case law can be pointed out in which the government's duty to investigate and provide information is brought up. The question has been posed, however, whether the positive obligations ensuing from the ECHR should result in farther reaching powers for the victim within the trial.[40]

One of the starting points of the Victim Support Act was that the claim for compensation is accessory to the criminal case and that it should not be allowed to dominate the trial. Now, 15 years later, the victim's role has unmistakably shifted to one of more participation, also during the examination in court, a role in keeping with the functions of the criminal justice system. In farther-reaching developments, the motto is still that the victim's role should be accessory to the criminal case and that the victim should not be able to make the trial go his or her own way, which motto has not lost any of its value.

The past period has taught that attention for both the accused and the victim can go together very well. They both deserve legal protection, and that of one does not have to go at the expense of that of the other.

---

38 See for example the Framework Decision of 15 March 2001, on the standing of victims in criminal proceedings, *OJEU* 2001, L82.

39 ECJ 16 June 2006, *Dutch Law Reports* 2006, 500 annot. M.J. Borgers.

40 F. Vellinga-Schootstra & W.H. Vellinga, *"Positive obligations" en het Nederlandse straf(proces)recht* (inaugural lecture Groningen), Deventer: Kluwer 2008, pp. 40–43 seem to answer this question in the affirmative. P.H.P.H.M.C. van Kempen, *Repressie door mensenrechten* (inaugural lecture Nijmegen), Nijmegen: Wolf Legal Publishers 2008, on the other hand, is very reserved about the role the ECHR is supposed to play for victims within the trial.

5. MORE POWERS FOR THE POLICE AND PUBLIC PROSECUTION SERVICE

In 1995, a parliamentary inquiry took place in the Netherlands into investigation methods. The reason was the use of unconventional investigation methods by the police. The results of this inquiry hit like a bomb; it became clear that the situation concerning the investigation methods used had got completely out of hand. It was therefore decided to lay down the investigative powers in statutory rules. This resulted in the introduction of the Special Methods of Investigation Act [*Wet bijzondere opsporingsbevoegdheden* (*Wet BOB*)], in which the powers of the police and Public Prosecution Service are extensively defined.

Afterwards as well, whether or not in relation to major reordering, numerous new rules were included in the Code of Criminal Procedure. This was usually necessary to allow the statutory powers to keep up with new possibilities for investigation. The statutory investigative powers have been constantly expanded further. Particularly after 11 September 2001, the police and Public Prosecution Service were given more powers in connection with counterterrorism. There are now many more and broader powers which should be able to meet the wishes of investigation practice. The many powers, however, have not made the legal system any simpler.

One could say that a proliferation of extensively defined powers was created in the Code of Criminal Procedure in the last decades, which have made the system rather complicated and obscure. If it is already difficult for an insider criminal jurist to follow, how will this be in day-to-day police practice? Manageability and efficiency, causes for concern in the evaluation of the Special Methods of Investigation Act,[41] have most likely not improved in the past years. Hope is now placed in the project Criminal Procedure 2011. In that year, several important legislative amendments are to take effect. In a letter to the Lower House, the Minister of Justice wrote that the

[41] The Special Methods of Investigation Act – final evaluation, Research and Documentation Centre (WODC), Research and Policy series, volume 222, pp. 253–255.

design of the current powers and investigative acts diverge strongly and are usually connected with time-related wishes and needs.[42] Restructuring, systematisation and streamlining are being pursued by 1 January 2011.

6. *FLEXIBLE REVIEW BY THE CRIMINAL COURT OF BREACHES OF PROCEDURAL RULES*

Breaches of procedural rules have not done any good to the image of the justice system. A persistent idea has arisen in society that breaches of procedural rules occur often and usually result in a favourable judgment for the accused: an acquittal or a bar to prosecution by the Public Prosecution Service. Current practice, however, is different.

The legislature recognised the problem of breaches of procedural rules and their penalisation in the '80s and '90s of the last century. This resulted for example in the Act of 14 September 1995 amending the Code of Civil Procedure (breaches of procedural rules) (*Wet vormverzuimen*),[43] by which many procedural nullities were abolished and Art. 359a CCP was included. This article gives the judge a review framework for penalising breaches of procedural rules, thus leaving a lot to the judge. The Supreme Court specified the frameworks in more detail in a summarising judgment.[44] The core could be summarised briefly as follows: a flexible review and penalisation by the criminal court judge, in which there is room for the most severe penalties on breaches of procedural rules – barring prosecution and excluding evidence – only by exception and subject to stringent requirements of justification.

When one looks at the rules on the exclusion of evidence, one discovers that their sharp edges have been removed through the years. A qualification can be indicated, certainly on three points. Firstly, a procedural irregularity can result in the exclusion of evidence only if it affects underlying substantive law as well. Secondly, evidence need not be excluded if the accused person has not been

---

42 Parliamentary Papers *II* 2007/08, 29 271, no. 7 p. 5.

43 Act of 14 September 1995, *Bulletin of Acts and Decrees* 441.

44 Supreme Court (HR) 30 March 2004, *Dutch Law Reports* 2004, 376 annot. YB.

directly affected by the irregularity (Schütznorm) and, lastly, the qualification applies that a penalty need not be imposed if the accused person's defence has not actually been harmed.

In my view, current practice evidences a balanced approach in which the possibilities for penalisation are weighed.[45] Many factors can be involved in such weighing. It is also an approach in keeping with the developments on this issue in other countries.[46] The judge still has to perform a balancing act on the bar. He or she has to strike a balance between making clear on the one hand that the prosecuting authority also has to obey the rules and, on the other, preventing accused persons from escaping punishment on insufficiently valid grounds if there is sufficiently reliable evidence.

7. *CONCLUSION*

Criminal procedure in the Netherlands has undergone major changes in the past 25 years. When one takes stock, it becomes clear what role Dutch judges, and thus also Supreme Court justices, have to fulfil. A criminal court judge has to balance – or even better – dance on a narrow tightrope between the abysses of the absence of legitimacy on the one hand and the absence of justice on the other. Without legitimacy he cannot operate, and justice is his aim.

A judge may be faced with a decision which will turn out badly for a party concerned, or which will not (immediately) please groups in society or administrators or politicians. The judge will have to make it clear that striving for justice entails that he sometimes has to convict when the vocal community demands acquittal and that he

---

[45] Mevis evaluates the course of the Supreme Court differently. He is of the opinion that the Supreme Court has sold out the penalisation and with that also the control over the lawfulness of the preliminary investigation and the importance of compliance with the rules and limits of powers by easing the penalisation. See P.A.M. Mevis, 'De evaluatie van de Wet-BOB en van de Wet herziening GVO en wat wij daarvan kunnen leren voor de herinrichting van het strafrecht', *Delikt en Delinkwent* 2005, 32 p. 459.

[46] See for example Y.G.M. Baaijens-van Geloven, 'De rechtsgevolgen (sanctionering) van onrechtmatigheden in het opsporingsonderzoek', in: Groenhuijsen & Knigge 2004, pp. 365–377 and R. Kuiper, 'De strafrechter en het vormverzuim: inspirerende rechtspraak van het Amerikaans Hooggerechtshof', *Rechtstreeks* 2008, no. 2.

must sometimes acquit when a conviction is demanded. He must practice justice in an individual case, even if the decision goes against firmly worded positions in society. A judge does not properly grasp his task if he automatically inclines his ear to those opinions.

Judges should be aware that this can cause tension. If they go against prevailing opinions, they will soon be reproached for living in an ivory tower. In order to maintain legitimacy nevertheless, judges should always explain in clear and understandable language how and why they arrive at their decisions. They should also know what is going on in society and take account of this in their decisions as one of the interests that should be weighed.

Briefly summarised, judges should perform their dance on the tightrope between legitimacy and justice with much dedication, perseverance, tenacity and constancy, without treading too much on the toes of their regular partner – society.

THE DUTCH SYSTEM OF LEGAL REMEDIES

Jan Watse Fokkens and Nathalie Kirkels-Vrijman[1]

1. INTRODUCTION

In the Netherlands, we assume that the system of legal remedies in criminal cases should serve roughly three purposes:[2]

1. To offer parties a possibility to bring decisions which in their view were erroneous or erroneously given before another judicial instance for a new judgment, which increases the chance of a correct and more acceptable final judgment;
2. To promote unity of law and monitor a correct course of criminal proceedings through possible assessment by a higher instance; and
3. To promote the authority of court judgments in society by offering possibilities to set aside erroneous decisions.

Two trends can be observed in the development of legislation and case law in the Netherlands in relation to the system of legal remedies in criminal cases.

Firstly, there has been a shift in the direction of more adversarial and responsive criminal proceedings. This tendency arose partly as a result of the effect of Strasbourg case law in Dutch criminal proceedings, and it is also reflected in the case law relating to breaches of procedural rules, illegally obtained evidence and the examination of witnesses. The more adversarial nature of criminal proceedings has been emphasised as well by the introduction of Art. 359(2) CCP (containing the obligation for a judge to justify why he or she departs from an explicitly substantiated position) and

[1] Procurator General at the Supreme Court (Hoge Raad) of the Netherlands and Professor of Criminal Law at the Vrije Universiteit in Amsterdam, respectively law clerk at the Supreme Court of the Netherlands.

[2] See J. De Hullu, *Over rechtsmiddelen in strafzaken* (diss. Groningen), Arnhem: Gouda Quint 1989, p. 165 and the Rapport van de Werkgroep hoger beroep en verzet, *Stroomlijnen in hoger beroep*, p. 27 ff.

Art. 359(3) CCP (no effect of the evidence is needed in the judgment if the accused has confessed to the offence charged). Other examples of this trend are: introduction of the progressive appeal procedure; introduction of mandatory documents on appeal to the Supreme Court; the case law relating to reasonable time-limits, which provides that if the accused and his or her counsel appeared at the hearing and did not invoke exceeding of the reasonable time-limit, the judge would not be required to show that he or she has checked whether the time-limit was exceeded;[3] the similar case law relating to reliance on incorrect service of the summons;[4] the more stringent requirements set by the Supreme Court on grounds for appeal in cassation and reduction of the number of ex officio appeals in cassation.

Secondly, there is a tendency to economise, centring on reducing the burden on the courts. Examples of this are limitations on the possibilities for appeal and cassation for summary offences, introduction of the leave system on appeal and the replacement of ordinary appeal in cassation by cassation as a special legal remedy in the interest of the law, as was done for example in the Surrender of Persons Act (*Overleveringswet*), the Traffic Regulations (Administrative Enforcement) Act (*Wet administratiefrechtelijke handhaving verkeersvoorschriften*), hereinafter referred to as WAHV, and the medical disciplinary rules.

The question is whether these tendencies are compatible with the purposes the system of legal remedies is supposed to serve. In the following, the main recent developments relating to the system of legal remedies and the bottlenecks these developments entail are addressed. In this regard, we shall limit ourselves to the legal remedies following a court judgment in the principal action: appeal and cassation. We shall not deal with notices of objection, appeals from court orders and suchlike. We shall however deal briefly with the developments concerning the special legal remedy of retrial.

---

[3] HR 12 June 2001, *Dutch Law Reports* (*Nederlandse Jurisprudentie*) 2001, 519.

[4] See e.g. HR 15 April 2008, *Dutch Law Reports* 2008, 453 annot. T.M. Schalken.

2. APPEAL

2.1. The Proposals in Criminal Procedure 2001 (*Strafvordering 2001*)

The streamlining of appeal is part of a gradual revision of our Code of Criminal Procedure (*Wetboek van Strafvordering*). Some of the revisions announced by the Minister of Justice in the General Framework for Revision of the Code of Criminal Procedure[5] have already been introduced.[6] These revisions are based largely on the proposals of the research project Criminal Procedure 2001. Concerning the system of legal remedies, which was brought up in the third interim report of the Criminal Procedure 2001 research project,[7] the most important proposal by the researchers was to arrive at a progressive appeal procedure. The judgment in the first instance is viewed in this context as the starting point of the debate on appeal. The appeal elaborates on the examination in the first instance and the hearing concentrates on the issues on which there is a difference of opinion. This would supposedly prevent unnecessary work. In principle, however, a new decision would be taken on the full range of questions in Art. 348 and 350 CCP, but the way in which attention is devoted to these questions would largely depend on the parties to the trial who would have to submit the grounds for appeal. A binding system of grounds of appeal, however, was not chosen. The grounds for appeal were only supposed to give direction to the examination. The appeal judge would retain his or her own responsibility for establishing the facts on appeal. These proposals by the researchers of Criminal Procedure 2001 have been implemented (in part) in the Appeal Procedures (Streamlining) Act (*Wet stroomlijnen hoger beroep*), which has meanwhile entered into effect.[8]

---

[5] *Parliamentary Papers (Kamerstukken) II* 2003/04, 29 271, no. 1.

[6] For the state of affairs, see the letter from the Minister of 27 February 2008, *Parliamentary Papers II* 2007/08, 29 271, no. 7.

[7] M.S. Groenhuijsen & G. Knigge (ed.), *Dwangmiddelen en Rechtsmiddelen. Derde interimrapport onderzoeksproject Strafvordering 2001*, Deventer: Kluwer 2002.

[8] *Bulletin of Acts and Decrees (Staatsblad)* 2006, 470.

2.2. The Progressive Appeal Procedure and its Disadvantages

The main recommendation of the researchers of Criminal Procedure 2001 which was adopted is the recommendation of a progressive appeal procedure with an accompanying system of grounds for appeal. Under Art. 410(1) CCP, the Public Prosecutor is required to submit a notice of appeal when bringing an appeal. The accused is not required to do so, but his or her appeal could be disallowed under Art. 416(2) CCP without further examination if the accused did not lodge written or oral objections to the judgment in the first instance. The appeal judge retains an independent responsibility for the extent and completeness of the examination in the light of the fixed questions he or she must answer pursuant to Articles 348 and 350 CCP. This follows from the Explanatory Memorandum as well as from Art. 415(2) CCP, which provides that the court of appeal must not only focus its examination on the objections, but also on what is otherwise necessary. In the Explanatory Memorandum, however, one can read that appeal must primarily relate to considerations and decisions against which the defence or Public Prosecution Service has objected and that, in practice, this means that the proceedings on appeal will concentrate on issues against which opposition has explicitly been lodged.[9] In response to a question from the members of the PvdA (Labour Party) in the Upper House of Parliament regarding how a type of system of grounds of appeal relates to the decision-making framework of Articles 348 and 350 CCP, the Minister remarked in his Memorandum of Reply that the court of appeal may consider issues regarding which no ground of appeal has been formulated, but that such ex officio examination will not always be conducted to its fullest extent, but will be limited and supplementary in nature.[10] According to the Minister, this could mean for example that in the absence of a defence by the accused, under certain circumstances, errors which might have been made in the preliminary investigation or the examination in the first instance do not necessarily have to result in annulment because the defence did

---

[9] *Parliamentary Papers II* 2005/06, 30 320, no. 3, p. 8.
[10] *Parliamentary Papers I* 2005/06, 30 320, C, p. 2.

not complain about them. This is in line with the development in the direction of more adversarial criminal proceedings already pointed out in the introduction. The way in which a criminal case is handled depends more and more on what the parties to the proceedings put forward as points for discussion. The circumstance that the judge pays less attention to issues that are not disputed may put the establishment of the substantive truth at risk. The judge will, after all, more easily assume that what is not disputed is correct.[11] This development could result in a lack of clarity as to what the ex officio duty of the judge actually is. The judge has the authority to intervene ex officio, but it will depend on the judge's attitude whether he or she exercises this authority often or hardly at all. The question is whether this is desirable from the viewpoint of legal equality.

This development also gives rise to the question of what this means for the funding of legal aid. The defence is expected to participate actively in the trial. Ever higher requirements are being set as well on the specification and substantiation of the defences or applications put forward by the defence. This increases the lawyer's responsibility.[12] Over and against the advantage for the accused of a 'tailor-made' trial and judgment, therefore, is the disadvantage that the accused's fate will depend more and more on a high quality defence. Because most accused persons are dependent on an assigned counsel, this means that legal aid expressly deserves attention in this context.

Besides in the system of grounds for appeal, the progressive nature of the appeal also comes to the fore in the amendment of the rules relating to the examination of witnesses which took effect on 1 January 2005.[13] Concisely stated, these rules entail that when witnesses are listed in the notice of appeal, the applicable criterion for

---

[11] See T.N.B.M. Spronken, *Verdediging: een onderzoek naar de normering van het optreden van advocaten in strafzaken* (doctoral thesis Maastricht), Deventer: Gouda Quint 2001, p. 150 and the literature listed there, and also A.M. van Woensel, 'Stroomlijning: voortbouwen, afbouwen en doortimmeren', in: P.G. Wiewel & R.E. de Winter (ed.), *Stroomlijning van het hoger beroep in strafzaken*, Nijmegen: Ars Aequi Libri, p. 26.

[12] See also Spronken 2001, pp. 146 ff.

[13] *Bulletin of Acts and Decrees* 2004, 579.

assessment of the application to examine these witnesses is whether not examining a witness could reasonably harm the accused's defence (Art. 410 CCP). If the witnesses are listed later, the applicable criterion is whether it is necessary to examine them, which criterion offers the judge a wider margin to reject an application than the criterion of the interest of the defence. In this case, there has been an overzealous tendency to streamline because the defence are not always able to have the full judgment at their disposal within the prescribed period of fourteen days from the filing of the appeal. If the addition to the abridged judgment is not available, the defence has no knowledge of the evidence used by the court, nor of the refutation of meritorious defences, which is usually not included in the abridged judgment. That is why the Dutch Supreme Court (Hoge Raad) radically amended these rules about a year after they had taken effect.[14] The Supreme Court's interpretation comes down to the obligation of the judge in determining whether it is necessary to call up a witness in cases where the application was filed after the period for submission of a document has expired to check whether the accused *was indeed able* to call up the witnesses within that period. The lack of a detailed judgment can be one of the reasons for the judge to rule that this was not possible. This interpretation is diametrically opposed to the Minister's opinions on this during the parliamentary debate,[15] which is of course an undesirable situation.

2.3. The System of Leave in Appeal Procedures

In departure from the recommendations of the researchers of Criminal Procedure 2001, in drafting the Appeal Procedures (Streamlining) Act, the legislature introduced a leave system for appeal in cases in which the accused was convicted of summary or serious offences carrying not more than four years imprisonment and in which no punishment or order was imposed other than one or more fines up to an aggregate maximum of € 500 (Art. 410a CCP). The background of this amendment is the limitation of the costs of

---

[14] HR 19 June 2007, *Dutch Law Reports* 2007, 626 annot. P.A.M. Mevis.

[15] *Parliamentary Papers II* 2003/04, 29 254, no. 8, p. 6.

the judicial system.[16] The president of the court of appeal decides on the basis of the notice of appeal and court documents submitted whether the hearing of the appeal is in the interest of the proper administration of justice. The judgment and report of the hearing in the first instance do not have to be worked out in detail.[17] If after studying the available documents, the president reaches the opinion that a hearing of the appeal is required in the interest of the proper administration of justice, the president will grant leave in an order in chambers. If the president decides that the appeal should not be heard, he or she will have to explain this opinion in a reasoned order in chambers.[18] No appeal to a higher instance is available against this order.[19] The presidents of courts of appeal have deliberately been given a broad weighing framework which does not limit their review to specific criteria.[20]

Even if leave is granted, the judgment and record of the hearing in the first instance do not have to be worked out in detail.[21] A progressive appeal procedure therefore does not apply to these cases. The question has, however, been posed in the literature whether this limitation of the appeal procedure is compatible with Art. 14(5) of the ICCPR, which reads: 'Everyone convicted of a crime shall have the right to his conviction and sentence being reviewed by a higher tribunal according to law.' This article in itself does not prohibit a leave system for hearing an appeal, but does set requirements on the quality of such a system. The lack of documents of the hearing of the case in the first instance means that the convicted person's possibilities to substantiate his or her objections and the leave judge's possibilities to substantiate his or her decision will be limited. According to Jebbink, this limitation goes too far, through which these rules do not to meet the requirements of Art. 14(5) ICCPR.[22] At present, an

---

16 See e.g. *Parliamentary Papers II* 2005/06, 30320, no. 3, p. 23.

17 Art. 365a (2), Art. 378 (2) first lines and under c and d and Art. 395(2) first lines and under c and d CCP.

18 Art. 410a (4) CCP.

19 Art. 410a (4) and 7 CCP.

20 *Parliamentary Papers II* 2005/06, 30 320, no. 3, p. 22.

21 *Parliamentary Papers II* 2005/06, 30 320, no. 3, p. 25.

22 W.H. Jebbink, 'Verlofstelsel in strafzaken: schijnrechtspraak in strijd met het IVBPR', *Delikt en Delinkwent* 2008, 59, pp. 849–864.

appeal to the Supreme Court is being heard against a refusal of leave. A complaint has also been filed with the Human Rights Committee on this matter.[23]

2.4. Abolishment of Unanimity Rules

In the context of streamlining the appeal procedure, the two unanimity rules were abolished. This concerns the rule that the court of appeal can convict an accused person who was previously acquitted by the district court only by a unanimous vote [Art. 424(1) (old) CCP] and the rule that an accused person who has appealed can be sentenced to a more severe penalty by a unanimous vote of the court of appeal only if the Public Prosecution Service has not appealed [Art. 424(2) (old) CCP].

The abolishment of the unanimity rule relating to conviction after acquittal is unfortunate, because this rule was an important guarantee for the quality of the court judgment. Cases where the accused was acquitted in the first instance and convicted in the second instance will often concern the question whether the evidence was convincing or not. The unanimity rule guaranteed that conviction would not be possible if the majority of the judges who ruled in the first instance and on appeal did not consider the evidence convincing. In our view, that guarantee was important because there are no criteria to answer the question 'convincing or not'. In other words: if an accused person is acquitted in the first instance and not all judges are convinced of that person's guilt on appeal, reasonable doubt will remain as to whether he or she is guilty. The idea that abolition of the unanimity rule is more in keeping with the progressive appeal procedure therefore does not appeal to us.

In connection with that progressive appeal procedure, the abolishment of the second unanimity rule is remarkable to the extent that increasing the sentence in case only the accused has appealed does not in itself fit in with that concept. Here, too, the unanimity rule could have continued to exist in order to express the exceptional nature of such a decision and to limit the possibility to take such a decision.

---

23 Mennen v. the Netherlands, Communication no. 1797/2008.

3. APPEAL IN CASSATION

In the research project Criminal Procedure 2001, no proposals were made yet for a drastic amendment of cassation proceedings. The researchers were of the opinion that appeal in cassation is of such great value in criminal procedure that a narrowing of the task of the Supreme Court merely to increase efficiency would be undesirable. The researchers expected that the effect of the proposals relating to appeal could lead to a reduction in the number of appeals in cassation. More suitable possibilities are also said to exist in the system to reduce the pressure on the Supreme Court, should this be unavoidable in the future.[24]

The report "*Versterking van de cassatierechtspraak*" (Strengthening of Supreme Court Jurisdiction), commissioned in 2007 by the Director for the Administration of Justice and Law Enforcement of the Ministry of Justice, has meanwhile been presented to the Minister of Justice. The Minister has now stated that he is in favour of the recommendations addressed to him.[25]

The conclusion of the report is that fulfilment of the Supreme Court's task in relation to the formation of law and legal protection needs to be adjusted. Experience teaches that a substantial number of the cases presented in cassation do not actually deserve the attention of the Supreme Court because no questions come up in them to which the answers are in the interest of legal unity or the development of law, while no important aspects of legal protection are brought up either. A proposal was therefore made to enable a 'selection at the gate'. A selection division should be charged with making a separation between cases that matter in cassation and cases that do not. In cases which are not suitable for hearing by the Supreme Court, the appeal will be disallowed. Such proposals are criticised for putting legal protection at risk. This is refuted in the report.

---

[24] See E.F. Stamhuis, 'De cassatierechter in strafzaken', in: M.S. Groenhuijsen & G. Knigge (ed.), *Afronding en verantwoording. Eindrapport onderzoeksproject Strafvordering 2001*, Deventer: Kluwer 2004, p. 422, raising the threshold is mentioned as a handle (see pp. 485–486).

[25] See the letter from the Minister of 27 March 2008, *Parliamentary Papers II* 2007/08, 29 279, no. 69 and the report of a written consultation, adopted on 4 July 2008, *Parliamentary Papers II*, 2007/08, 29 279, no. 78.

Legal protection also remains a function of cassation proceedings. But in appeals in cassation that are mainly aimed at individual legal protection, a decision by the Supreme Court is necessary only if a party could have suffered a significant loss through errors of the lower court. In this way, the Supreme Court can focus its attention on matters which are important for the quality of the judicial system.

The proposals are in line with measures taken earlier to limit the workload of the Supreme Court, such as excluding appeal in cassation in cases of minor offences and WAHV cases and the introduction and ever broader application of Art. 81 of the Judiciary (Organisation) Act (*RO*), which makes it possible to dismiss an appeal in cassation on the grounds that the appeal need not be discussed because it does not contain any questions that have to be answered in the interest of legal unity or the development of law. Thanks to the introduction of the mandatory drafting of documentation by counsel, there have been no more unsubstantiated appeals in cassation.

A limitation of the task the Supreme Court views as reserved for itself is also evident from the case law of the Supreme Court. For instance, increasingly less use is made of the possibility to quash judgments ex officio. The Supreme Court will quash a judgment without an appeal only if serious errors were made.[26] Furthermore, ever higher requirements are being set on the appeals filed. An example of a case in which this clearly came to the fore is a case in which a complaint was made that the court of appeal had wrongfully rejected a request to examine a witness.[27] The Advocate General drew the conclusion that the court of appeal had applied an incorrect criterion and that the appeal had been brought justifiably. The Supreme Court nevertheless ruled that the complaint was not about the criterion applied by the court of appeal, nor about the reasons

---

[26] For a survey of the case law after introduction of the obligation to submit documentation, see: C.J. van der Wilt & M.K.T. Tjiong, 'Ambtshalve cassatie in strafzaken na invoering van de schriftuurverplichting', *Delikt en Delinkwent* 2006, 16, pp. 303–319.

[27] HR 21 October 2008, *Dutch Law Reports* (*Nederlandse Jurisprudentie*) 2008, 610 annot. P.A.M. Mevis.

for rejecting the request referred to in the notice of appeal. The appeal therefore failed to recognise that the issue of whether the court of appeal had wrongfully rejected the request cannot be examined in cassation, and for that reason, according to the Supreme Court, the appeal was faulty.

The limitation proposed in the report of the duty of the Supreme Court to safeguard the interests of legal unity and the development of law, with attention in addition to legal protection if errors have clearly been made on that point, is the right development. Only in this way could the Supreme Court continue to contribute towards a good administration of justice. At the same time, this development gives points of reference to give ex officio cassation a clear place in the future. The report argues for a broader use of cassation in the interest of the law so that important legal questions can be brought before the Supreme Court. The use of ex officio cassation in cases in which ordinary appeal in cassation has been brought is in line with this. This is appropriate if an error was made in a case on an issue of importance to the development of law or which puts legal unity is at risk. Outside this, the Supreme Court can limit itself to what is put forward by the parties in cassation.

4. RETRIAL

It emerges from the foregoing that the need to reduce the workload of the Supreme Court results in many cases being dealt with summarily. On the other hand, with respect to review, proposals were made to expand the duty of the Supreme Court. A bill to amend the rules relating to review was being prepared at the time this paper was written. It provides for an increase of the grounds for review. According to the bill, review will be possible not only in the event of a new factual circumstance, but also if there is otherwise a *fact* that *was not known* to the judge at the time of the examination in court which, in itself or in connection with the evidence supplied earlier, does not seem to be compatible with the judgment. Among other things, this amendment sees to it that new expert insights into facts which were known to the judge who passed the first judgment can constitute a new point of law in certain circumstances.

Furthermore, a possibility is created for an investigation if there are clear indications that there may be grounds for a retrial. The investigation is intended to provide clarity on that issue. The former accused who has been convicted of a crime which, according to its statutory definition, carries a prison sentence of twelve years or more and which has seriously shocked the legal order, can have his or her counsel request the Procurator General to launch such an investigation. The Procurator General must allow the request unless (a) there are insufficient indications that there may be a ground for retrial, or (b) the investigation requested is not necessary.

The proposed rules also provide for input from 'third parties'. The Procurator General can (and must in certain cases) obtain advice on the desirability of a further investigation from a committee to be formed for that purpose. In conducting further investigation, the Procurator General can be assisted by an investigation team composed of investigating officers and possibly members of the Public Prosecution Service or experts who were not previously involved in the case. Such further investigation can also be conducted by order of the Supreme Court.

This proposed widening of the possibilities for the Supreme Court to examine a criminal case in retrial proceedings is somewhat at odds with the limitation of the role of the Supreme Court in cassation proceedings discussed above. It remains to be seen in particular whether the possibility of further investigation into any fresh fact would have consequences for the way in which the appeal in cassation is judged in cases in which the accused denies the charges. At any rate, it will have to be seen whether more requirements should be set on the grounds of the judicial finding of fact in such cases than have been set up to now. A situation in which an appeal in cassation against the grounds of the judicial finding of fact is dismissed in order to start an investigation shortly afterwards into the correctness of the conviction on the basis of facts which were already known at the time of the cassation proceedings should be avoided as far as possible. It can be noted in this context that the ECtHR exercises much less restraint in reviewing factual decisions than the Supreme Court.

The aforementioned bill also makes retrial possible to the disadvantage of the former accused, a subject on which opinions diverge. We will leave this out of consideration here, although we do want to state that a new point for attention has recently been brought up, namely the extent to which the State's obligation to protect the victim should be a reason to make retrial possible to the accused's disadvantage.[28]

5. CONCLUSION

In the developments discussed above in relation to the system of legal remedies for criminal cases in the Netherlands, two tendencies can be observed, namely the shift in the direction of more adversarial and responsive criminal proceedings and the tendency to economise. Tested against the purposes of legal remedies as described at the beginning, not all developments can be considered positive. Limitation of the possibilities to institute a legal remedy because of – in brief – insufficient importance is, however acceptable. In cases of little importance, after all, a possible error, however undesirable it may be, does not have unacceptable consequences for the convicted person. In this context, however, we do want to note that we are under the impression that adequate account is not always taken of consequences a criminal conviction of a crime can have for a convicted person, completely apart from the sentence. These could for example be the limitation of possibilities to hold certain jobs because of such previous conviction. That aspect deserves more attention than it has received, for example upon introduction of the restricted leave system on appeal.

We have reservations about the restriction of ex officio review in appeal and cassation proceedings. Although there is formally no question of a restriction, the courts and the Supreme Court limit themselves more and more in practice to what has been put forward on the part of the defence or the Public Prosecution Service.

---

28 In this connection, see the inaugural lecture of F. Vellinga-Schootstra & W.H. Vellinga, *'Positive obligations' en het Nederlandse straf(proces)recht*, Deventer: Kluwer 2008, p. 43 ff.

In our view, the question of the judge's own responsibility as criminal proceedings change deserves thorough reconsideration. With respect to the Supreme Court, the report on the strengthening of Supreme Court jurisdiction ("*Versterking van de cassatierecht-spraak*") offers points of reference for a reassessment of ex officio cassation.

On one point we can be clear: the requirement of unanimity for a judicial finding of fact after acquittal should not have been dropped. This is also remarkable at a time when so much attention is being paid to wrongful convictions and there has been a widening of the retrial rules.

THE JUDGE IN THE PRE-TRIAL INVESTIGATION

Stijn Franken[1]

1. THE NARROW MARGINS OF THE DEBATE

The debate in the Netherlands upon the organisation of the (pre-trial) investigation in criminal cases is one of small steps. Truly new points of view are relatively rare. The arguments presented do not change essentially in the course of the years. Diverse insights and outcomes are mainly the result of a difference in the legal-political weighing of interests which in themselves are not at issue. It is self-evident that the passage of time is a relevant factor in this context: at a given moment, more or less weight may be attributed to a specific argument than before, particularly because of changing circumstances. This could give cause to reconsider choices made earlier. Consequently, it is not even surprising that positions are taken in the current debate which show similarities to positions also defended in a somewhat dimmer and more distant past, but which subsequently seemed to be outmoded.

In my opinion, such a pattern is recognisable in the Dutch debate upon the role of the examining magistrate in the pre-trial investigation. The tasks and responsibilities of a judge at this stage of the criminal proceedings are also connected with the positions of other participants in the proceedings and with the rules and practice of the trial. As a consequence, room for too rash changes of course is limited in a certain sense: a different view of the place of the examining magistrate in the pre-trial investigation would after all have repercussions on the role of the Public Prosecution Service and the defence and on the relationship between the preliminary investigation and the trial.[2] At the same time, within those narrow margins, a

---

[1] Professor of Criminal Law and the Law of Criminal Procedure in Utrecht and lawyer in Amsterdam. The manuscript of this chapter was finished in the end of 2008.

[2] See also P.P.J. van der Meij, *'De wankele status van de rechter-commissaris in strafzaken'*, *Nederlands Juristenblad* 2008, pp. 2444–2450.

new weighing of interests could result in the legislature reverting to a position taken not too long ago:

> In the past years, partly as a result of several legislative amendments, the involvement of examining magistrates in pre-trial investigations in criminal cases has decreased. Examining magistrates have taken some distance from investigations and have less of a view of what goes on in them. I consider this undesirable, in view of the great importance of judicial involvement in preliminary investigations.[3]

Such importance lies in the progress, balance and completeness of the pre-trial investigation. According to the legislature, the current proposals to strengthen the position of the examining magistrate are for the purpose of providing more legal protection – by expanding the possibilities of the accused to request the examining magistrate to conduct certain investigative acts – as well as a more expeditious hearing of cases in court. To achieve this, the formal frameworks of the preliminary judicial investigation (*gerechtelijk vooronderzoek*) and the mini-instruction (*mini-instructie*) will be abolished. Their place will be taken by general provisions which enable examining magistrates to develop activities in the pre-trial investigation, on demand by the Public Prosecution Service, at the request of the defence or ex officio. In addition, a material strengthening is pursued in terms of sufficient capacity, quality and support. Examining magistrates will thus be better equipped to exert more influence on pre-trial investigations than has been the case in the past years and in departure from positions taken fairly recently by the legislature. To achieve this goal an examining magistrate, who has to conduct some investigation in a case, ought to have, at any rate, the court documents at his or her disposal.[4]

---

[3] Explanatory Memorandum to the Draft Bill of the Examining Magistrates (Strengthened Position) Act (*Wet versterking positie rechter-commissaris*), p. 1, also for the following.

[4] On the interpretation of the words "any investigation", see also J. Hielkema, '*De rechter-commissaris in strafzaken: leidender of lijdelijker?*', in: A. Harteveld, D.H. de Jong & E. Stamhuis (red.), *Systeem in ontwikkeling* (*Knigge-bundel*), Nijmegen: Wolf Legal Publishers 20005, esp. pp. 270–271.

2. THEORY AND PRACTICE

The arguments used to support the intended strengthening of the examining magistrates' position are not new. That is not surprising, as already noted. It was pointed out, for example in the context of the research project *Strafvordering 2001* (Criminal Procedure 2001) that in the debate conducted at the end of the 80s and beginning of the 90s of the last century upon the framework of the preliminary judicial investigation, positions were relied on which had already been brought up for discussion at the time the Code of Criminal Procedure was drafted.[5] This concerns the legal-political argument that the engagement of examining magistrates guarantees impartiality and objectivity, and the pragmatic argument that efficient settlement is served by assigning a major role to examining magistrates not only in a number of coercive measures, but also in the (pre-trial) investigation of the facts. It is remarkable that both opponents and proponents of the preliminary judicial investigation find support for their diverse positions in these arguments.

In the 21st century, those legal-political and pragmatic arguments are called progress, balance and completeness in the pre-trial investigation. The difference from two decades ago is that the knot is cut differently than at the time: the intention now is to abolish the preliminary judicial investigation. General provisions will be laid down on the investigative duties of examining magistrates, not linked to the procedural structures of the preliminary judicial investigation and mini-instruction. In my opinion, this in itself is pure gain. The debate upon the organisation of the pre-trial investigation in criminal cases should not primarily be about procedural frameworks.

That position can be explained briefly on the basis of the vicissitudes of the preliminary judicial investigation, At the time the Code of Criminal Procedure was drafted, the legislature intended to place the focal point of the pre-trial investigation on the preliminary

---

[5] M.S. Groenhuijsen, '*Het vooronderzoek in strafzaken. Algemeen deel*', in: M.S. Groenhuijsen & G. Knigge (ed.), *Het vooronderzoek in strafzaken. Tweede interimrapport onderzoeksproject Strafvordering 2001*, Deventer: Gouda Quint 2001, p. 45, also for the following and with a more detailed listing of sources.

judicial investigation, which made the examining magistrate responsible for the progress, quality, scope and depth of the pre-trial investigation. It is therefore logical that the legal status of the accused was largely based on this procedural framework. The rules of the preliminary judicial investigation, including the provisions with a strong legally protective image, nevertheless quickly lost their importance through hearsay case law. This case law not only shifted the focal point from the trial to the pre-trial investigation, but also resulted in a gradual dismantling of the preliminary judicial investigation and the current dominance of the criminal investigation by police officers, under the authority of the Public Prosecution Service. Consequently, the express link between notions of legal protection and the preliminary judicial investigation is in fact outmoded. This development has only been strengthened by unlinking the exercise of powers from this investigative framework in a series of legislative amendments.[6] If one acknowledges that it is not very fruitful to give shape to the accused's legal status in the pre-trial investigation in a concept that hardly plays a meaningful role in practice any more, it is logical to think about a new design which is less exclusively linked to a procedural framework. Nowadays, therefore, it is mainly feelings of nostalgia and wishful thinking that can still argue against the proposed abolition of the preliminary judicial investigation. In themselves, those feelings can be well understood, but they may not be decisive.

In my opinion, the question should be mainly: at what times is the engagement of a judge necessary or at any rate desirable in the pre-trial investigation in criminal cases, with a view to the different interests at stake? Separating this from a discussion of the procedural framework makes it is easier to approach the core of this matter, but a different risk lurks. The independence and impartiality attributed to judges are very strong arguments. Those qualities stand out when a solution to problems or a guarantee in keeping with new developments is sought. In the course of the years, for instance, examining magistrates have been saddled with numerous duties

[6] A.E. Harteveld & E.F. Stamhuis, '*De rechterlijke bemoeienis met het strafvorderlijk vooronderzoek*', in: Groenhuijsen & Knigge 2001, p. 497 et seq. See also Hielkema 2005 and Van der Meij 2008.

which they did not yet have in 1926. An example of them can be taken from the special categories of witnesses. In the statutory rules on threatened witnesses, for example, or on the witnesses with whom prosecution authorities want to make agreements in exchange for the statements to be made by those witnesses, an important role is invariably set aside for examining magistrates. Their status supposedly entails that they are the officials designated to determine that special position of witnesses and subsequently to examine them. With the same reliance on independence and impartiality, it is considered necessary to obtain the examining magistrate's opinion before far-reaching investigation methods such as wiretapping and recording confidential communication can be used.

These examples are intended to make it clear that it is tempting to assign the examining magistrate as many duties as possible in the pre-trial investigation. After all, no serious opposition is expected to the engagement of an impartial official at that stage of the criminal proceedings. The question is nevertheless how realistic it is to employ examining magistrates for a series of diverse assignments. In that context, I have already discussed the way in which examining magistrates function in practice and with that the realistic value of the ambitions attached to their actions.[7] It is an important step forward that the legislature is now paying attention to this by stating that an improvement of the statutory rules is not sufficient and that it is important as well for examining magistrates to have enough manpower, quality and support available.

I wholeheartedly endorse both the proposal to abolish the procedural frameworks of the preliminary judicial investigation and the mini-instruction and the importance attached to material support. But this will not suffice. It is urgently necessary to reduce the range of duties of examining magistrates, and that real choices are thus made. This has not been done to date. The legislature is actually hobbling between two ideas. On the one hand, it argues that the criminal investigation by police officers, under the authority of the Public Prosecution Service, is the only procedural framework for the pre-trial investigation of crimes. It ensues from this that the public

---

[7] A.A. Franken, *'De rol van de rechter-commissaris: tussen ideaal en praktijk'*, *Delikt en Delinkwent* 2006, 14, pp. 266–276.

prosecutor would then be put in charge of the pre-trial investigation and that the examining magistrate would (only) be a judge in the pre-trial investigation rather than an examining magistrate. On the other hand, it is stated that examining magistrates should be involved in the pre-trial investigation more often than now, because their independent actions guarantee a balanced investigation which can also reduce the burden on the trial judge. To my mind, however, enhancing the quality of the pre-trial investigation by saddling examining magistrates with even more work than they already have is not realistic and at any rate does not reflect much insight into the practice of criminal procedure.

3. *THE DUTIES OF THE EXAMINING MAGISTRATE*

It is therefore a good idea to review some duties of the examining magistrate. In the first place, he or she is expected to give an opinion on the lawfulness of taking a suspect into police custody and to decide on a demand for pre-trial detention for a period of (a maximum of) 14 days. The need for judicial review of deprivation of liberty shortly after a suspect has been arrested is not at issue. Judicial intervention is, after all, prescribed in Art. 5(3) ECHR. The case law of the Dutch Supreme Court (Hoge Raad), however, charges the examining magistrate with an additional duty: reviewing the procedural rules on arrest and police custody while relying on the closed system of legal remedies exclusively reserved for examining magistrates.[8] That additional assignment has not been without criticism. One of the objections to it is connected with the limited possibilities for examining magistrates in the short space of time available to them to recognise problems in this area and study them in depth if necessary. This reservation is in line with the general concerns about the role of examining magistrates in reviewing police custody and in deciding on pre-trial detention.[9] As a rule, files are not supplied until

[8] See for example HR 8 May 2001, *Nederlandse Jurisprudentie* 2001, 587 annotated by JR; HR 30 March 2004, *Nederlandse Jurisprudentie* 2004, 376 annotated by YB; HR 22 June 2004, *Nederlandse Jurisprudentie* 2004, 561 annotated by PMe and HR 13 June 2006, *Nederlandse Jurisprudentie* 2006, 623 annotated by Klip.

[9] See for example D.V.A. Brouwer & W.H. Jebbink, '*Wie behoedt ons voor de rechter-commissaris?*', *Nederlands Juristenblad* 2002, pp. 393–398 and N. van der Laan, '*De*

shortly before indictment and they are sometimes so voluminous that it is an illusion to think that the examining magistrate can study them completely in a few hours. This means that a more in-depth assessment of the incriminating evidence and grounds necessary for pre-trial detention can be made only at a later stage, by the court sitting in chambers which decides on the subsequent stages of pre-trial detention. A solution to such problems can be found at most in the increased material support of examining magistrates, of which the legislature has held out the prospect.

The second duty for examining magistrates is to assess demands (by the Public Prosecution Service) for an investigation into telecommunications and for recording confidential communication. In this respect, examining magistrates manifest themselves as authorising judges. The division of tasks among the public prosecutor, the examining magistrate and the trial judge in this context has been the subject of several rulings. In a case in which the lawfulness of a telephone tap was at issue, the Dutch Supreme Court ruled:[10]

> Initially, it is up to the public prosecutor to judge whether a suspicion exists within the meaning of Art. 126m (1), of the Code of Criminal Procedure and whether the investigation urgently demands the recording of data traffic. In the latter review, the principles of proportionality and subsidiarity play a part. Should there be a question of whether an authorisation can be granted, an examining magistrate must subsequently review whether the above-mentioned statutory requirements have been met. Lastly, it is up to the trial judge to assess the lawfulness of the use of the authority. In the legal system, in a case like this in which the examining magistrate granted an authorisation in advance, such an assessment contains an answer to the question whether the examining magistrate could reasonably have arrived as his or her opinion on that authorisation.

Therefore, in succession, the public prosecutor, the examining magistrate and the trial judge must form an opinion on the telephone

---

mantel der liefde van de rechter-commissaris in strafzaken', *Nederlands Juristenblad* 2006, pp. 993–998.

[10] HR 21 November 2006, *Nederlandse Jurisprudentie* 2007, 233 annotated by PMe. See also HR 11 October 2005, *Nederlandse Jurisprudentie* 2006, 625 and regarding this case law J.W. Fokkens & N. Vrijman, *'De rechterlijke toetsing van het gebruik van bijzondere opsporingsbevoegdheden'*, in: *Kruijstocht door het strafrecht* (*liber amicorum P.W. van der Kruijs*), The Hague: Sdu Uitgevers 2008, pp. 15–28.

tap. The marginal review by the trial judge described by the Dutch Supreme Court, is closely connected with the engagement of the examining magistrate. It can be concluded from this that the trial judge is expected to conduct a more penetrating review of the use of special investigative powers if the examining magistrate is not involved. This immediately gives rise to the question whether the examining magistrate, as authorising judge, is indeed of added value in terms of legal protection. According to the Dutch Supreme Court, because the examining magistrate's role can result in a less penetrating review by the trial judge, this is not at any rate self-evident. Moreover, practice shows that examining magistrates ultimately play a very small part in the review of special investigative powers.[11] There is a big difference between the rationale of his or her engagement and its actual effect. The practice does not meet the objective of the condition included in the law for authorisation in order to subject the use of far-reaching powers to a critical judicial opinion. The theory is nice, but in practice the image looms of the examining magistrate as a rubber stamp. Authorisations on the stationery of the public prosecutor's office, as they occur now and then, are a poignant example of this. At most, a certain preventive effect can still be attributed to the prescribed authorisation. After all, it cannot be entirely ruled out that the investigating officers, under the responsibility of the public prosecutor, will be restrained in requesting, for example a telephone tap by the prospect of judicial supervision.[12] It may work that way, if only now and then. But this is not visible to, let alone verifiable by the outside world. Consequently, I cannot find a strong argument in this in favour of the examining magistrate as authorising judge.

In the third place, examining magistrates have a number of independent investigative powers assigned primarily to them because of their far-reaching nature. A search of the home or office of professionals entitled to privilege is an outstanding example of this. In cases where it is not possible to wait for the examining magistrate to take action, the public prosecutor or, if necessary, the assistant

[11] See A. Beijer et al., *De Wet bijzondere opsporingsbevoegdheden – eindevaluatie*, The Hague: Boom Juridische uitgevers 2004, especially pp. 164–168 and pp. 173–177.

[12] In that sense, see Beijer et al. 2004, p. 175.

public prosecutor may, however, search those premises with an authorisation from the examining magistrate. This alternative, which is laid down in Art. 97 of the Dutch Code of Criminal Procedure, is interpreted in different ways:[13]

> In larger court districts, during the daytime, the examining magistrate often proves to be occupied with witness examinations, indictments and suchlike. For this reason, authorisations are more likely to be issued during office hours, and outside office hours, the search is more likely to be conducted by the examining magistrate him or herself. In smaller court districts, the practice is sometimes reversed. It is more likely that they will have time to search during the daytime. Authorisations are more likely to be issued there outside office hours, because it takes more time for the examining magistrate to get there, as proved to be the case in one court district. There are also differentiations according to the gravity of the offence. The day of the week may also determine whether examining magistrates are available or not and therefore an authorisation is more likely to be issued.

Once again, a difference can be seen between the rationale of the engagement of an examining magistrate and legal practice. Elements such as time of the day and travelling distance prove to be decisive, not the idea that the far-reaching nature of a search compels the engagement of an examining magistrate.

In the fourth place, examining magistrates have a duty as protecting judges. I want to deal briefly with this. In this capacity, the examining magistrate acts as an investigative judge who in a certain sense takes over the tasks of the trial judge in relation to threatened and protected witnesses. For this purpose, the compensation idea is relied on which ensues from the Strasbourg case law on Art. 6 ECHR. The idea is that because the defence is given the opportunity to question a special witness in proceedings under the authority of the examining magistrate, shape can be given to the right to examine witnesses. This may be correct in theory, but practice usually showes otherwise. Most questions intended for a threatened witness remain unanswered out of fear that the answers will reveal the identity of

---

[13] Erasmus University Rotterdam, *Evaluatie Wet herziening GVO*, (Evaluation of the Preliminary Judicial Investigations (Amendment) Act), The Hague: Ministry of Justice 2004, Research and Documentation Centre Notebooks (*WODC-Cahiers*) 2004–11, p. 20.

the witness. Most questions intended for a protected witness remain unanswered out of fear that the answers will endanger state security. Instead of being able to manifest him or herself as impartial and independent, during these examinations the examining magistrate is necessarily on the short leash of the public prosecutor or the General Intelligence and Security Service (AIVD) officer or state advocate.

Lastly, examining magistrates carry out investigative acts in the context of the preliminary judicial investigation, at the suspect's request in connection with a mini-instruction or after referral by the trial judge. This mostly concerns examining witnesses. Much value is often attached to this task. Charging an examining magistrate with the examination of witnesses would give the pre-trial investigation a more adversarial character and more possibilities would arise for the defence to collect exculpatory material. Compared to an examination by police officers, an examination by the examining magistrate would also be more objective and impartial in nature and therefore guarantee a higher quality. In this way, the examining magistrate could also take work off the hands of the trial judge. Finally, it should be noted that examining magistrates have possibilities which police officers do not have: they can swear in witnesses and give an order to have witnesses brought before the court who are unwilling to appear. These alleged benefits, however, must contend with the examining magistrate's overfull agenda. He or she often lacks time to comply quickly with a request from the defence or an instruction from the trial judge to examine several witnesses. In addition, the hollowing out of the preliminary judicial investigation seems to have a considerable effect on the way in which examining magistrates conduct witness-examinations. They often have limited knowledge of the case in which the witnesses are examined. That is why many examining magistrates suffice with taking the statement and asking a few questions as an introduction or for clarification, and leave the actual interrogation to the defence (or, as an exception, to the Public Prosecution Service). An active examining magistrate, who takes the lead in examining witnesses, is the exception rather than the rule. He or she sometimes does not go beyond the role of a minutes secretary.

4. *NOT MORE, BUT LESS AND BETTER*

The differences between the ideals attached to the engagement of examining magistrates in the pre-trial investigation on the one hand, and practice as it has developed in the course of the years on the other, are in many respects exemplary of the well-known distinction between *law in books* and *law in action*. All aspects of their range of duties can be defended by relying on the impartiality and independence ascribed to examining magistrates. A proposal could even be made to involve examining magistrates more intensively, because their engagement presumes a guarantee of quality. All this may be theoretically correct, but practice often shows otherwise. In my view, an actual strengthening of the position of examining magistrates can be brought about only by reducing their duties and responsibilities. Examining magistrates should not be engaged more often, but they should be able to make their mark more emphatically at the times their appearance is indispensable through a concentration of work: not more, but less and especially better.

This is not the place to sketch the contours of a new, limited role of examining magistrates in pre-trial investigations in criminal cases with any degree of precision. As stated above, their position cannot be viewed separately from that of the public prosecutors, the defence and the trial judges. A scaling down of the activities of examining magistrates is not a goal in itself, but should be embedded in a developed view of the organisation of the pre-trial investigation and in the relationship between this phase and the trial. This is also how I understand Mevis, who has argued in favour of a coordinated system of decision-making and supervision, in which the relationship between the public prosecutor, the examining magistrate and the trial judge in reviewing coercive measures is made explicit.[14] I present only a few rough ideas here, which need to be developed and thought through in more detail.

---

[14] Mevis in his note under HR 21 November 2006, *Nederlandse Jurisprudentie* 2007, 233. See also Schalken's note under HR 24 April 2007, *Nederlandse Jurisprudentie* 2008, 145.

The core of these ideas is that that more justice could be done to the qualities of examining magistrates, if they concentrate on their role in review and decision-making. The legal-political argument that the engagement of examining magistrates guarantees an impartial and objective pre-trial investigation has less meaning in the current spirit of the times when it comes to their investigative duties. Nowadays, this objective can also be met in a different way than through an active investigative role of examining magistrates. Moreover, such alternatives could meet the pragmatic argument that it is handy and efficient for trial judges if work is taken off their hands by a thorough pre-trial investigation.

I realise that an investigative role of examining magistrates will not be abolished straight away. In the context of the research project *Strafvordering 2001* (Criminal Procedure 2001), a comment was made for example that it is undisputed that it must be possible to charge the magistrate in the pre-trial investigation in some way with the performance of certain investigative acts.[15] As far as I am concerned, this is not necessarily self-evident. In a certain sense, the idea that the examining magistrate should not investigate is even in keeping with the starting point on which the special investigative powers are based: a clear division of responsibilities means that the public prosecutor is the undisputed leader of the investigation in the pre-trial stage and that the examining magistrate should not become too intensely involved in it.[16] Examining magistrates who conduct their own investigations distort that image and therefore do not immediately help to create the desired clarity.

That is not all. Because occasional arguments such as travelling time and day of the week are (or may be) decisive in answering the question whether a search will be conducted under the direction of an examining magistrate or with the latter's authorisation, examining magistrates also in fact demonstrate the relative value of the argument that they are actually indispensable for an impartial investigation in the pre-trial stage. If such considerations are a reason for

---

[15] Groenhuijsen 2001, p. 46.

[16] See for example P.A.M. Mevis, '*De evaluatie van de Wet-BOB en van de Wet herziening GVO*', *Delikt en Delinkwent* 2005, 32, pp. 452–466 and Fokkens & Vrijman 2008.

outsourcing the investigative work to a public prosecutor or assistant public prosecutor, something at any rate can indeed be detracted from the argumentative value of the legal-political argument. Furthermore, it is not true that the examining magistrate is demonstrably better qualified as an investigator than, for example police officers. The office is not the primary determinant of the quality of, for example, the questions posed to a witness and the recording of his or her answers. I am of the opinion that knowledge of the file, attitude and input of the parties to the trial are more important for an adequate formulation of the question. It is also high time for the dated manner in which statements are now recorded as a rule by a reporting officer or by an examining magistrate to be replaced by a verbatim report of the hearing, using technological facilities.

Against that background, it is not so difficult to think of alternatives to the engagement of the examining magistrate as an investigator. I limit myself here to the examination of (regular) witnesses. One option is, for example to examine more witnesses in court. The advantages of this are evident, but entail a change in the relationship between the pre-trial investigation and the trial. If the starting point is that no essential changes should be made to this, one could consider possibilities to have witnesses examined by police officers in the presence of the defence (and, if desired, the Public Prosecution Service).[17] If such an examination is tape recorded, worked out word by word and clear rules have been agreed for the organisation of the examination, this will not necessarily produce fewer results in terms of establishing the truth than an examination under the direction of an examining magistrate. All sides may have to get accustomed to this, and it could cause problems in the beginning. The Strasbourg case law on legal assistance for a suspect prior to or during a police interrogation, however, shows that defence lawyers will inevitably end up in the preserves of investigating officers.[18] In that sense,

---

[17] A possibility is also to charge one of the trial judges with the examination of witnesses, with the consent of the defence and Public Prosecution Service, and in their presence. This has been provided for on appeal, but not yet in the first instance.

[18] ECHR 27 November 2008, Appl. no. 36391/02 (Salduz versus Turkey) and ECHR 11 December 2008, Appl. no. 4268/04 (*Panovits v. Cyprus*). In more detail: Matthias Borgers, '*Een nieuwe dageraad voor de raadsman bij het politieverhoor?*',

possible cold feet in the contacts between the police and the bar will have to disappear quickly, no matter what.

In my opinion, with provisions such as these – which, of course, have to be worked out in more detail – the requirements of progress, balance and completeness of the investigation can be met on at least the same level as now when examining magistrates are engaged as investigating judges. If examining magistrates are released from their investigative activities, they will also be able to concentrate on their other duties. More time can be set aside, for example for decisions on pre-trial detention and their preparation. The position of the examining magistrate as authorising judge for telephone taps and recording confidential communication should be examined more closely, and especially in relation to the responsibilities of the public prosecutor and trial judge in that respect, whereby it could be meaningful to concretise and specify the requirements of proportionality and subsidiarity. Finally, the examining magistrate could assume more of the role of an arbitrator. In that capacity, for example, he or she could deliberate on the question whether a warrant should be issued to bring a witness before the court. With some creativity, the issue of the swearing-in of a witness could be placed under this heading. Important for the role of an arbitrator is mainly the proposal by the legislator to give the examining magistrate the authority to call up the suspect and public prosecutor to appear before him or her "for the proper course of the investigation". In such a meeting, examining magistrates, having heard the parties to the proceedings, could take decisions on the progress and organisation of the pre-trial. That is a task par excellence in which they could live up to all the qualities attributed to them as examining magistrates.

The gap between the theory and practice of engaging examining magistrates can be narrowed. A limitation of their range of duties and the introduction of alternatives which are in line with the current spirit of the times could contribute to this. Saddling examining magistrates with even more assignments and expectations would ultimately only widen the gap. That is not the way to go.

Nederlands Juristenblad 2009, pp. 88–93 and Taru Spronken, '*Ja, de zon komt op voor de raadsman bij het politieverhoor!*', *Nederlands Juristenblad* 2009, pp. 94–100.

SOME MAIN FINDINGS OF 'STRAFVORDERING 2001' AND THE SUBSEQUENT REFORM OF DUTCH CRIMINAL PROCEDURE

Marc Groenhuijsen[1]

1. INTRODUCTION

The current Dutch Code of Criminal Procedure (CCP) entered into force in 1926. That is quite some time ago. Hence, one would expect that the basic structure of this Code reflects the socio-economic and political features of the Dutch society as it existed in the first quarter of the 20th century. The truth of the matter is, however, that the roots of the CCP are even much older. They can be traced back to the previous Code of Criminal Procedure, of 1838. Imagine the circumstances that were obtaining back then. We are talking about a society in which transport of people usually took place on horseback. Bicycles had not yet been invented, not to mention motor vehicles. There was a huge gap between life in the cities and towns on the one hand and the countryside on the other. Travelling at night was outright hazardous. To name but one other example: our small country had several different time-zones which were only in 1909 replaced by a single national time.[2] This kind of conditions directly impacted on some of the specific provisions in the CCP. Some of the time limits for pre-trial custody, for instance, can only be comprehended in the light of the fact that in those days it could take more than a day to transfer a suspect to a place where he could be interrogated by a public prosecutor.[3]

It does not need any explanation that things have changed dramatically since the first half of the 19th century. Contemporary

---

[1] Professor of criminal law, Department of Criminal Law, Tilburg University.

[2] A. van Hulzen, *De wereld van eergisteren. Nederland tussen de jaren 1900–1920*, Den Haag: Kruseman 1983.

[3] Example derived from Jolande uit Beijerse, *Op verdenking gevangen gezet. Het voorarrest tussen beginselen en praktische behoeften*, diss. Rotterdam, Nijmegen: Ars Aequi Libri 1998.

society hardly has anything in common with the situation that existed 150 years ago. Yet, despite the countless differences, there is one crucial factor of continuity. I am referring to the intrinsic purpose of a national Code of Criminal Procedure and a small number of core values it embodies.

How can we outline the supreme underlying objectives of a CCP? In short, the ulterior objective of a CCP is of a dual nature. On the one hand, criminal procedure serves the purpose of protecting society by effectively fighting crime. On the other hand – and at the same time – its goal is to protect individual citizens against excessive use of power by the government. It follows that the CCP has an ambivalent relationship with the phenomenon of power. The Code has specific provisions *creating* legal power for officials to combat crime. But in doing so it also *limits* power, since any governmental action which is not legitimized by a statutory mandate can no longer be considered acceptable.

During the last decades of the 20th century, a consensus has emerged that the CCP had become dysfunctional in connection with both main objectives of criminal procedure.[4] As far as crime control is concerned, the general sentiment was that the CCP had become too restrictive. Its content was deemed to be overly formalistic and the specific powers conferred on law enforcement agencies did not meet the demands of contemporary society. Alternatively, the goal of protecting individual citizens' rights was not fully attained either. Several kinds of practices had been developed which are hardly reconcilable with the concept of a fair trial. Consequently, Dutch criminal procedure was reprimanded by the European Court for Human Rights in a significant number of cases where the minimum standards of the European Convention had not been observed.[5]

The first question to address, then, is how we ended up in a situation where neither one of the primary objectives of criminal

---

[4] T.M. Schalken, *Strafrecht als systeem van rechtsbetrekkingen*, inaugural address Amsterdam, Arnhem: Gouda Quint 1987.

[5] Examples are the Kostovski case (ECHR 20 november 1989, *Nederlandse Jurisprudentie* 1990, 245) and Lala case (ECHR 22 september 1994, *Nederlandse Jurisprudentie* 1994, 733).

procedure were adequately served by the CCP. This will be covered in the next section, which is also about the interim solutions that were chosen to defuse the problem. Section 3 will then move on to describe the research project 'Strafvordering 2001'. It will provide insight into the objective of the project, the methods used, and the results that were attained. In section 4, the governments' response to the research findings will be outlined. On a higher level of abstraction, section 5 is about some general trends that can be discerned in the recent development of Dutch criminal procedure. The final part of this chapter, section 6, contains some concluding observations.

2. *MAIN REASONS FOR DYSFUNCTIONAL CODE AND AD HOC SOLUTIONS*

When we turn to the question what made the Code dysfunctional, it is important to look for root causes. It is not the content of specific provisions where the main shortcomings are hidden. Rather we must identify more structural or systematic features of the Code that have proved to be anachronistic.

The first problem in this connection is the fact that the Code builds on an obsolete conception of crime. The designers of the 1926 Code conceived of crime as a relative rare phenomenon. For them, crime is an inconvenience, committed occasionally by an individual perpetrator. The Code offers solid solutions for dealing with this kind of events. Modern day society, however, looks completely different in this respect. Crime has taken massive proportions. On top of that, the nature of crime has changed dramatically. First, there is a small group of persons who commit crime with an incredibly high frequency. Rough estimates indicate that a minority of some 25% of the perpetrators is responsible for some 75% of the crimes committed. Obviously, to a large extent this can be attributed to drug related serial crime – whereas the entire problem of illegal narcotics was completely absent at the time when the current Code was introduced. One step further, we might observe the emergence of crime committed by larger groups of perpetrators, corporate crime, cross border crime and organised crime. It is obvious that the solutions the Code provides for traditional crime do not always fit the challenges posed by the modern manifestations of crime.

The second area of friction is caused by the fact that the Code proceeds from the assumption that every case which is solved by the police needs to be brought to court.[6] In other words: the prosecutor was not supposed to have any discretionary power in disposing of a case. Settlement out of court, for instance, was not part of the system. Again, developments during the 20th century forced law enforcement officials to introduce alternative practices. Vast numbers of crimes can only be processed by adopting more informal approaches, such as settlements out of court. Needless to say that he basic structure of the Code was not designed to easily accommodate these novel procedures.

A third item that needs to be mentioned concerns the relative weight or importance of the various stages in the criminal procedure. According to the designers of the Code, the trial stage was supposed to be all important. Like in most countries, the principle of immediacy would have to apply.[7] The judge was supposed to take a decision based on the evidence that was presented in court. These fundamental choices underlying the basic structure of the Code were virtually shattered by a single verdict by the Dutch Supreme Court, issued less than one year after the Code entered into force. In this case, the Supreme Court ruled that hearsay evidence (statements *de auditu*) is admissible as a basis for convictions.[8] This has had tremendous impact on the way ordinary trials have been conducted. Ever since this landmark decision by the Supreme Court, it has become normal to record statements by victims, witnesses and experts during the pre-trial stages. Either the police or an examining magistrate will take down a deposition. The recorded statement will then be included in the case-file. This file becomes the main source of information for the court. Witnesses are rarely called to give oral testimony in open court. Two implications are immediately clear. First: the preliminary stages of the procedure become more and

---

[6] On this: J.F. Nijboer, *De doolhof van de Nederlandse strafwetgeving*, Groningen: Wolters-Noordhoff 1987 and M. Hildebrandt, *Straf(begrip) en procesbeginsel*, Deventer: Kluwer 2002.

[7] Dorothé Garé, *Het onmiddellijkheidsbeginsel in het Nederlandse strafproces*, diss. Maastricht, Arnhem: Gouda Quint 1994.

[8] Supreme Court (hereinafter: HR) December 20, 1926, *Nederlandse Jurisprudentie* 1927, 85.

more important. The information collected during these stages is included in the case file and can be hard to challenge or refute during the actual trial. Secondly: the advantage of this *modus operandi* is great benefits in terms of efficiency. In The Netherlands, it is not unusual to have 8 or 9 serious cases (felonies) tried in a single day. On the other hand, it is obvious that the inner structure of the Code was not at all designed to dispose of cases in this manner.[9]

Next, a fundamental problem was caused by the fact that the Code basically provides for one single unified procedure to deal with all different kinds of crime and all different kinds of defendants. The most serious cases are governed by more or less the same provisions as the more average cases.[10] And from a procedural point of view, according to the Code it does not make a difference whether the defendant confesses the crime or denies any involvement in the alleged criminal acts. The latter example is particularly conspicuous, given the fact that in many jurisdictions in situations where there is a confession the real trial will be replaced by a sentence hearing. In actual practice, though, it should not be surprising that in cases where the defendant denies the charges much more emphasis is laid on evidential issues. Alternatively, when there is a guilty plea, the bench will automatically shift most of its attention to the question which sentence would be appropriate. But again: the Code does not provide a solid basis for this kind of logical differentiation in conducting the trial.

The list seems endless, but there are more anomalies that need to be referred to. Many of the provisions in the Code are linked to the 'judicial preliminary inquiry'. For the drafters of the Code, this was an important instrument to protect a due process. The involvement – indeed: the leading role – of an examining magistrate was supposed to protect the interests of a fair trial. Consequently, the use of many coercive powers was restricted to situations where a judicial preliminary inquiry had been requested. Over time, however, this kind of

[9] W.P.J. Pompe, 'Vooronderzoek of eindonderzoek beslissend?', in: *Vijf opstellen van Willem Pompe*, Zwolle: W.E.J. Tjeenk Willink 1975, pp. 55–64.

[10] To avoid misunderstandings: less serious cases can be tried by a single judge whereas the more severe cases are usually tried by a panel of three judges. However, the procedure to be followed – and the level of legal safeguards – is more or less invariable.

inquiry became marginalised. It was only used in a tiny minority of cases (approximately 4%). In these circumstances, it quickly became dysfunctional to link up coercive powers with the use of a judicial preliminary inquiry. Here was another example where a new systematic foundation for specific provisions was called for.

One of the cornerstones of the Code of 1926 was that criminal procedure starts when there is a 'reasonable suspicion' that a crime has been committed. When this threshold is taken, the police have powers to investigate. From this moment on, a suspect has rights which can be exercised in his defence. Since the advent of organised crime, however, more and more situations arose when there was a dire need for law enforcement agencies to act *before* a crime had been committed. The need for a kind of pre-emptive strike became even more apparent after the terrorist attacks of September 2001. This was all translated into new powers for the police at a stage when there was not yet probable cause. Again, the basic assumptions underlying the Code had to be reconsidered in this new light.

Finally, the Code presupposes a certain institutional position of the main actors involved in criminal justice. The judiciary, the prosecutor's service and the police are the main government bodies that interact in criminal procedure. There can be no doubt that these bodies have changed beyond recognition since the Code entered into force. The body of prosecutors, for instance, has autonomously extended its discretionary powers by gradually shaping and executing a full fletched *policy* on when and how to enforce criminal law. This policy directly impacted the work of the police in as far as it specified categories of crime which needed to be prioritised in investigation. Simultaniously, prosecutors issued policy guidelines on what levels of sentences they would request the court to impose, thereby undeniably affecting sentencing practices of the bench. Further developments in the institutional ties between the main actors became visible when the police organisation professionalised in a way that was sometimes hard to supervise for the prosecutor's service. In short, the mutual relationships between the judiciary, the prosecution service and the police have undergone evolutionary changes. These changes had not been sufficiently absorbed in the content of the Code, thus undermining the cohesion of its inner structure.

Since 1926, three main instruments have emerged in order to deal with the many changes which have occurred in society. Each of them was meant to cope with new and additional demands emanating from constantly evolving circumstances.

The first instrument is the case law from the Supreme Court. A prime example is a series of decisions in which the Supreme Court acknowledged so-called 'principles of proper procedure'. These are unwritten principles of law which provide guidance in the interpretation of specific provisions in the CCP.[11] According to these principles, prosecutors are precluded from acting in a capricious way. They should furthermore respect the principles of proportionality and subsidiarity and when they have raised reasonable expectations on the part of the defence (like in relation to a decision not to prosecute), these expectations must be met. A second example is the introduction of an exclusionary rule. Even though the Code did not have any provision to this effect, the Supreme Court held that illegally obtained evidence is not admissible to support a conviction.[12]

The examples supports the argument that case-law is better suited to protect legitimate interests of the defence than to safeguard effective law enforcement. The latter objective can be served more adequately by legislative means. That is exactly what happened. Ever since 1926, our jurisdiction has been virtually inundated with countless amendments to the CCP. It is not useful to provide an overview of the main pieces of reform that were gradually introduced. Suffice it to mention that just in the year 1993 no less than 200 articles in a Code comprising a total of some 600 articles were changed.[13] Other years show similar numbers. So it is obvious that many attempts were made to keep up with the rapidly changing demands in an environment in constant motion. The problem, however, was that it appeared to be impossible to maintain an adequate

---

[11] C.P.M. Cleiren, *Beginselen van een goede procesorde*, diss. Leiden, Arnhem: Gouda Quint 1989.

[12] HR June 26, 1962, *Nederlandse Jurisprudentie* 1962, 470. Like in many other countries, the exclusionary rule has been modified and refined in subsequent decisions by the Court. The details are irrelevant for the purpose of this chapter.

[13] D. van der Landen, 'Technische fouten bij recente wijzigingen van het Wetboek van Strafvordering', *Nederlands Juristenblad* 1994, p. 618.

level of coordination. The large number of partial adaptations of the Code led to patchwork. The many hundreds of new provisions were not driven by a coherent philosophy or by a unifying perspective. The end result was a Code which lacked a solid systematic foundation.

In order to remedy this absence of systemic coherence, the government decided to appoint a Committee charged with 'reassessing' all the interests that are at stake in criminal procedure. The Committee was to adopt a comprehensive approach.[14] During the years of its existence, from 1989 till 1993, it published 10 reports on some vital parts of the Code.[15] The reports contained a large number of recommendations, quite a few of which were actually accepted by the government and parliament. Nevertheless, the ensuing new modifications of the CCP did not bring the kind of shift that was hoped for. In fact, with hindsight, the conclusion probably must be that the entire operation made things worse. Instead of solving the problem, it rather compounded the situation. This was primarily caused by the composition of the committee. In order to preserve some sense of fairness, the Minister of Justice appointed members from all the main interest groups and stakeholders within the criminal justice system. Representatives from the judiciary, senior prosecutors, prominent members of the bar association, the director of the probation service, someone with a background in victim support, and a handful of academics. It is highly unlikely that a committee comprised of representatives of stakeholders will easily agree on a shared vision on criminal procedure. So, instead of shaping a comprehensive view on what a CCP should look like, the committee did its utmost to agree on compromise solutions for a range of very specific issues that needed to be addressed. It was commendable that they in fact did manage to rally behind a wide range of

[14] The Committee was named after its chairperson, mr. Moons, a former president of the Supreme Court.

[15] The results of the Committee work have been collected in: *Herziening van het gerechtelijk vooronderzoek. Een rapport van de Commissie herijking Wetboek van Strafvordering*, Arnhem: Gouda Quint 1990; G.J.M. Corstens (ed.), *Rapporten herijking strafvordering 1990–1992*, Arnhem: Gouda Quint 1993; G.J.M. Corstens (ed.), *Rapporten herijking strafvordering 1993*, Arnhem: Gouda Quint 1993.

recommendations. But like before, the proposals submitted to the government lacked a broader systematic perspective, so it added to the existing fragmentation rather than providing a unifying philosophy.

3. *THE RESEARCH PROJECT 'STRAFVORDERING 2001'*: SCOPE, METHOD AND MAIN FINDINGS

In 1997, a group of researchers from Groningen University and from Tilburg University submitted a proposal to the Ministry of Justice. After some negotiations, the Minister of Justice commissioned a project in which the researchers were mandated to address the following central question:

How would a Code of Criminal Procedure look which:

- meets contemporary needs and corresponds to state of the art doctrinal views;
- is coherent in the sense that it offers a systematic approach of criminal procedure;
- is connected to developments on a European level?

Quite a complicated question. The research group started work in 1998.[16] The methodology of the project was rather straightforward. The first thing to do is define some basic assumptions. That means: one needs to spell out a vision on the nature and the purpose of having a codified body of rules governing criminal procedure. Next the group needed to identify the main interests which have to be served by a revised Code. An articulated conception of the interests that need to be served and balanced is inevitable to subsequently justify a number of substantive choices which will carry the project to its end. I will now briefly clarify these three consecutive steps.

---

[16] The Group was headed by prof. Geert Knigge (Groningen) and myself (Tilburg). The other members of the team were Alex Harteveld, Anita den Hartog, Nico Kwakman, Marleen Laméris and Evert Stamhuis from Groningen and Yvonne Baaijens and Joep Simmelink from Tilburg. The group was supplemented occassionaly by individual researchers from other universities.

The first one is about defining the basic assumptions underlying the project. The researchers proposed that a CCP needs *flexible* provisions, allowing the parties room to navigate in a purposeful way. This is a very fundamental preliminary option. In theory, there are many ways of looking at the functionality of legal rules. It is possible to aim for an exhaustive normative structure with specific instructions for as many situations as can be imagined. The researchers preferred the exact opposite. Since it is by definition impossible to provide specific solutions for concrete future problems, it is more appropriate to provide a normative framework. The framework will have to be constructed in a way which allows the participants to balance competing interests in a pre-structured way. In other words: the Code does not provide an outcome for each and every question that can surface, but it does provide guidance in the manner in which unforeseen questions can be structurally tackled.[17]

As an extension of the idea of having flexible provisions, which allow the key players to act in a purposeful way, the researchers dug deeper into the question of how to conceive of strategies that qualify as 'purposeful'. This notion presupposes a general idea of why we have (rules of) criminal procedure. For here, the researchers suggested that the main objective of criminal procedure is to provide for an *adequate response* to crime. It is inevitable to phrase this in somewhat general terms. But there can be no misunderstanding that there is added value to accepting the 'adequate response to crime' as an overriding consideration in explaining why we adhere to a Code of Criminal Procedure. It is important to notice that this conception of the overriding objective of criminal procedure transcends the traditional point of view, according to which criminal procedure is just ('merely') the means to apply substantive criminal law. In our view, criminal procedure represents a value in and of itself. The implications of this view will be demonstrated in more detail in a moment.

The third and final preliminary assumption is of a somewhat different nature. It dictates that new coherent ideas on criminal

[17] Geert Knigge came up with the briljant metaphor of a CCP as a 'rubber band': G. Knigge, 'Een wetboek van elastiek', *Delikt en Delinkwent* 2000, pp. 222–232.

procedure need to take account of the international dimension. Contemporary criminal justice cannot do without an international perspective. This perspective comprises at least three component parts. The first is the case law of the European Court of Human Rights in Strasbourg. Over the past decades, the Court has provided guidance as to the minimum standards which must be observed in every domestic legal order, no matter the level or the nature of the crimes which have to be deterred and regardless what kind of (terrorist) threats are perceived to be in the air. Secondly, modern day criminal procedure needs to be equipped for effective international cooperation, both on the police level and in terms of judicial cooperation.[18] And finally, it is assumed that the central research question cannot be adequately tackled without adopting a comparative approach. Nowadays, it is no longer contested that fruitful research is only feasible by scrutinising other jurisdictions for original and successful solutions which might provide inspiration for designing similar practices in the Netherlands.

The next step, according to the proposed methodology, is to list the main interests which need to be served by a new and coherent CCP.

The first one of these is self evident and hardly needs any explanation or clarification: we want a fair and expeditious trial. It is conceded that there can be debate as to the precise delineation of the concept of 'fairness', but the principle as a bottom line benchmark stands firm. Similarly, it is contestable when exactly the standard of 'undue delay' is either met or violated, and one can argue that some expedited procedures are too fast for the defence to prepare adequately, but there is consensus about the fact that the general interest is served by having the trial completed within as little time as possible.

The second main interest that was identified is less obvious. It is a corollary of the general objective of criminal procedure to provide 'an adequate response to crime'. The researchers argued that the goal

---

[18] To this end, the concept of mutual recognition was discovered and developed. Potentially classic source on this: Jannemieke Ouwerkerk, *Quid Pro Quo? A comparative law perspective on the mutual recognition of judicial decisions in criminal matters*, Antwerp: Intersentia 2011.

of providing an adequate response can never be attained if the interests of all persons involved in the procedure are not properly taken into account. Traditionally, this was taken to mean that a CCP should balance interests of the defence and the prosecutor. Period. The researchers of 'Strafvordering 2001' felt this represents too narrow a view. They insisted that interests of 'third parties' also need protection in the Code. As a consequence, it was proposed that separate parts of the Code would have to deal with the position of the victim and the position of witnesses. These chapters would have to provide a comprehensive set of norms. Victims and witnesses should not exclusively be regarded in an instrumental way, that is, as individuals who can assist the government in procuring convictions (by reporting the crime, by giving testimony, etc.). The novel element here is that victims and witnesses were also depicted as individuals with needs and interests of their own, which need to be served and protected during the course of proceedings. Some of these needs can be acknowledged by awarding them procedural rights of their own. Hence the idea of creating separate chapters in the Code detailing the rights and obligations of these 'third parties'.

Finally, a more mundane consideration. The researchers introduced the concept of cost-efficiency as one of the interests that deserve attention in its own right. Every criminal justice system is inevitably handicapped by limited capacity. Capacity is by definition not unlimited because of available financial resources. The basic question will then be how to allocate insufficient funds in the best way possible. From this starting point the researchers have argued that resources should primarily be spend where the stakes are highest. To be more specific: in principle, you spend more resources in cases where there is reason to do so, either because of the severity of the case or because of special circumstances.[19] Conversely: legal

[19] The project has been criticised for entering financial considerations into the equation. Some academics have claimed that financial resources do not belong to the realm of principles which determine the systematic coherence of a CCP: C.H. Brants, P.A.M. Mevis & E. Prakken (eds.), *Legitieme strafvordering. Rechten van de mens als inspiratie in de 21e eeuw*, Antwerpem/Groningen: Intersentia 2001, pp. 1–21; and more specifically C.H. Brants, P.A.M. Mevis, E. Prakken & J.M. Reijntjes, 'Op zoek naar grondslagen', in: C.H. Brants c.s., *Op zoek naar grondslagen. Strafvordering 2001 ter discussie*, Den Haag: Boom Juridische uitgevers 2003, p. 25.

protection should not be offered (automatically) in situations where nobody is actually in need of it.

Articulating basic assumptions and the interests that need to be served are preliminary undertakings. Once that has been completed, the real task at hand is to make substantive choices and arrive at the main proposals. It is impossible to present a full picture of all the results that have been reached in the project. It took four heavy volumes to elaborate the main findings.[20] I will confine myself to briefly explain the three most conspicuous ideas that emerged from the project. Conspicuous, because it is this set of three ideas which form the heart of the framework that is to provide systemic coherence to a future CCP.

The proposals to explain concern *a.* the role of the judge in court; *b.* the interaction between the parties in the procedure; and *c.* a three track model of adjudication.

When it comes to the role of the judge in court, there are basically two models to choose from. The judge is either positioned as a referee, whose main responsibility is to make sure that the parties observe the rules of the game, or, alternatively, the judge is the leading authority in the fact finding process. In 'Strafvordering 2001', the latter option has been recommended.[21] According to the researchers, the judge[22] is responsible for a complete and careful trial. He has to decide whether all relevant material – either incriminating or exculpatory, aggravating or mitigating – has been presented in full.

---

[20] M.S. Groenhuijsen & G. Knigge (eds.), *Het onderzoek ter zitting. Eerste interimrapport onderzoeksproject Strafvordering 2001*, Groningen 1999 (463 pp); idem, *Het vooronderzoek in strafzaken. Tweede interimrapport onderzoeksproject Strafvordering 2001*, Deventer: Gouda Quint 2001 (755 pp); idem, *Dwangmiddelen en rechtsmiddelen. Derde interimrapport onderzoeksproject Strafvordering 2001*, Deventer: Kluwer 2002 (978 pp); and idem, *Afronding en verantwoording. Eindrapport onderzoeksproject Strafvordering 2001*, Deventer: Kluwer 2004 (602 pp).

[21] Which is in line with the obtaining Code. This recommendation is not really controversial. The researchers also proposed to keep to the tradition of having only professional judges (the Netherlands is one of few countries where no laymen participate in trying criminal cases). This has been challenged by some scattered academics and by some (predominantly right wing) politicians, but at present it does not look like major changes are to be expected.

[22] This can be a single judge or a panel of three judges.

If a gap is noticed, further investigation must be ordered. The judge has the power to determine which of the witnesses shall be heard in open court. If a witness or an expert testifies, the judge takes the lead in questioning – the prosecutor and the defence will only play a secondary part in questioning. The researchers conceive of adjudication as being more than just deciding the case: it also involves *communication*. An integral part of the job description of the judge is to be *responsive* to the parties. The CCP must contain a framework provision holding that when a party makes a well reasoned request or takes a position on fact or on law, the judge will either grant the request and agree with the point of view that was expressed, or he will expressly and supported by written arguments explain why he rules differently. The researchers refer to this general principle as a manifestation of a prominent feature of the trial as they see it: the trial as a structured form of dialogue – dialogue among the parties and dialogue between the parties and the judge.

The second main proposal is to better articulate the effects of the interaction between the participants in the trial. Maybe this sounds somewhat fuzzy or unclear, but in actual fact this touches the very heart of the kind of the reform the researchers are seeking. It aims at bringing more focus in a criminal trial. It is meant to avoid wasting time.

So how is 'the interaction between participants' defined and what benefits does it offer? The kind of interaction the researchers have in mind is closely linked to the concept of accountability. The idea is that a trial can be better focused by addressing the precise issues that keep the prosecutor and the defence apart. This can only be achieved if and when the parties disclose their positions at a relatively early stage of the proceedings.

The core essence of this proposal is that the prosecutor and the defence will to a large extent determine the agenda of the trial. Of course, in this respect the stage is set by the indictment. In the indictment the prosecutor spells out the charges brought against the defendant and in doing so he delineates the *objectum litis*. Next, the defence makes it clear whether or not there are elements in the indictment which are contested. If that is the case, it follows that the attention of the judge will be focused on the disputed parts of the accusation. Evidence concerning these items will be scrutinised with particular care. If the defence makes it clear that the facts of the charges are not challenged – like in a guilty plea in the USA – the agenda of the trial will be affected. It leads to a relatively 'quick check' of the evidence by the court, and the main focus of the trial will be redirected to the question of proportionate and appropriate sentencing.

This kind of interplay between the prosecution and the defence effectively introduces some elements into our trials which do compare to the adversarial systems in common law countries. For instance, it promotes an open 'dialogue' between the parties, under the supervision of the court. One example of this is the proposal by the research group to introduce[23] a preliminary hearing in court to determine and agree on how the actual trial should be prepared and conducted. This session comes close to what some American States refer to as a 'status hearing'. The hearing offers the parties an opportunity to express wishes as to the number of witnesses they want to see summoned and it offers a platform to discuss the desirability of additional investigative actions. All of this serves to be able to better plan the trial and avoid surprises which would lead to adjournment of trials and the unavoidable subsequent delays (not to speak of wasting valuable time of all professionals involved).

Another example would be to encourage the presence of the accused during trials. In The Netherlands, we have a tradition of having relatively many trials *in absentia*. While this practice offers some obvious advantages in terms of efficiency, it clearly compromises the quality of proceedings, because it precludes any kind of direct dialogue between the defendant and the court. Hence the research group proposes to reduce the number of trials by default. One concrete measure to this effect is to allow for pre-trial detention on the ground that this would ensure the presence of the accused during court proceedings.[24]

The proposed provisions on the content of the final verdict of the court are also aimed at promoting interaction between the

---

[23] Or rather: 'formalise', since this was already practised by some courts on an informal basis, without any foundation in the CCP.

[24] Naturally, this would only be allowed if some additional conditions are met; for the sake of the purpose of this chapter I can leave these details unreported.

parties involved. According to the research group, the reasoning of decisions taken by the court should again focus on the areas which have been disputed by the prosecutor and the defence. And if one of the parties has put forward a position which is on the one hand of crucial importance for the outcome of the case and is on the other hand declined by the court, the latter would need to carefully explain why it could not accept that point of view.

This approach is pursued with unwavering consistency until the very end of the proceedings. In the Netherlands, there are relatively large opportunities for a convicted person to challenge the outcome in a higher court. For instance, in every case where a custodial sanction has been imposed, there is a right to appeal. Under the existing CCP, an appeal would lead to a complete and full new trial. Almost as if nothing had been decided before. The research group felt this was wrong. It conceived of the appellate stage as a continuation of the trial in first instance. With the same underlying idea of structuring the proceedings as a streamlined dialogue between the parties under the supervision of the court. In operational terms this meant that a convicted person who appeals a judgment must argue with some precision which elements of the verdict he wants to challenge on appeal. The superior court can subsequently suffice with a scant review of all the other parts of the first verdict and can focus its attention on the specifically contested areas. Naturally, the court of appeals only has to give a reasoned ruling on this limited set of issues.

In this way and along these lines the research group has attempted to introduce some well tested and useful elements of an adversarial trial in an otherwise still moderately inquisitorial type of procedure.

The final main result that needs to be recorded here is the proposal to introduce a three track-model of adjudication. As noted before, the existing CCP basically prescribes a single unifying way of trying defendants. Whether the accused confesses or denies charges, whether the indictment concerns grave criminal acts or minor crimes, the Code provides for only small differentiations in the way of dealing with these facts. The research group was convinced a three track-model would be a superior way to acknowledge the vast differences that exist between the various charges a criminal justice system has to process. The idea behind is that we should spend the resources in a balanced way: that is, capacity of the justice system must be prioritised proportionate to the level of the interests of the accused and of the society that are at stake.

The first track is designed to adjudicate cases in which a long prison sentence might be imposed. The procedure in these cases is elaborate in the sense that it offers a larger number of legal safeguards for defendants than are available under the current CCP. Like before, these facts can only be tried by a panel of three judges. However, unlike the existing situation, the proposal of the research group holds that the principle of immediacy shall be restored to a large extent. The current practice of only hearing oral evidence in exceptional circumstances, shall be abolished. Instead, it is recommended that questioning witnesses in open court should be the rule rather than the exception. Implementing this proposal would amount to a major shift in the features of Dutch criminal procedure.

The second track is meant for cases of moderate severity. The researchers defined this category as crimes for which a penalty of no more than six months incarceration might be expected. The procedural rules guiding this track are very similar to the ones which apply under current legislation. This implies adjudication by a single judge and a time-efficient organisation of the trial, with heavy reliance on the case file and widespread use of hearsay evidence (*testimonium de auditu*, as recorded in affidavits and statements to the police).

Perhaps the most far reaching innovation concerns the proposed third track. It is intended to provide an adequate way of processing the vast number of less serious offenses, where no imprisonment is called for in case of conviction. During the past decades, these situations were largely dealt with by way of settlement out of court. The concept of settlement meant that it was mainly an agreement between the prosecutor and the offender. The substance of this arrangement was that the prosecutor promised to drop the case if and when the offender met certain conditions, most prominently among those paying a fine. Because it was an agreement, there was an element of voluntary consent involved. The latter point is exactly the main difference with the third track. According to this newly suggested procedure, the prosecutor will no longer offer a deal to the offender, but he will have the power to unilaterally impose a financial penalty.[25] What the arrangement comes down to, is essentially the following. A part of the administrative branch of government[26] can impose a penal sanction. The order in which the prosecutor makes use of that power, is directly enforceable without any interference or prior approval of a judge. Should the (presumed) offender disagree with the order, he can appeal to a court of law. In order to dissuade evidently unfounded appeals, the offender's appeal shall only be admissible if he pays an amount of money up front, which will be reimbursed if his complaints are succesful. When the case reaches the court in this way, the judge will see whether there is enough evidence to warrant conviction and he will check if the penalty is not excessive (that is: disproportionate to the seriousness of the crime). He can also increase the fine (*reformatio in peius* is possible). When the court sustains the order by the prosecutor, the offender will have one more opportunity to challenge this: he can turn to the Supreme Court, which will see whether legal errors have been made.

4. *HOW DID THE GOVERNMENT RESPOND TO THESE FINDINGS?*

4.1. Introduction

It is a well known fact that many large scale proposals on reform of the criminal justice system do not fare well. In recent history, one of the most dramatic of such experiences in the Western hemisphere

---

25 Such was the original idea, after the first year of the project had run its course. In subsequent stages, the central notion of unilaterally imposing a penalty was also examined in connection to other penal sanctions like community service and revoking a driver's license. This has led to a rather sophisticated system. For fines above a designated threshold and for other more serious sanctions, additional procedural safeguards can be added to the procedure. Among these is an obligation for the prosecutor to question the offender, during which interview the offender can be seconded by legal counsel. As far as the level of the fines is concerned, the researchers proposed to distinguish between ordinary crime and economic crime, and between individual offenders and legal persons as offenders. For each category a different ceiling was suggested.

26 This is a very sensitive designation. According to the Dutch Constitution, the prosecution service is part of the judiciary. 'Real judges' are in doctrinal writings

relates to the work of the 'Review of the Criminal Courts of England and Wales', which was carried out between 1999 and 2001 by a Committee chaired by Sir Robin Auld. The final product ('The Auld Review'), issued in 2001, was 686 pages long and included no less than 328 concrete recommendations. In its initial press release, the British government appeared to hail this achievement: 'It was welcomed by the government as an important contribution towards establishing modern, efficient criminal courts, that have fewer delays, are in touch with the communities they serve and respond to the needs of their users. The Auld Review fits in with the current review of sentencing and police reform to provide a criminal justice system that is respected, efficient and seen to deliver.'[27] Sir Robin Auld must have been pleased with this acclaim. During subsequent years, though, very little action was visible and at the time of our conference in November 2008, Sir Robin Auld had to conclude that virtually all of the Auld Review had ended up in some civil servants desk drawers and in government archives.

In The Netherlands, things turned out quite differently.[28] Shortly after the publication of the final volume with results from the research project, the Minister of Justice wrote a letter to the Parliament in which he announced a major legislative programme based on the findings of 'Strafvordering 2001'. The initiative was

---

referred to as the 'sitting judiciary', whereas prosecutors are part of the 'standing judiciary'. However, since the Minister of Justice is politically responsible for every act of the prosecutors office, and can be held to account by parliament for any such acts, in actual reality the position of the prosecution service can be described as part of the executive branch of the government.

[27] LCD press notice 342/01, date: 8 October 2001. According to the same press release, the Lord Chancellor, Lord Irvine, said: 'The government is grateful to Sir Robin Auld for his very substantial and important review of the criminal courts at every level. He offers a stimulating vision of what a modern criminal justice system should be…'. The Home Secretary, David Blunkett, said: 'The Auld Review is a vital part in our programme of reform of the criminal justice system.' The Attorney General, Lord Goldsmith, said: 'These and his many other important recommendations make a radical and thoughtful contribution to the process of reshaping the criminal justice system for the future, and are deserving of the widest consultation and most careful consideration.'

[28] One of the most important sources of information on the government's response to 'Strafvordering 2001' is the inaugural address delivered by Tijs Kooijmans at Tilburg University on March 18, 2011: *Dat is mijn zaak!*, Tilburg 2011.

labelled 'General Framework Reform Code of Criminal Procedure'.[29] Subsequently, a long list of separate Acts have been introduced to Parliament, all aiming to reform the CCP in a way that consistently corresponds with the body of ideas underlying the recommendations of the research group. During the following years, quite a few of these amendments have been adopted and entered into force, while others are still pending in the legislative process.

In the parliamentary year 2007–2008, the Minister of Justice took stock of what had already been achieved and announced the next steps in further reforming criminal procedure.[30] His communication culminated in the announcement of 'Strafvordering 2011', a highly creative working title for the complete package of reformist legislation in this area. It refers to the intention of the Ministry of Justice to have this part of the recodification process completed by the year 2011.

I will now list the more significant pieces of legislation which have directly emanated from the research project 'Strafvordering 2001'.

4.2. Disposal by the Public Prosecutor

In line with the recommendation to introduce a 'third track' as outlined above, an Act was introduced – and adopted[31] – which gave the prosecutor the power to unilaterally impose criminal sanctions. This is possible in cases where a crime has been committed which is punishable by law with a prison sentence of up to six years. This disposition can involve a fine, a compensation order, a community service order (with a maximum of 180 hours), or revoking a driver's license. Additionally, asset forfeiture and directives concerning future behaviour of the offender can also be included. Community service orders and depriving the offender of the permit to drive a motor vehicle is only allowed when the perpetrator is personally

---

29 *General Framework Reform Code of Criminal Procedure*: *Parliamentary Papers II* 2003/04, 29 271, nr. 1.

30 *General Framework Reform Code of Criminal Procedure*: *Parliamentary Papers II* 2007/08, 29 271, nr. 7.

31 *Parliamentary Papers II* 2004/05, 29 849; *Bulletin of Acts and Decrees* (*Staatsblad*) 2006, 330. The Act went into force in 2008.

heard by the prosecutor and the former has indicated his willingness to comply with the penalty. Fines and compensation orders exceeding an amount of € 2000 can only be imposed after the offender is interviewed by the prosecutor in the presence of a defence lawyer. The disposition by the prosecutor can be challenged within 14 days, which will then lead to a full and ordinary trial.

The Act deviates from the proposals of 'Strafvordering 2001' on a number of specifics. These details need not be elaborated here.[32] I just draw attention to two of the discrepancies. One is that the completely passive perpetrator will automatically be punished in the third track of 'Strafvordering 2001', while a judicial check will take place according to the ideas of the government in case the offender doesn't execute, for example, the community service order. Secondly, when an offender does challenge the order issued by the prosecutor, he will enter the 'normal' court system, with all available remedies. This means that he can get a court decision, he has the right to appeal that decision, and after that he can appeal to the Supreme Court. To some, this might look like it takes away an awful lot of the gains in efficiency which justified this kind of proposals in the first place.

4.3. Promoting Dialogue between Parties and Bench

A distinct feature of 'Strafvordering 2001' was to borrow carefully selected elements of an adversarial system which can be productively accommodated within the environment of a trial which retaines a more moderately inquisitorial nature. Apparently, this idea was also appealing to the legislative.

In 2005, the 'Act on confessing defendants' entered into force. This Act includes two provisions which are directly inspired by the idea to stimulate more productive substantive dialogue between the parties and the judge.

The first one of these is about the reasoning of a court verdict. In the old days, the reasoning was governed by requirements in the

---

32 For a more detailed discussion, see M.S. Groenhuijsen & J.B.H.M. Simmelink, 'Het wetsvoorstel OM-afdoening op het grensvlak van juridische techniek en strafprocessuele uitgangspunten', in: A.H.E.C. Jordaans c.s. (eds.), *Praktisch strafrecht. Liber amicorum J.M. Reijntjes*, Nijmegen: Wolf Legal Publishers 2005, pp. 171–196.

CCP which did not distinguish between confessing defendants and those who denied all charges. Now this has changed. According to the amended law, it is no longer deemed to be necessary to explain at length why the court finds the accused guilty if he himself admits the charges brought against him. In these instances, simple references to the incriminating pieces of evidence will suffice, without elucidating the precise content of these relevant statements and documents.

The second reform to be pointed out here concerns a new provision on the type and kind of arguments brought forward by the parties which need to be addressed explicitly in the courts' verdict. In the 2005 Act a full sentence was added to the existing article 359, section 2 CCP. Basically, it holds that if and when either the defence or the prosecutor puts forward 'a particularly reasoned point of view' which is not accepted by the court, the latter will have to explain its reasons for declining this point of view in the written verdict. In other words: when a party has extensively argued a specific point,[33] and the court adopts a different position, than this needs explicit explanation and justification. It is obvious that this new provision contributes to the dialogue between the parties and the bench.[34]

4.4. Victims

Another area where the proposals by 'Strafvordering 2001' have been accepted virtually chapter and verse by the government is the reform on behalf of victims of crime.

Like in many countries, during the last decades the position of victims within criminal procedure has been a topic of volatile debate in The Netherlands. In 1992, the Terwee-Act entered into force, with new rights for those victims who endeavoured to claim damages

---

33 The point of view that needs to be addressed explicitly may concern a dispute about the facts of the case, or a point of law or an observation on the required or appropriate level of punishment (e.g. mitigating or aggravating circumstances). In its case law, the Supreme Court has provided guidelines as to what exactly is to be considered as a 'particularly reasoned point of view' in article 359, section 2 CCP: Supreme Court April 11, 2006, *Nederlandse Jurisprudentie* 2006, 393.

34 See J.W. Fokkens, 'De wijziging van art. 359 lid 2 Sv: een stap op weg naar een contradictoir strafproces', in: A. Harteveld, D.H. de Jong & E. Stamhuis (eds.), *Systeem in ontwikkeling. Liber amicorum Geert Knigge*, Nijmegen: Wolf Legal Publishers 2005, pp. 139–149.

from the offender during the criminal procedure (this is usually referred to as the 'adhesion procedure'). It should be noted, though, that even after this improvement of the standing of victims in the various stages of the criminal procedure, the victim still only had legal rights when he performed in a derived capacity: like someone reporting a crime, or as a witness, as a civil claimant, etc. The CCP still did not include a single identifiable right for the victim a such.

This was altered in 2005, with the introduction of the 'victim impact statement'. In cases of severe crime, the victim was henceforth allowed to orally explain to the court in what way the crime had affected him or her.[35, 36]

The latest and most comprehensive development here is the 'Act on the strengthening of the position of the victim in criminal procedure', which came into force on Januari 1, 2011.[37] The Act provides for a wide range of new victims' rights. It reflects the recommendation made by 'Strafvordering 2001' to create a separate chapter in the CCP neatly listing the most important rights victims shall have throughout the criminal procedure. Prominent among these are the right to be treated correctly (i.e. with respect for their dignity), the right to receive information about the progress of the case, the right to inspect the case-file and legal assistance. The new chapter in the CCP with dedicated victims' rights is important from two angles. One is a *symbolic* one. Having an entire chapter solely dealing with

35 This particular victims' right was first recommended in the first interim report of 'Strafvordering 2001' (p. 47, p. 271). When the government refused to take immediate action in this direction (understandably so, since the Minister of Justice wanted to wait for the project to be completed and then consider a comprehensive set of balanced measures), the proposal on the victim impact statement was 'hijacked' by a member of Parliament, Boris Dittrich, who introduced a bill of his own, which ultimately led to the amendment to the CCP that was adopted as a law dated July 21, 2004 (*Staatsblad* 2004, 282), entering into force on January 1, 2005.

36 Interestingly, the victim impact statement was at first predominantly opposed by the judiciary. They cautioned that the v.i.s. might lead to emotial trials, that it would cause delays and unequality in sentencing, and that it might even go against the best interests of victims. In the end, none of these drawbacks materialized. See Kim Lens c.s., *Het spreekrecht in Nederland: een bijdrage aan het emotioneel herstel van slachtoffers?*, Tilburg: INTERVICT 2010.

37 The Act had a long and bumpy Parliamentary history. The initial governmental proposal was bombarded with amendments by Parliament, and in the end it took quite a while after the adoption of the Act before it could enter into force. For the records, see *Parliamentary Papers II*, 30 143.

the position of the victim, finally places the victim on an equal footing with the other participants in the criminal procedure (the defendant, the prosecutor, the examining magistrate, witnesses and experts[38]). That is a meaningful way to acknowledge victimisation: it is an expression of social solidarity indicating that the victim should no longer be alienated from the criminal trial. Secondly, this catalogue of victims' rights also has a distinct *legal* effect. The new provisions were necessary to finally comply with the requirements of EU law. In 2001, the EU adopted its Framework Decision on the Standing of Victims in Criminal Proceedings.[39] Even though the Framework Decision is supposed to contain only minimum standards, subsequent evaluation reports[40] indicated that *none* – I have to repeat: *none* – of the member States fully complied with its provisions. It looks like the blancs noticed by the European Commission have been filled by the amendments of the CCP as per Januari 1, 2011.

Two additional observations are called for. The first one is that the current Dutch system can be considered to represent 'best practice' as far as the enforcement of a compensation order is concerned. Up until 1992, any claim for damages that was awarded by the court, had to be executed by the victim himself. In a majority of cases, this led to a complete failure to actually regain any money. Starting with the Terwee-Act of 1992, the government took over the responsibility making the offender pay the amount of the compensation order. The result was that over 75% of these orders became effective. However, that still left almost a quarter of the victims with empty hands. Under the new rules the government will pay the relevant amount of money up front to the victim and will then proceed to recover the sum from the offender.[41] This is a revolutionary step forward; an example for many other jurisdictions to follow.

The second remaining observation is a sobering one. Now that the Netherlands has finally reached a legislative level of sophistication

---

[38] I will deal with the position of expert momentarily.

[39] 15 March 2001, 2001/220/JHA.

[40] The most recent one is the '*Report from the Commision pursuant to Article 18 of the Council Framework Decision of 15 March 2001 on the standing of victims in criminal proceedings* (*2001/220/JHA*), Brussels, 20.4.2009, COM(2009)166 final.

[41] During the First stage this arrangement is limited to compensation orders pertaining to violent crime and sexual crime. There is also a ceiling (a cap) to the size of the damages dealt with in this way.

that is apparently required by the existing Framework Decision, the European Commission has decided that it is time for the next step. In May of 2011, the Commission proposed a 'legislative package' with several additional, highly aspirational victims' rights, which will have to be transposed into domestic legislation in the member States. Most prominent part of this package is a *'Proposal for a Directive of the European Parliament and of the Council establishing minimum standards on the rights, support and protection of victims of crime'*.[42] I seriously doubt the wisdom of this approach. It would have made more sense to insist on adequate Union-wide implementation of – and compliance with – the old standards before insisting on new ones which are clearly unattainable by a majority of the member States.

4.5. Mandatory Blood Sample Testing

When a woman has been sexually abused, or when a violent crime has taken place where body liquids of the perpetrator and the victim have been in direct contact, the result can be that the victim is extremely anxious of having contracted a dangerous contagious disease. For quite a long time, this kind of understandable and legitimate fears could not be adequately addressed within our system of criminal procedure.[43] An Act of November 2009 changed this deplorable situation.[44] This Act provides for mandatory testing of suspects in criminal cases to see whether they have been infected with AIDS/HIV, dangerous types of Hepatitus and similar diseases specified in an accompanying Order in Council. The presumed offender will first be asked by the prosecutor to voluntarily submit to a test. If he refuses, he can then be ordered to be tested, following a written authorisation by the examining magistrate.[45] The victim is entitled by law to request the prosecutor to make use of these powers. If a test is carried out, the results will be disclosed 'as soon as

---

42 Brussels, 18 May 2011, COM(2011) 275 final.

43 The only remedy available for these victims was to go to civil court. It goes without saying that this route was hazardous and expensive and hence not very attractive for victims.

44 Act of November 12, 2009 (*Staatsblad* 475), which entered into force on July 1, 2010 (preparatory documents under number 31 241).

45 The specifics can be found in articles 151[e]–151i CCP.

possible' to both the suspect and the victim. In case of a negative outcome, the prosecutor can repeat the same process after a period ranging from three to six months. When there is a positive result (i.e. infection) and it turns out that the victim is infected with the same disease, the prosecutor has the power to charge an expert with the question to see whether there is a causal link between the crime and the infection suffered by the victim.

This is an important new instrument to protect the interests (i.e. the peace of mind) of crime victims. The significance of this reform lies in the fact that traditionally coercive powers can only be used within the framework of criminal justice if it can contribute to the fact finding process pertaining to criminal charges.[46] This new legal power serves a completely different, unrelated objective. It fits with one of the overarching basic assumptions underlying 'Strafvordering 2001', stipulating that the main objective of criminal procedure is to provide for an overall *adequate response to crime*. It should not come as a surprise that the new Act on mandatory blood sample testing is a carbon copy of the recommendations made by the research group.

4.6. Streamlining of the Appeals Procedure

On July 1, 2007 a new milestone was achieved in reforming Dutch criminal justice along the lines suggested by 'Strafvordering 2001'. On this day an Act 'on streamlining the appeal stage' of criminal proceedings entered into force.[47]

As noted before, filing an appeal used to lead to a complete, comprehensive second trial, at the level of the court of appeals. This amounted to a waste of a lot of time and energy, since many of the procedural moves and interim-decisions which had not been contested, were repeated again without having any added value.

---

[46] The only other goal which justifies the use of coercive powers is to secure the presence of persons or goods. Hence the existence of pre-trial detention and confiscation powers.

[47] Act of October 5, 2006, coming into force on July 1, 2007. Preparatory documents under nr. 30 320. More on this in P.G. Wiewel & R.E. de Winter (eds.), *Stroomlijning van het hoger beroep in strafzaken*, Nijmegen: Ars Aequi Libri 2007.

The present Act aims to avoid unnecessary duplication of judicial inquiries. The party lodging an appeal will have to state the grounds for his dissatisfaction with the rulings in first instance, and the trial on appeal will then focus on these specific complaints. It suffices to repeat the same example mentioned before: when the defendant appeals the verdict because he feels the sentence is too severe, the court of appeals can deal with any evidentiary issue in a perfunctory way and move very quickly to the facts and circumstances that should determine the proper penalty in the case.[48]

A further reduction of workload was achieved by an adjoining Act which allows for more cases to be tried on appeal by a single judge instead of a panel of three judges. This innovation is also in conformity with the advice provided by 'Strafvordering 2001'.

However, in reforming the appeal stage of proceedings, the changes in the CCP deviate in one important respect from the views expressed in 'Strafvordering 2001'. In minor cases, i.e. where there has been a conviction to a fine of a truly minor amount of money (≤ € 500), a system of 'leave to appeal' was introduced. In these cases the presiding judge of the court of appeals will see whether or not a new, second trial would 'serve the interests of a proper administration of justice' (article 410a CCP). If the answer is in the affirmative, he will order the case to be tried on appeal. If the presiding judge finds that no genuine interest of justice is at stake, he will give a reasoned ruling to this effect. This ruling counts as a final decision on the appeal.[49]

---

[48] Vellinga correctly poses the question whether an opportunity has been missed to even further turn the appellate stage into an adversarial kind of procedure. He feels that a truly consistent approach would have led to a situation in which the trial would be started by the party explaining his objections to the outcome in first instance, to be followed by a rebuttal by the other party, an exchange of views which would form the basis for further inquiries to be made by the court: W.H. Vellinga, 'Hoger beroep in verandering', *Trema* 2007, pp. 74–84; also see Kooijmans 2011, p. 57.

[49] Both the ECHR (22 Februari 2011, appl.nr. 26036/08, Lalmahomed v. the Netherlands) and the Human Rights Committee of the United Nations (27 July 2010, Communication no. 1797/2008, Mennen v. The Netherlands) have judged that certain aspects of this leave to appeal violate the accused's right to a fair trial.

4.7. Experts

The large number of recommendations made by 'Strafvordering 2001' are built on quite a few interfaces. One of the recurrent propositions by the research group was that the legal position of all the main players in criminal procedure should in broad term be defined in separate chapters of the CCP. As in the case of victims and witnesses, the same recommendation was made in connection to the role of experts.

Traditionally, the CCP was virtually silent on quality standards for experts and expert-witnesses. This even came to the point of the standard joke among Dutch legal professionals, holding that "an expert is everyone carrying a briefcase who is more than ten miles from home".

All of this changed with the adoption and subsequent introduction of the 'Act on experts in criminal cases'.[50] The CCP now stipulates that quality standards shall be laid down in an Order in Council and that rules will be elaborated on the way compliance with these quality standards can be monitored. There is a separate package of requirements a written report by an expert must comply with. The expert has to give and explain the reasoning underlying his report, the method he has used reaching his conclusions, he must explain the extent of the reliability of this method and the results which it has yielded, and he must provide information about his own ability in using this method (article 51l CCP). On top of that, a national register is being compiled, comprising all experts who have been accredited. If a prosecutor or a judge wants to make use of the services of an expert not included in the National register, that is only allowed when it is explicitly argued why the relevant person can be labelled as an expert in the relevant field (article 51k CCP).

5. *REFLECTION ON GENERAL TRENDS*

In the preceding sections, I have outlined the main results of the research project 'Strafvordering 2001' and the governments'

[50] Act of January 1, 2009 (*Staatsblad* 33), entering into force on October 1, 2010.

response to these findings. It is obvious that the project has been quite influential. Looking back, it is appropriate to try to put the developments which have been detailed into perspective. Taking stock of the overall reform of criminal procedure during the past decade, I have identified three main trends.

The first general trend can be summarised as follows. Where new legislation deviated from the proposals by 'Strafvordering 2001', generally speaking the adopted provisions have been more repressive (i.e. more focused on crime control) than the researchers have recommended. There are quite a few examples to illustrate this trend.

In the preceding section, the changes in the appeals procedure have already been mentioned. While many of the new provisions were mirror images of the proposals of 'Strafvordering 2001', there was one conspicuous exception. The novel kind of 'leave to appeal' procedure (article 410a CCP) in cases of lesser importance is distinctly different from what the researchers had in mind. There can be no doubt that it constitutes a more government oriented regime, which compromises defendants' rights which were hitherto considered to be fair and reasonable.

Another example concerns the approach adopted in connection with terrorist acts. Now, it has to be submitted that the research project was well under way when the attacks of 9/11 took place. The basic choices had been made, the main structural elaborations were in place, and the notion of establishing specific procedural rules to deal with acts of terrorism was completely alien to the established lines of reasoning. In actual reality, though, the events of 9/11 propelled the international legal community into action. The European Union adopted a Framework Decision on this subject matter, obliging its member states to adapt their domestic systems of criminal law and criminal procedure.[51] Hence, after the completion of our research project, the Dutch legislation was amended to deal with this specific type of crime. In criminal procedure, two elements stand out to demonstrate how individual defendants' rights were curtailed. The first one is about pre-trial detention. Whereas in

[51] Framework Decision of 13 June 2002 on combating terrorism (as amended by Council Framework Decision 2008/919/JHA of 28 November 2008).

ordinary cases the maximum period of custody would be 90 days, for terrorist crimes the duration was extended to a maximum of nothing less than two years (article 66, section 3 CCP). The other significant part of the more repressive system in this area is about what common law systems would probably refer to as 'disclosure'. In short, during pre-trial stages defendants in cases of terrorist activities can be precluded from inspecting the case file for a prolonged time. The respective provisions diverge from the rules pertaining to 'ordinary' suspects to such an extent that it has even been argued in the academic literature that they are at odds with the case-law of the European Court of Human Rights.[52]

The second main trend that I have identified somewhat relates to the first one. To be very brief: the zero-sum concept of 'Strafvordering 2001' did not materialise. The idea of our project was to find some resources within those parts of the criminal justice system where the existing level of safeguards looks disproportionate, and then spend these savings elsewhere in the system, in areas where additional protection for defendants and others is really needed. The bottom line has been explained in previous sections. Since our CCP traditionally did not acknowledge what in many countries would be called the difference between a 'real trial' and a 'sentence hearing', the researchers argued that quite a few procedural provisions on fact finding are redundant in cases where the defendant confesses to the charges. More generally speaking, the researchers wanted the bench only to address issues which keep the prosecution and the defence apart. That would safe time. That would assure meaningful use of scarce capacity of the court system. Thus the basic proposition of 'Strafvordering 2001'.

In actual practice, a large number of our proposals which make the system operate cheaper and more efficient have been accepted. A readily available example is the introduction of the 'third track' mode of disposition of cases as discussed in the previous sections.

---

[52] T. Kooijmans & J.B.H.M. Simmelink, 'Het recht op kennisneming van de processtukken in het Wetsvoorstel tot verruiming van de mogelijkheden tot opsporing en vervolging van terroristische misdrijven', *Delikt en Delinkwent* 2006, pp. 1107–1126, with additional references.

On the other hand, though, the proposals which would have required new investments by the government have largely been rejected or ignored. The most conspicuous example of this mechanism concerns the fate of the so-called 'first track'. As was presented in the above, the first track is about cases where a long prison sentence is expected to be imposed. According to the research team, the presently obtaining way of organising a trial in these cases offers too little safeguards in terms of legal protection of the defendant. 'Strafvordering 2001' argued for restoration of the principle of immediacy in the first track. Instead of a trial based to a large extent on the case file, it should be standard practice to summon incriminating witnesses to court in order to give oral testimony. None of this happened. The plea for more procedural safeguards in the most serious cases fell on deaf ears.

The third main trend can be described as follows. Not all parts of the reform of the criminal procedure during the past couple of years have been inspired by "Strafvordering 2001'. Unsurprisingly, there have also been major innovations and changes which have been driven by completely unrelated sources.

As far as I can see the most prominent example of this is caused by the occurrence (or rather: the revelation) of several miscarriages of justice. Some of the most notorious of these incidents are known as the 'Schiedam murder case', the 'Putten murder case' and the case of 'Lucia de Berk'.[53] These sad cases have led to an avalanche of criticism, both by the public at large and in particular by experts from the world of science.[54] Massive criticism forced the government to

---

53 In our country, there is the custom to refer to defendants in criminal trials by their initials only. So the latter case was always mentioned in the media as the case against 'Lucia de B.". Only after she was finally acquitted, she took the public stage under her full name: Lucia de Berk.

54 The intensity of the criticism might be explained by the fact that in the Netherlands, we were not used to the phenomenon of exposed miscarriages of justice. To illustrate this, I recall that even as recent as during the early 1990-tees, three of the most prominent scholars in law and psychology solicited so-called 'suspect' cases from the defense bar. One might expect that quite a lot of dirt would turn up. However, during the entire project they were not able to show a single instance of wrongful conviction. See H.F.M. Crombag, P.J. van Koppen & W.A. Wagenaar, *Dubieuze zaken: de psychologie van strafrechtelijk bewijs*, Amsterdam: Contact 1994 (second revised edition).

respond by taking measures which are supposed to reduce the risk of new mistakes being made or to correct court decisions which can be demonstrated to be wrong. Here are the most important reforms of criminal procedure emanating from these developments:

First, the government decided on a comprehensive programme to reinforce the process of investigation.[55] The programme is designed in order to improve the quality of the fact finding process, particularly in its early stages. Quite often, the police will have a suspect and focus to a large extent on collecting incriminating evidence. Now, according to the new internal rules, it becomes mandatory to systematically organise dissent within the organisation. This means that officers within the force will be demanded to take a critical look at the investigation and to see if there are other leads which may have to be followed. Making the same point from another angle, it is now considered to be 'state of the art' police work to always reckon with the potential validity of 'different stories', i.e. alternative scenarios exonerating the suspect. Needless to say, all of this is intended to avoid police investigations from being (mis)guided by some sort of 'tunnel vision'.

The initial stage of any investigation is quite often decisive for its final outcome. Hence, it is imperative that mistakes are prevented during the first crucial parts in the criminal procedure. Special attention must be payed to the interrogation of the defendant by the police. Some of the miscarriages of justice were partly – or mainly – based on a confession by the suspect which later on turned out not to correspond to the facts.[56] Consequently, new administrative rules were introduced to systematically caution against false admissions of guilt. As part of this parcel, police were instructed to videotape interviews with defendants in serious cases. On top of that, experiments were initiated in several cities in which a defence lawyer was allowed to be physically present during the first police interview with the suspect. Ironically, right when these experiments were running, Dutch policy makers were overtaken by external forces.

---

55 *Versterking opsporing en vervolging naar aanleiding van de Schiedammer parkmoord* (OM/Politie/NFI 4 november 2005).

56 This was particularly hurting in the Schiedam-case.

In 2008, the Strasbourg Court of Human Rights issued judgements in the cases of Salduz and Panovits.[57] In the Netherlands, it was argued by some academics that these decisions held that all suspects had the right to be physically assisted by a defence attorney during the first interview by the police.[58] Others interpreted the Court's rulings in a different, a more restricted way.[59] The Dutch Supreme Court brought a temporary end to the confusion by ruling that adolescents had an unqualified right to have an attorney present during the police interrogation, whereas in adult cases a right to consult defence counsel prior to the interview would suffice.[60] After more debate, the government circulated a draft amendment to the CCP on this issue (on 15 April 2011). According to this proposal, the right to have a lawyer present during the police interview will be extended to adults who are suspected of having perpetrated a crime punishable by a maximum of no less than six years imprisonment. This can only be refused by the police 'in the best interest of the investigation'. The defendant can waive this right only after consulting an attorney. For juveniles, the proposal holds that *every* suspect shall consult a lawyer before the first police interview. These developments make it abundantly clear that the provisions on how to conduct police interviews with defendants have moved way beyond the horizon of the research project 'Strafvordering 2001'.

Another emergency measure responding to the exposure of some embarrassing miscarriages of justice was the creation, in 2006, of a special Commission (the so-called CEAS) to re-examine cases which had been closed for a longer time. In very serious cases (maximum penalty 12 years plus) where someone is convicted and his prison sentence is still pending, a 'professional' with some involvement in

---

[57] ECHR 27 November 2008, appl.nr. 36391/02 (Salduz v. Turkey); ECHR 11 December 2008, appl.nr. 4268/04 (Panovits v. Cyprus).

[58] T. Spronken, 'Ja, de zon komt op voor de raadsman bij het politieverhoor!', *Nederlands Juristenblad* 2009, pp. 94–100; A.J.M. de Swart, 'Enkele ontwikkelingen na *Salduz/Panovits*: toch nog een advocaat bij het politieverhoor?', *Nederlands Juristenblad* 2010, pp. 223–226; idem, 'Update *Salduz*-doctrine. Toch nog een raadsman bij het politieverhoor? Part II', *Nederlands Juristenblad* 2010, pp. 2692–2695.

[59] M.J. Borgers, 'Een nieuwe dageraad voor de raadsman bij het politieverhoor?', *Nederlands Juristenblad* 2009, pp. 88–93; idem, 'De ijdele hoop van *Pishchalnikov* en *Brusco*', *Nederlands Juristenblad* 2010, pp. 2818–2819.

[60] Supreme Court 30 June 2009, *Nederlandse Jurisprudentie* 2009, 349.

the case[61] who has doubts about the outcome, can send a 'signal of a wrongful conviction' to the Commission. The Commission has a separate 'chamber' which decides on the admissibility of the case. If this chamber decides that there is sufficient reason for further inquiries, it will refer the case to a panel of three experts drawn from a large pool, which will then substantively review the entire process of investigation and prosecution which has transpired during the proceedings leading up to the conviction.[62] The review includes personal interviews with the police and with prosecutors who have handled the case. It can also take the form of hearing outside scientific (forensic) experts. At the end of its mandate, the panel will submit its report to the Board of Directors of the Prosecution Service.[63] The report will be made public. Subsequently, the Prosecution Service will determine what happens next. After five years of operation, it can be concluded that the recommendations made by the various panels have been accepted by the prosecution. In some cases this has resulted in additional revision procedures and ultimately in the release of a wrongfully convicted person.[64]

The final reform that was not propelled by the findings of 'Strafvordering 2001' concerned an extension of the revision procedure.[65] Revision is – by nature – a very special instrument. It means that a fully completed criminal case, in which all legal remedies have been exhausted, will be reopened. Needless to say, one ought to be very careful in making this instrument available. Otherwise, no

---

[61] According to the explanatory notes accompanying this admistrative regulation, the professionals include police, prosecutors, members of the National Forensic Science Service, or academics who have studied the case. Defence attorneys and the convicted person are precluded from approaching the Commission.

[62] Note that the review concerns investigation and prosecution: the Commission does not have the power to review the trial or any other judicial act (like the verdict). The panel of three experts is usually composed of a senior prosecutor (at the appellate level), an academic, and a former senior police officer.

[63] This Board has created the entire structure of the Commission.

[64] The work of the Commission was evaluated after three years. See J. de Ridder, C.M. Klein Haarhuis & W.M. de Jongste, *De CEAS aan het werk. Bevindingen over het functioneren van de Commissie Evaluatie Afgesloten Strafzaken 2006–2008*, Den Haag september 2008.

[65] A summary of the proposals and more specific references can be found in *Nederlands Juristenblad* 2008, pp. 1776–1777.

serious criminal case would ever come to an end. Yet, against the background of the previously mentioned miscarriages of justice and in light of the operation of the CEAS, the government felt that the existing conditions for having a revision procedure were too restrictive. In 2008, it was proposed to allow some more leeway. Most importantly, the production of new expert evidence will be somewhat easier accepted as a ground for reconsidering the case, if and when there is 'a considerable likelihood' that the court would have given a different verdict had it been aware of this new information. A second major change is that after a revision procedure has been opened, there will be new opportunities to investigate the case. Until now, the 'retrial' had to be conducted solely on the basis of the factual evidence collected during the initial investigation. Then there was a fundamentally new idea incorporated in the reform proposals. Traditionally, the revision procedure served exclusively to the benefit of the convicted person. Now it was suggested that revision also be possible in order to reverse an acquittal of the defendant. In very serious cases, where new and very convincing incriminating evidence (DNA, for example) has been found, the government feels that – under strict conditions – a new trial should no longer be categorically excluded.[66]

6. *CONCLUSION*

We are at the end of a long story. From inception to completion, the research project 'Strafvordering 2001' ran for some six years. It has been a unique academic endeavour. In legal research; this kind of teamwork is very rare. The results of the project went way beyond our expectations. Take the sheer size of it. It took four volumes and close to 3000 pages to report our findings. To put things into perspective: the bulkyness of the output became a separate cause for critics to complain about. They argued – never in print, but back stage – that the magnitude of our reports prevented ordinary academics from seriously studying the soundness of our recommendations. With hindsight, I feel there is some merit in this argument.

[66] Once again, the details of this proposition are not relevant to elaborate.

Probably, the project leaders would have been wise to condense the main findings in a small book of some 200 pages. That would have greatly benefitted the accessibility of the results.[67]

Perhaps the material was too rich in scope and in detail for the average professional in criminal law. It most certainly was well received by the lawmakers it was aimed at. As detailed in the preceding sections, 'Strafvordering 2001' has been uncommonly influential. The main line of reasoning as outlined in the project has proved to be convincing for our government and for our parliament.[68] During the years following the reports, many recommendations were incorporated in new Acts and Statutes amending the CCP in a systematic way. As a result, today the internal structure of the CCP looks much more coherent than it did a decade ago.

Of course, reform of criminal procedure is an ongoing process. It never stops. The demands of a dynamic society require flexible responses by the criminal justice system. In the previous sections, we have seen that this process tends to overemphasize the requirements and values of crime control. The other side of the coin, i.e. the protection of legal safeguards ensuring a due process of law, is apparently less self evident. Hence it is of paramount importance to continue to advocate maintaining a proper balance between the two perspectives.

Finally, I have to point out that reforming criminal procedure entails more than just amending the CCP. It is relatively easy to adopt new provisions, but it is infinitely more difficult to make them work as intended and to avoid unintended and undesirable side-effects. This is probably the real challenge for the immediate future. Our goal should be to have a Code of Criminal Procedure which meets contemporary needs and which is at the same time functional and well functioning.

---

[67] Likewise, it would have been fitting to publish a similar book to disseminate the content of the project in English.

[68] I once more refer to the *Algemeen kader herziening Wetboek van Strafvordering* (General Framework for Reform of the Code of Criminal Procedure), *Kamerstukken II* 2003/04, 29 271, nr. 1; and *Kamerstukken II* 2007/08, 29 271, nr. 7.

THE EXTRAJUDICIAL DISPOSAL OF CRIMINAL CASES

Tijs Kooijmans[1]

1. INTRODUCTION

Traditionally, in the system of the Dutch law of criminal procedure, it is the criminal court which has ultimately been charged with the disposal of offences. That system, on which the Dutch Code of Criminal Procedure (*Wetboek van Strafvordering*) (hereinafter referred to as CCP) is based – in which the criminal court judge, not only on the basis of the results of the preliminary investigation (conducted by different authorities), but also on the basis of the examination he conducted independently in court, forms an opinion on the criminal case presented by the Public Prosecution Service – is a manner of disposal which is not still used in all cases by far. Corstens states that of the total of approximately 257,000 court cases disposed of in 2007, about 40% were disposed of by the Public Prosecution Service, for example through settlement penalties and conditional dismissals.[2] Characteristic of these disposal modalities, which can be considered forms of out-of-court settlement of criminal cases, is that they are based on consensus.[3] In other words, these are manners of disposal in which the consent or cooperation of the accused is needed.

On 1 February 2008, the range of extrajudicial disposal modalities was expanded. On that date, part of the Public Prosecution Service

---

[1] Professor of criminal law, Department of Criminal Law, Tilburg University.

[2] G.J.M. Corstens, *Het Nederlands strafprocesrecht*, sixth impression, Deventer: Kluwer 2008, pp. 11–12.

[3] A settlement penalty (Art. 74 Dutch Criminal Code (*Wetboek van Strafrecht*)) entails that the public prosecutor can set conditions prior to the start of the trial to avoid criminal prosecution for summary offences and for crimes carrying imprisonment not exceeding six years according to their statutory description. A conditional dismissal (Art. 167(2) and Art. 244(3) and Art. 245(3) CCP) entails that the Public Prosecution Service, while setting certain conditions, can postpone the decision on (further) prosecution that has to take place for a certain period determined therein. Unlike the settlement penalty, a conditional dismissal can be applied to any offence.

(Settlement) Act (*Wet OM-afdoening*) entered into effect.[4] In essence, the Public Prosecution Service (Settlement) Act comes down to an adjustment of the legal basis of the extrajudicial disposal of criminal cases.[5] Whereas the legal structure of the still existing settlement penalty as referred to in Art. 74 of the Dutch Criminal Code (hereinafter: CC) entails that – if the accused fulfils the settlement conditions – the Public Prosecution Service refrains from (further) prosecution, and the settlement penalty therefore serves to avoid (further) prosecution,[6] the concept of the 'punishment order' as referred to in Art. 257a CCP introduced by the Public Prosecution Service (Settlement) Act is a form of actual prosecution. At the same time, the punishment order is a form of sanctioning. This means that unlike the settlement penalty, the punishment order entails a (positive) opinion on the accused's guilt of an offence.[7] Whereas the settlement penalty included in the Criminal Code precedes the decision on (further) prosecution, the punishment order is the result of the decision to prosecute. In this state of affairs, unlike in the 'classical' system of the law of criminal procedure, the criminal court is in principle no longer involved in the case, unless the accused proves to

---

[4] Act of 7 July 2006 amending the Criminal Code, the Code of Criminal Procedure and several other Acts relating to the out-of-court settlement of offences (Public Prosecution Service (Settlement) Act) (*Wet OM-afdoening*), *Bulletin of Acts and Decrees* (*Staatsblad*) 2006, 330.

[5] Cf. *Parliamentary Papers II* 2004/05, 29 849, no. 3, pp. 2–3 and 14 and, in this regard, J.H. Crijns, 'Rationaliteiten achter de Wet OM-afdoening', in: C.P.M. Cleiren et al. (ed.), *Op zoek naar samenhang*, Deventer: Kluwer 2006, pp. 51–70, esp. pp. 54–56. See also T. Kooijmans & S. Meijer, 'De positie van het openbaar ministerie in de executiefase na inwerkingtreding van de Wet OM-afdoening', *Delikt en Delinkwent* 2007, 35, pp. 446–464, esp. pp. 447–448; T. Kooijmans, 'De strafbeschikking in verkeerszaken', *Verkeersrecht* 2007 (Kooijmans 2007a), pp. 201–207, esp. p. 201 and T. Kooijmans, 'Note 5.1 to art. 257a–257h', in: A.L. Melai & M.S. Groenhuijsen et al. (ed.), *Het Wetboek van Strafvordering*, Deventer: Kluwer sa, pp. 1–116 (supplement 160, April 2007) (Kooijmans 2007b). This paper was taken partly from the three latter publications.

[6] The settlement penalty will gradually be abolished.

[7] See Art. 257a lid 1 CCP and *Parliamentary Papers II* 2004/05, 29 849, no. 9, as well as G.T.J.M. Jurgens, 'Harmoniseren of integreren? De strafbeschikking en de bestuurlijke boete vergeleken', in: L. Loeber (ed.), *Het wetsvoorstel OM-afdoening en de verhouding tussen strafrechtelijke en bestuursrechtelijke handhaving. Preadviezen Vereniging voor wetgeving en wetgevingsbeleid 2006*, Nijmegen: Wolf Legal Publishers 2007, pp. 35–37.

want his or her case to be settled by the criminal court. So there has been a fundamental turnaround in the Dutch law of criminal procedure which requires consideration in more detail.

In this paper, attention is devoted to the historic backgrounds which ultimately led to the introduction of the punishment order (Section 2). The accent is placed on the proposals made by the Criminal Procedure 2001 (*Strafvordering 2001*) research group.[8] Next, several main features of the Public Prosecution Service (Settlement) Act are discussed (Section 3). Following this, it will be possible to bring to light and assess some differences between the proposals by the Criminal Procedure 2001 research group and the Public Prosecution Service (Settlement) Act (Section 4). The paper ends with a conclusion (Section 5).

2. *HISTORIC BACKGROUNDS OF THE PUNISHMENT ORDER*

2.1. Knigge's Preliminary Advice

The extrajudicial disposal of offences has undergone a constant development in the Netherlands, which seems to have gained momentum in the last two decades. On 1 September 1992, the Traffic Regulations (Administrative Enforcement) Act (*Wet administratiefrechtelijke afdoening van inbreuken op bepaalde verkeersvoorschriften*) (henceforth: WAHV) entered into effect.[9] This Act has, as it were, removed a number of traffic violations from criminal law and disposed of them under administrative law. It is thus characteristic of this Act that the administrative authority imposes a sanction on the party subject to its jurisdiction. The idea is that if the party does not agree with the sanction imposed and wants to challenge it, that party will have to take action on his own account.

That WAHV system, which is geared to administrative law, must have inspired Knigge when he issued preliminary advice to the Dutch Lawyers Association in 1994. This author proposed making a further distinction in criminal proceedings into three different

[8] See also the papers by G.J.M. Corstens and M.S. Groenhuijsen in this collection.

[9] Act of 3 July 1989, *Bulletin of Acts and Decrees* 1989, 300.

tracks.[10] The point of departure in his reasoning which resulted in this proposal is an inquisitorial model of the law of criminal procedure. In such a model, the public prosecutor, as a magistrate, is co-responsible for the result of the trial. According to Knigge, the position of the public prosecutor shows a certain similarity to that of an administrative body: as is the case for the Public Prosecution Service's decision on prosecution, an impartial weighing of interests should also be expected of administrative bodies, which can then be subjected to the judgment of the court. Knigge extends this reasoning fairly consistently in two senses.

Firstly, this author poses the rhetorical question of whether the concept of the settlement penalty does justice to the magistrate's status of the Public Prosecution Service in extrajudicial disposal. In Knigge's view, the Public Prosecution Service's own responsibility for this form of disposal would better come into its own if the authority to impose a settlement penalty were converted into the authority to impose fines by order or by 'punishment order'. It would then be the accused who could appeal to the court against this punishment.[11] In the law of administrative procedure, this is also called the 'beeper system'.[12] The difference from administrative disposal is that, in Knigge's view, the imposition of punishment by the Public Prosecution Service remains embedded 'in the greater whole of criminal proceedings'. In this situation, the Public Prosecution Service does not become an administrative body, but maintains its magistrate's status.

Nevertheless, it should be borne in mind, which brings us to Knigge's second point of reasoning, that the abolishment – perhaps better: conversion – of the settlement penalty advocated by Knigge would result in the introduction of a 'procedure with an administrative law slant'. If the public prosecutor imposes a fine 'by order', the accused can appeal to the court. The subject of the court's judgment

10 G. Knigge, 'De strafvordering in het geding', in: *Herbezinning op (de grondslagen van) het Wetboek van Strafvordering* (Handelingen Nederlandse Juristen-Vereniging 1994–I), Zwolle: W.E.J. Tjeenk Willink, pp. 37–116, esp. pp. 59–60 and 75–78.

11 G. Knigge, 'De strafvordering in het geding', in: *Herbezinning op (de grondslagen van) het Wetboek van Strafvordering* (Handelingen Nederlandse Juristen-Vereniging 1994-I), Zwolle: W.E.J. Tjeenk Willink, pp. 37–116, esp. pp. 59–60.

12 See G. Knigge, 'De verkalking voorbij', *RM Themis* 2000/3, pp. 83–96, esp. p. 86.

is the order given by the public prosecutor. This centres on the objections put forward against the order.[13] Although, according to this author, the sentence imposed is based on the 'magistrate-like' opinion of the public prosecutor, it is not primarily the accused's behaviour which is reviewed by the court on the basis of the procedural issues contained in Art. 348 and 350 CCP[14], but, in Knigge's view, the order appears to be the main subject of review.

Considering the core of this author's proposal, it would therefore introduce an administrative law procedure in criminal law, no matter how much the magistrate's status of the Public Prosecution Service and the 'greater whole of criminal procedure' might play a part.

2.2. The Korthals Altes Committee

A bit more than a year after Knigge had brought his position to light, the Committee for the Review of the Instruments of Law Enforcement (commissie Heroverweging Instrumentarium Rechtshandhaving) – named the Korthals Altes Committee after its chairman – published its final report in August 1995.[15] The committee was given the task of making practical proposals for the enforcement of rules and regulations otherwise than by criminal law and for the replacement of custodial sentences by alternatives.[16] In its final report, the Committee suggested that after a certain time, the settlement penalty should be converted *ipso jure* into an enforceable decision, unless the accused lodges 'objection' during that time – which objection should be

---

[13] G. Knigge, 'De strafvordering in het geding', in: *Herbezinning op (de grondslagen van) het Wetboek van Strafvordering* (Handelingen Nederlandse Juristen-Vereniging 1994-I), Zwolle: W.E.J. Tjeenk Willink, pp. 37–116, esp. pp. 75–76.

[14] Art. 348 CCP contains four 'procedural' issues on which the criminal court must form a judgment based on the indictment and the examination in court: the validity of the summons; the jurisdiction of the court; whether or not prosecution is barred and the question whether there are reasons to suspend prosecution. Art. 350 CCP contains four 'substantive' questions: Have the charges been proved? What offence does the finding of fact constitute? Is the accused is liable for punishment? What sanction should be imposed?

[15] Commissie Heroverweging Instrumentarium Rechtshandhaving, *Het recht ten uitvoer gelegd. Oude en nieuwe instrumenten van rechtshandhaving*, The Hague: Ministry of Justice 1995.

[16] *Parliamentary Papers II* 1995/96, 24 802, nos. 1–2, p. 9.

linked with the provision of security equal in the amount (of a substantial part of) the settlement penalty – and brings the case before a court.[17]

According to the memorandum '*Rechtshandhaving en veiligheid*' ('Law enforcement and safety') the then cabinet, together with the Committee, were of the opinion that this proposal had an attractive side, entailing that an 'expensive and time-consuming call upon the judge' would be made only if the accused took action to that effect. In this view, the accused would not be able to continue to sit still, waiting to see if the judge would indeed proceed to prosecute. Although, in principle, the cabinet did not reject the proposal, they expressed the suspicion that this would further complicate the system of extrajudicial disposal. Besides disposal on the basis of the WAHV, there was also a settlement penalty that could be offered by the Public Prosecution Service and, in the case of certain summary offences and minor crimes, by the police. In the system recommended by the Committee, in addition to this, for a certain number of crimes to be determined, the possibility would be introduced to convert the settlement penalty offered by the Public Prosecution Service – the proposal did not relate to the police settlement penalty – into an enforceable decision. The Committee's proposal related to offences which would also be eligible for a police settlement penalty, as well as minor crimes which, in the Committee's proposal, were classified as 'misconduct'. All in all, this would do little to make institution of the settlement penalty clear to citizens. The cabinet stated that it intended to 'prepare a legislative proposal which [...] provides the possibility for a settlement penalty to become enforceable *ipso jure*'.[18]

The Explanatory Memorandum to the Public Prosecution Service (Settlement) Act stated that the positions taken by the Korthals Altes Committee, and the government's positions in relation to them, had given a strong impetus to the rethinking of the legal

[17] Commissie Heroverweging Instrumentarium Rechtshandhaving, *Het recht ten uitvoer gelegd. Oude en nieuwe instrumenten van rechtshandhaving*, The Hague: Ministry of Justice 1995, pp. 35–37.

[18] *Parliamentary Papers II* 1995/96, 24 802, nos. 1–2, pp. 61–63.

framework of extrajudicial disposal. The Public Prosecution Service (Settlement) Act is largely the result of this. The government, however, questioned the dogmatic concept of the enforceable settlement penalty proposed by the Committee. The government rightly typified the settlement penalty as an offer by the Public Prosecution Service, the acceptance of which is evident from fulfilment of the relevant conditions. In the government's view, this makes the settlement penalty a type of 'agreement' between two parties. Regarding the enforceable settlement penalty, the government derives the existence of this 'agreement' and its enforceability from the circumstance that the accused has not objected to a proposal by the Public Prosecution Service. According to the government, this cannot be 'properly defined or justified legally'. In other words, the Korthals Altes Committee were hobbling between two ideas by, on the one hand, wanting to maintain the disposal modality of the settlement penalty based on 'consensus' and, on the other, providing the government with an instrument to enforce the settlement penalty, while – as will be argued under 3 below – the legislature had cut the knot by way of the Public Prosecution Service (Settlement) Act in the sense that with the punishment order, the possibility was introduced (for a government authority other than the criminal court) to impose sanctions unilaterally. This choice, which independently justifies the introduction of the punishment order, is appealing in itself. The same, however, cannot be said of the argument the government already used in 1996 that the legal concept proposed by the Korthals Altes Committee would do little to make the institution of the settlement penalty clear to citizens.

In itself, the government was right in 1996 when it stated that the proposed enforceable settlement penalty would also contribute towards an (even more) obscure set of extrajudicial disposal modalities. It remains to be seen, however, whether this problem would be avoided by introducing the punishment order. Today as well, disposal on the basis of the WAHV still exists as a separate modality. Under the regime of the Public Prosecution Service (Settlement) Act, under the conditions referred to in (and pursuant to) Articles 257b and 257ba CCP, investigating officers and bodies or persons charged with public duties can issue punishment orders. Conditional dismissal can also be maintained. This small overview alone makes it clear that the introduction of the punishment order has not resulted in a more transparent system.[19]

2.3. 'Towards a Safer Society'

In the safety programme 'Towards a safer society' (*'Naar een veiliger samenleving'*) of 16 October 2002, the government announced that it would circulate a legislative proposal which was intended to re-regulate extrajudicial disposal.[20] This proposal centred on several aspects. First of all, more room should be made for settlements by the Public Prosecution Service 'in cases that lend themselves for this'. The government had 'cases' in mind 'in which there was no lack of clarity about the offence and sanction'. Consequently, more crimes would receive an appropriate and timely response, which would also relieve the burden on the capacity of the criminal courts to hold hearings. The cabinet specifically had in mind an expansion of the so-called 'public prosecutor's model' of community service in juvenile law; introduction of more disposal modalities for the Public Prosecution Service, such as shorter disqualification from driving; always making settlement by the Public Prosecution Service possible where the court would otherwise only impose a fine; and increasing efficiency by making settlement by the Public Prosecution Service enforceable for a category of cases to be determined later.

The government gave a quantitative argument to support this policy intention.[21] The enforceability of settlements by the Public Prosecution Service could substantially relieve the judiciary. The government estimated that in three fourths of the cases, the settlement penalty was paid to the Central Judicial Collection Agency (CJIB), thus no payment was made in approximately one fourth of the cases. With respect to the latter cases, the starting point was that

---

[19] See further P.A.M. Mevis, 'Strafbeschikking openbaar ministerie, WAHV en "kleine ergernissen"', *Delikt en Delinkwent* 2004, 24, pp. 353–368 and ditto, 'Bestuurlijke boete in Absurdistan', *Ars Aequi* 2005, pp. 580–587.

[20] *Parliamentary Papers II* 2002/03, 28 684, no. 1, p. 26.

[21] See also *Sancties in perspectief. Beleidsnota inzake de heroriëntatie op de toepassing van vrijheidsstraffen en vrijheidsbeperkende straffen bij volwassenen*, The Hague: Ministry of Justice 2000, p. 35.

the accused would be summoned. The cabinet were of the opinion that if the initiative to try cases were left to the citizens, the number of cases brought before the courts would be substantially reduced. Because in WAHV cases, in which such a model was already used, the court is engaged by the person concerned in about 4% of the cases, the cabinet estimated that the percentage of cases in which the accused would protest to the court against a settlement by the Public Prosecution Service was between 4% and 25%: 'In that case, therefore, substantial savings are still possible.' From this reasoning based on quantitative data and estimates, the cabinet concluded that a legislative amendment was important.

More or less parallel to these political developments, in the period round the turn of the millennium a large-scale research project was conducted which also contributed towards the introduction of the punishment order: the Criminal Procedure 2001 (*Strafvordering 2001*) research project.[22]

2.4. Criminal Procedure 2001: The Three-Track Model

It was already noted in 2.1 above that Knigge had proposed the introduction of a 'three-track model' in criminal law in 1994. A similar proposal was formulated several years later by the 'Criminal Procedure 2001' ('*Strafvordering 2001*') research group.[23] In that proposed model, a distinction is made between 1) proceedings in which the gravity of the offence requires hearing by a three-judge division, 2) proceedings in which the gravity of the offence allows for hearing by a single judge and 3) an extrajudicial procedure in which the authority is conferred on the Public Prosecution Service to impose

[22] For the background and content of this project, see the paper by M.S. Groenhuijsen in this collection.

[23] A.R. Hartmann, '*Buitengerechtelijke afdoening*', in: M.S. Groenhuijsen & G. Knigge (ed.), *Het onderzoek ter zitting. Eerste interimrapport onderzoeksproject Strafvordering 2001*, Deventer: Kluwer 2001, pp. 59–90; G. Knigge, '*Dwangmiddelen en rechtsmiddelen. Algemeen deel*', in: M.S. Groenhuijsen & G. Knigge (ed.), *Dwangmiddelen en rechtsmiddelen. Derde interimrapport onderzoeksproject Strafvordering 2001*, Deventer: Kluwer 2002, pp. 15–17 and 26–36; A.R. Hartmann, '*Buitengerechtelijke afdoening II*', in: M.S. Groenhuijsen & G. Knigge (ed.), *Dwangmiddelen en rechtsmiddelen. Derde interimrapport onderzoeksproject Strafvordering 2001*, Deventer: Kluwer 2002, pp. 79–198.

sanctions. The object of making this distinction is to coordinate procedural guarantees to what is actually at stake.[24]

The proposed introduction of three-track proceedings was based, among other things, on a quantitative argument. According to the research group, the Dutch criminal law system in which the starting point was a trial in the sense of an obligation to try with a view to punishment,[25] was 'creaking everywhere' because of the enormous increase in the number of criminal cases to be dealt with. On the one hand, this led to a hollowing out of the guarantees relating to the immediacy principle.[26] For instance, it no longer proved possible to examine all witnesses at the trial, which resulted in a style of conducting proceedings which the researchers labelled as substandard. At the same time, this style of conducting proceedings for simple summary offences was often 'too much of a good thing'. In the research group's view, the downside of this development was that holding on to the trial as the starting point had resulted in the acceptance of an unus judex as a necessary evil and in the introduction and expansion of the possibilities to dispose of criminal cases extrajudicially, the object of which, with a view to the aforementioned starting point, could not be punishment.[27]

The quantitative argument referred to above does not stand alone, but is closely connected with a more substantive argument. In the view of the Criminal Procedure 2001 research group, the settlement penalty, which they termed 'improperly designed' as an extrajudicial disposal modality, is not a punishment, but a 'buyout

---

[24] See also *Parliamentary Papers II* 2004/05, 29 849, nr. 7, p. 34 and *Parliamentary Papers II* 2003/04, 29 271, no. 1, pp. 8 and 12–13.

[25] For an extensive treatment, see M. Hildebrandt, *Straf(begrip) en procesbeginsel* (thesis Rotterdam), Deventer: Kluwer 2002 and J.F. Nijboer, *De doolhof van de Nederlandse strafwetgeving*, Arnhem: Gouda Quint 1990.

[26] J.F. Nijboer, *Strafrechtelijk bewijsrecht*, fifth impression, Nijmegen: Ars Aequi Libri 2008, p. 70, defines the immediacy principle as the whole of rules and principles for the purpose of ensuring that the court giving judgment uses as many authentic sources of information as possible itself, which have all been brought up and reviewed in court – after hearing the arguments on both sides – whereby, as far as persons are concerned (accused, witness, expert) the oral form – the person is present and makes an oral statement – prevails over the written (report, police report etcetera). See also D.H.R.M. Garé, *Het onmiddellijkheidsbeginsel in het Nederlandse strafproces* (thesis Maastricht), Arnhem: Gouda Quint 1994.

[27] Knigge 2002, pp. 15–16.

payment' by which prosecution and trial are avoided, which is hardly compatible with the public, law enforcing function of criminal law. Moreover, a shortage of legal protection would arise because the chosen construct (of the 'buyout payment') does not require a guaranteed establishment of guilt. Nor would the construct be very efficient if the settlement penalty offered is not accepted.

Characteristic of the three-track model proposed by the Criminal Procedure 2001 research group is that the question of which procedural track is chosen depends on the actual gravity of the offence and the appropriate sanction to be imposed for it, all of which would be at the public prosecutor's discretion. Only 'simple offences' could be eligible for use of the third track – extrajudicial disposal. These, apparently, would mainly be offences that used to be disposed of by a settlement penalty.[28]

Against the background of the foregoing, it is not surprising that the Criminal Procedure 2001 research group proposed integrating conditional dismissal and the settlement penalty in the 'third track'.[29] Furthermore, the research group was rightly of the opinion, referring to the provisions of Art. 113 (3) of the Dutch Constitution and Art. 5(1)(a) of the ECHR,[30] that there is no room for the extrajudicial imposition of custodial sentences (including alternative detention[31] in so far as imposed without judicial intervention).[32] It ensues logically from this train of thought that only the court may be charged with alternative detention. In the research group's view, non-custodial sentences could indeed be imposed by the Public Prosecution Service in the third track. In this view, if the accused did not agree to the sanction imposed, he could bring the case before the court, which would assess the case in its entirety.

---

[28] Hartmann 2001, pp. 70–71.

[29] Hartmann 2001, p. 71; Knigge 2002, pp. 27–30.

[30] Art. 113(3) of the Constitution reads: 'A custodial sentence may be imposed only by the judiciary.' Art. 5(1)(a) ECHR reads: 'Everyone has the right to liberty and security of person. No one shall be deprived of his liberty save in the following cases and in accordance with a procedure prescribed by law: (a) the lawful detention of a person after conviction by a competent court'.

[31] Concisely stated, alternative detention is a form of detention that can be enforced if the convicted person fails to comply with a pecuniary sanction imposed on him or her.

[32] Knigge 2002, pp. 29 and 32.

3. THE MAIN ASPECTS OF THE PUBLIC PROSECUTION SERVICE (SETTLEMENT) ACT

3.1. Introduction

It can be concluded from the foregoing that the Public Prosecution Service (Settlement) Act has had a long and multifaceted preliminary stage. In summary, it can be stated that the extrajudicial disposal of criminal cases has enjoyed extensive political as well as broad academic interest since the period in which the CC of 1886 was drafted and particularly in the last decades.[33] The background of this is partly the overburdening of the criminal justice system. The synergy between, mainly, the political and academic points of view ultimately resulted in the Public Prosecution Service (Settlement) Act.

This section deals in more detail with some main aspects of the Public Prosecution Service (Settlement) Act.[34] Firstly, attention is devoted to the question in which cases and on what grounds a punishment order can be issued. Next, the guarantees attached to the issue of the punishment order are examined. Afterwards, the possibility of the accused to challenge the punishment order is discussed. Finally, the possible consequences are dealt with of the circumstance that the sanction imposed by a final punishment order in some cases cannot be enforced.

3.2. The Punishment Order: Cases and Grounds

The public prosecutor can issue a punishment order on the basis of Art. 257a(1) CCP if he establishes that a summary offence was committed or a crime which, according to its statutory description, carries imprisonment not exceeding six years. Just like the police had the authority before the Public Prosecution Service (Settlement) Act

---

[33] See further, with reference to sources, P. Osinga, *Transactie in strafzaken* (thesis Tilburg), Arnhem: Gouda Quint 1992; G.J.M. van den Biggelaar, *De buitengerechtelijke afdoening van strafbare feiten door the Public Prosecution Service* (thesis Maastricht), Arnhem: Gouda Quint 1994; Hartmann 2001, pp. 59–90 and W.H. Vellinga, 'Van handhaving van verkeersregels naar regels van strafrecht en strafprocesrecht', *Verkeersrecht* 2006, pp. 317–326.

[34] See also extensively M. Kessler & B.F. Keulen, *De strafbeschikking*, Deventer: Kluwer 2008.

entered into effect (and still have it) to propose a settlement penalty for certain summary offences and simple crimes, the Public Prosecution Service (Settlement) Act now provides a basis for investigating officers (not being public prosecutors) also to issue punishment orders for summary offences and simple crimes carrying imprisonment not exceeding six years, provided these crimes were committed by persons at least eighteen years of age.[35] Furthermore, persons or bodies charged with public duties – henceforth referred to as administrative bodies – on the basis of Art. 257ba CCP have been given the authority to issue punishment orders. It is striking that the law does not contain any limitations regarding the cases in which this authority can be exercised. It must be assumed nevertheless that this authority will not extend beyond the above-mentioned limitations set on public prosecutors in Art. 257a CCP.[36]

In the cases referred to above, the authorities in question may issue a punishment order. This gives rise to the question of the basis on which this authority can be exercised. Art. 257a(1) CCP gives the start of an answer to this question as well. This paragraph requires 'establishment' that the summary offence or crime was committed. Two aspects require further attention here.

First of all, the statutory formulation seems to suggest that it only needs to be established that the accused committed an offence and that the authority that issues the punishment order does not have to check whether the accused is criminally liable for that offence. In other words, the text of the Act gives the impression that it does not have to be checked whether there is a ground of justification or a ground of excuse. That suggestion, however, is incorrect.[37] The formulation of Art. 257a(1) CCP is based on an amendment adopted by the Lower House.[38] According to its explanatory notes, the amendment is for the purpose of 'embedding more clearly in the text of the Act that the punishment order is based on an establishment of guilt'. In this light, it must be assumed that the establishment that the

35 Art. 257b CCP.
36 In this sense also Kessler & Keulen 2008, pp. 111–112.
37 In this sense also Kessler & Keulen 2008, pp. 7–8.
38 *Parliamentary Papers II* 2004/05, 29 849, no. 9.

accused committed an offence also contains the question whether a ground for exemption from criminal liability is present.

Secondly, the question arises of how the term 'establish' should be interpreted. As discussed above under 1, the punishment order is a form of sanctioning, which means that the punishment order contains a (positive) judgment on the accused's guilt of an offence.[39] The question in this regard is what standard of evidence applies. The Dutch law of criminal procedure has an evidentiary system which could be described as a 'negative-legal' evidentiary system (a system in which one is innocent until proved guilty).[40] It is a 'legal' system because evidence may be furnished only by way of the articles of evidence referred to in the Act.[41] Furthermore, in many cases the requirement of 'double confirmation' applies. This means that the charges may not be declared proved on the basis of only one article of evidence.[42] The evidentiary system is 'negative' because the judge may not declare the offence charged proved if the evidence has not convinced him or her that the accused committed the offence. In other words, this concerns the question whether the offence charged has been proved beyond reasonable doubt on the basis of the evidence. These requirements of legality of the evidence and the judge's conviction pertain to the judgment given by the judge. Do these requirements now apply as well to the 'establishment' by the public prosecutor that an offence was committed, which establishment then results in the issue of a punishment order?[43] No attention was

---

[39] See also J.G. Cabboort & J.P. Quist, 'De Wet OM-afdoening in civilibus. Civielrechtelijke complicaties van de onherroepelijke strafbeschikking', *Verkeersrecht* 2008, pp. 338–342.

[40] Corstens 2008, pp. 665–666.

[41] This concerns the judge's own perception, statements by the accused, statements by a witness, statements by an expert and written documents (Art. 339 CCP).

[42] Nijboer 2008, pp. 82–83. This concerns, e.g. a single statement by the accused, by the witness and written documents that do not have the formal status of official documents. Conversely, on the basis of Art. 344 (2) CCP a finding of fact can indeed be based on a single official report by an investigating officer. See also B. de Wilde, 'Bewijsminimumregels als waarborgen voor de waarheidsvinding in strafzaken?', in: J.H. Crijns, P.P.J. van der Meij & J.M. ten Voorde (red.), *De waarde van waarheid. Opstellen over waarheid en waarheidsvinding in het strafrecht*, Den Haag: Boom Juridische uitgevers 2008, pp. 269–294.

[43] Cf. J. Crijns & P. van der Meij, 'Over de grenzen van de materiële waarheidsvinding', in: R. Haveman & H. Wiersinga (ed.), *Langs de randen van het strafrecht*, Nijmegen: Wolf Legal Publishers 2005, pp. 45–69, esp. pp. 66–68.

paid to this in the parliamentary debate on the Public Prosecution Service (Settlement) Act. It appears nevertheless that the question must be answered in the affirmative. The requirements of legality of the evidence and conviction already apply to the judge when he or she declares a *summary offence* proved. So it would not be logical to set less stringent requirements on a public prosecutor who wants to dispose of a *crime* by way of a punishment order. Furthermore, in this context, the above-mentioned circumstance is significant that the issue of a punishment order – just as the pronouncement of a conviction by the criminal court judge – is linked with the imposition of criminal sanctions. This circumstance means that relatively strict requirements must be set on the legitimating basis of such sentencing – which basis can be found in the establishment that the offence was committed – regardless of which authority establishes this. This has consequences. If the punishment order is issued on the basis of an offence discovered when the accused was caught in the act by an investigating officer – it may be assumed that the punishment order will be issued mainly in such situations – there is no problem. The investigating officer can give an account of his or her observation of that offence in an official report, which constitutes sufficient legal evidence. But this can be different in other cases (for example in the event of an anonymous telephone call to the police that a person has committed an offence). There is not yet sufficient legal evidence in that case and, against the background of the foregoing, no punishment order may be issued.

3.3. Guarantees Concerning the Issue of a Punishment Order

Various sanctions can be imposed by a punishment order that encroach upon the financial position of the accused or upon his or her personal freedom.[44] It is self-evident that the issue of a punishment order is subject to guarantees. Art. 257c CCP provides for several guarantees. They can be distinguished further, for example according to the time at which a guarantee is effected or according to the requirement of proportionality.

---

[44] Art. 257a (2–3) CCP.

If the time at which the relevant guarantee is applicable is taken as the starting point, one sees that the public prosecutor's obligation to examine the accused[45] exists prior to the issue of the punishment order. A written report is made of such an examination of the accused.

Art. 257c (2) CCP contains an elaboration of the proportionality principle. This is the obligation to examine the accused while he or she is assisted by counsel, if the public prosecutor intends to issue a punishment order containing payment obligations on the basis of a fine and/or compensation order which separately or together amount to more than two thousand euros. According to the Explanatory Memorandum, this procedure is in line with the practice of the settlement penalty. There are two reasons for continuing this practice. In the first place, such amounts will usually be imposed for more serious offences, which may give rise to more questions in connection with the evaluation of the act and its punishability. In the second place, larger interests are involved in such amounts. The idea is that extrajudicial imposition of high payment obligations should be limited to cases in which the accused is assisted by counsel. Legal assistance must therefore provide a certain compensation for the (absence of the) guarantees provided by disposal by the court.[46] This starting point nevertheless needs some refining, in two senses.

3.4. Objection to the Punishment Order

The issue of a punishment order is an act of prosecution which, as a rule, entails the imposition of a punishment. This necessitates the possibility for the accused to have his or her criminal case judged by the court. This possibility exists for the accused: on the basis of Art. 257e CCP, the accused can object to a punishment order. Such an objection must be lodged with the public prosecutor's office mentioned in the punishment order within the period set by law.

---

[45] Art. 257c (1–2) CCP. See further J.W. van der Hulst, 'Horen door het OM', *Verkeersrecht* 2008, pp. 333–337.

[46] *Parliamentary Papers II* 2004/05, 29 849, no. 3, pp. 30, 31 and 33. See also *Parliamentary Papers I* 2005/06, 29 849, C, pp. 34–37. See further Kooijmans 2007b, note 5.6.

Subsequently, in accordance with Art. 257f CCP, the public prosecutor informs the court of the objection, unless he withdraws the punishment order. The court then judges the criminal case in its entirety. Appeal and appeal to the Supreme Court are possible within the limits set by the law.

The Dutch Minister of Justice rightly showed that he was aware of the above-mentioned need for the possibility to subject a punishment order to the judgment of a court, and he was guided in this by the starting point that the possibility to appeal in court against the punishment order should not be obstructed by the formulation of requirements that could keep the accused from turning to the court. Partly in this light, the Minister considered the procedure in accordance with Art. 6 ECHR: 'It can be concluded from ECHR case law that an extrajudicial 'preliminary procedure' would not encounter objections, provided an appeal to the court is possible which meets the requirements of the Convention.'[47] According to the Minister this is the case for the Public Prosecution Service (Settlement) Act.

It is however, open to doubt whether the generous possibility professed by the Minister to object to the punishment order in court would be experienced as such by the accused in practice. Immediately after the passage cited above, a comment is made in the Explanatory Memorandum that 'just as in the current judicial system, it is possible to see to it in a different way that the case is not brought before the court.' The Minister refers here to the practice in which it is customary that in the cases in which a settlement penalty is offered (in vain), a heavier punishment is demanded and – if the accused fails to appear – imposed in court. According to the Minister, this practice can be continued fully under the regime of the punishment order.[48] The Minister developed this position in more detail in the Further Memorandum of Reply to the Upper House.[49] Referring to

47 *Parliamentary Papers II* 2004/05, 29 849, no. 3, p. 42. J.H. Crijns, 'Het wetsvoorstel OM-afdoening: een wolf in schaapskledij', *Sancties* 2004, pp. 225–236, esp. p. 232 mentions as an 'unmistakably positive effect' of the new provisions that it is beyond any doubt that Art. 6 ECHR applies to the authority to issue a punishment order.

48 *Parliamentary Papers II* 2004/05, 29 849, no. 3, p. 42. Cf. *Parliamentary Papers II* 2004/05, 29 849, no. 17, p. 27. See also *Parliamentary Papers I* 2005/06, 29 849, C, pp. 10–11 and 26.

49 *Parliamentary Papers I* 2005/06, 29 849, E, pp. 5–7. See also *Parliamentary Papers I* 2005/06, 29 849, D, pp. 4–5.

the case law of the European Court of Human Rights, the Minister argued that the circumstance that by using a legal remedy, the accused de facto risks a heavier penalty if he or she does not have any well-founded, substantive objections is not incompatible with Art. 6 ECHR.[50] He also referred to the notion that the criminal court may attach consequences to the accused's attitude for the sentence to be imposed. In this regard, the Minister had in mind 'generally accepted objectives of the application of criminal law, such as general and special prevention'. According to the Minister, it is desirable and justified in principle, with a view to special prevention, to impose a somewhat heavier penalty on an accused person who has lodged objection but has not been heard from and fails to appear at the hearing, or appears but has no substantive objections concerning the establishment of the facts or sentencing than on an accused person who appears at the hearing, conducts his or her defence there and whose attitude shows that he or she is susceptible to criminal correction.

This reasoning is not convincing, partly because it is based on a complete disregard of the distinction in legal character between the settlement penalty on the one hand and the punishment order on the other.[51] Whereas the settlement penalty, to the extent relevant here, is characterised by its, in principle, voluntary nature for the accused, the punishment order must be considered as unilateral and, in principle, binding application of a sanction by the government. This has consequences. By way of the punishment order, a punishment is imposed which – in the perception of the public prosecutor – does justice to the actual circumstances of the case and which, unlike the settlement penalty, cannot be considered as a form of buyoff of the criminal case by the accused. This means that the punishment imposed by a punishment order must be in accordance with the customary manner of sentencing. The fact that Art. 6 ECHR does not oppose certain restrictions on the right of access to the courts does not alter this.

---

[50] ECHR 27 February 1980, *Nederlandse Jurisprudentie* 1980, 561 (Deweer); ECHR 2 March 1987, *Nederlandse Jurisprudentie* 1991, 165 with notes by EAA (Monnell & Morris) and ECHR 21 September 1994, *Nederlandse Jurisprudentie* 1995, 463 (Fayed).

[51] Kooijmans 2007a, p. 204 and Kooijmans 2007b, note 5.8.

Groenhuijsen and Simmelink rightly comment in this regard that the customary manner of sentencing is the standard point of departure for the imposition of a punishment (in the event of a punishment order) in individual cases. Together with these authors, it should be strongly emphasised not only that this framework fails to provide a legal ground for the application of a reduction on the basis of the accused's consent to extrajudicial disposal or an increase due to failure to appear at the hearing, but also that an increase in the severity of the sentence by the criminal court judge (purely because objection was lodged) is at odds with the nature of objection against the punishment order.[52] Increasing the severity of the sentence on the mere basis that objection was lodged and the accused subsequently failed to appear is the unjustified price of invoking a legal guarantee. That legal guarantee already consists of the circumstance that the judge fully assesses the criminal case (after an objection to that effect made by the accused), irrespective of the position the accused chose after lodging objection.

3.5. Impossibility of Enforcement

If an objection is lodged in good time against a punishment order, the punishment order cannot be enforced. That situation should be distinguished from the circumstance that – without objection having been lodged – the punishment order has not been or cannot be enforced. For example, community service has been imposed by a punishment order, but the person concerned has not complied with that punishment. In such a case, the system of the Public Prosecution Service (Settlement) Act presumes that a summons will still be issued.[53] This is sometimes also referred to as 'prosecution in stages'.[54] Summoning means that the case will be investigated in its

---

52 M.S. Groenhuijsen & J.B.H.M. Simmelink, '*Het wetsvoorstel OM-afdoening op het grensvlak van juridische techniek en strafprocessuele uitgangspunten*', in: A.H.E.C. Jordaans et al. (ed.), *Praktisch strafrecht* (Reijntjes-bundel), Nijmegen: Wolf Legal Publishers 2005, pp. 171–196, esp. p. 188.

53 This follows (a contrario) from Art. 255a CCP, entailing that only a fully enforceable punishment order has the consequence that the accused cannot (in principle) be tried again for the same offence. See also *Parliamentary Papers II* 2004/05, 29 849, no. 3, pp. 18 and 65.

54 *Parliamentary Papers II* 2004/05, 29 849, no. 3, p. 19.

entirety by the criminal court. To prevent the court from giving an enforceable judgment in addition to a punishment order issued for the same offence, the Act provides that in such a case (in the case of a summons), the punishment order will no longer be enforceable.[55] The enforcement that has already started will then be suspended or stayed. Further, in such a case, the punishment order is in principle set aside.[56] At first sight, this body of rules seems to be based on the assumption that a punishment order can relate to only one offence. In that case, the punishment order cannot be enforced any more at all and it is set aside (in principle) in its entirety. A punishment order can nevertheless relate to several offences.[57] If the sanctions relating to only a part of those offences cannot be enforced (completely), a summons will have to be issued only for those offences, and the comments just made will apply only to that extent.

The logical next step in summoning is that, as a rule, the criminal court gives judgment on the case. If the court acquits the accused, discharges him from further prosecution or convicts him, it sets aside the punishment order. In this context, it does not make any difference whether the court is involved in the case because the accused lodged objection,[58] or that the court is called upon to give judgment because the punishment order cannot be enforced (completely).[59]

The question has been posed in the literature whether, for example from a systematic viewpoint, a more balanced approach would be to have the impossibility to (completely) enforce a sanction imposed by a punishment order followed by a so-called 'conversion procedure'.[60] This is an elaboration on the proposals by the Criminal Procedure 2001 research group.[61] The core of those proposals comes down to the fact that the court should examine whether an imposed fine can be converted into alternative detention. In that examination, the guilt of the accused person should be discussed as well. If the court rules that the public prosecutor should not reasonably

[55] Art. 255a (3) CCP.
[56] Art. 354a CCP. See *Parliamentary Papers II* 2004/05, 29 849, no. 3, pp. 19 and 78.
[57] *Parliamentary Papers II* 2004/05, 29 849, no. 3, pp. 4, 76 and 81.
[58] Art. 257f (4) CCP.
[59] Art. 354a CCP.
[60] Groenhuijsen & Simmelink 2005, pp. 188–191.
[61] Knigge 2002, pp. 31–34 and Hartmann 2002, pp. 169–175.

have disposed of the case by a fine, it would have to rule that the imposition of that fine was in conflict with the principles of due process and reject the demand for that reason.[62]

The approach chosen in the literature, in which a conversion procedure can systematically be better embedded in the legal system than the 'prosecution in stages' chosen by the legislature, is appealing.[63] It should be taken into consideration that, on the one hand, the accused has the opportunity to protest at law against the punishment order by lodging objection and, on the other, that if the accused does not use that possibility, the system of the Public Prosecution Service (Settlement) Act entails that the sanctions imposed will become final. The latter circumstance in turn demands a regime in which, as a result of such finality, enforcement can be compelled. A new, 'full dress' procedure in criminal cases is not in keeping with this. In addition, the issue of a summons for an offence for which a final punishment order has already been issued could be at odds with the ne bis in idem principle.[64]

4. *SIMILARITIES AND DIFFERENCES BETWEEN CRIMINAL PROCEDURE 2001 AND THE PUBLIC PROSECUTION SERVICE (SETTLEMENT) ACT*

Under 2 and 3 above, the main features were discussed of the proposals by the Criminal Procedure 2001 research group and the Public Prosecution Service (Settlement) Act. That description now provides the opportunity to bring to light several similarities and differences between those proposals.[65]

---

62 Hartmann 2002, p. 175 proposes in respect of so-called 'performance sanctions' (sanctions requiring the accused's cooperation), eliminating enforcement problems by giving the public prosecutor the authority to attach the resolutive condition to the sanction order that the accused must comply with the order. If the community service subsequently fails, in this approach, the public prosecutor will still be at liberty to summon the accused, invoking the resolutive condition.

63 For further substantiation of this position, see Kooijmans 2007, note 5.9.

64 Cf. however Art. 255a (1) CCP: 'If a punishment order was issued against the accused which has been fully enforced, he or she may not be tried again (...) for the same offence.' This paper is not the place to deal further with the question whether the requirement that the punishment order is fully enforced is justified.

65 On the similarities and differences between the proposals of 'Strafvordering 2001' and the Public Prosecution Service (Settlement) Act, see M. de Graaf,

The punishment order shows similarity to the third track proposed by Criminal Procedure 2001 to the extent that the core idea of both modalities is that the construct of consent is abandoned in favour of that of unilateral sentencing.[66] Both the research group and the Minister are of the opinion that the guarantees for the accused can be given more adequate shape in such a system, because they can be made dependent on what is at stake for the accused. In that way, a differentiation would be made in regime, which would partly depend on the severity of the (intended) sanction. Also derived from the proposals by the research group is the introduction of the possibility to give the accused instructions in the punishment order which, should they not be followed, would result in the accused being summoned before the criminal court. Finally, the existing criminal law and criminal procedure framework was also a guideline for the research group in incorporating the third track. The research group assumed that if a legal remedy were instituted against the punishment order, the criminal court would judge the case in its entirety on the basis of the questions of Art. 348 and 350 CCP,[67] based on the description of the facts in the contested order.[68] On this point, therefore, the research group differs from the proposal by Knigge discussed above under 2.1 to make the order issued the main subject of judicial review and not the behaviour of the accused to be assessed in accordance with Art. 348 and 350 CCP.

Not only similarities exist between the proposals by the Criminal Procedure 2001 research group and the Public Prosecution Service (Settlement) Act, but also differences. In the Explanatory Memorandum, the following differences are put forward.[69]

The first difference lies in the degree to which a connection is sought with the existing framework of criminal law and criminal procedure. For instance, in the system of the Public Prosecution

'Doelmatigheid boven rechtmatigheid', *Delikt en Delinkwent* 2003, pp. 811–829 and Groenhuijsen & Simmelink 2005, pp. 175–176.

[66] *Parliamentary Papers II* 2004/05, 29 849, no. 3, pp. 52–55 and *Parliamentary Papers I* 2005/06, 29 849, C, p. 33.

[67] Cf. footnote 14.

[68] Hartmann 2002, p. 185. Initially, the research group seemed to keep its options open on this issue: Hartmann 2001, pp. 73–74.

[69] *Parliamentary Papers II* 2004/05, 29 849, no. 3, pp. 53–55.

Service (Settlement) Act, the consequence of the circumstance that the fine imposed in a specific case (in which no objection has been lodged) cannot be enforced is that the criminal case – just as under the regime of the old law – can be brought before the criminal court in its entirety. Conversely, as stated above under 3.5, in Criminal Procedure 2001, a so-called conversion procedure was chosen. In that procedure, on the one hand, the court only has to answer the question of the accused's guilt and, on the other, the question whether the fine can be converted into a prison sentence. Should the judge be of the opinion that the public prosecutor should not reasonably have disposed of the case with a fine, he or she will have to rule that its imposition was in conflict with the principles of due process and reject the demand for that reason. In the system of the Public Prosecution Service (Settlement) Act, such an assessment of the fine, which has an administrative law slant according to the Minister, was not chosen. According to his taste, the central point of the Public Prosecution Service (Settlement) Act should be that 'justice is done to the offence in the court judgment'.

The following difference relates to the legal remedies available to the accused. Criminal Procedure 2001 proposes only making appeal to the Supreme Court available against the judgment of the court of first instance. The effect of this, the Minister rightly decided, would be that the possibility to have the case judged by another court deciding questions of fact is made dependent on the question whether the Public Prosecution Service starts prosecution by a summons or by a punishment order. The Minister noted that this issue is especially important in relation to the higher fines and disqualification from driving. The Code does not provide for the possibility to appeal against low fines.[70] The Minister also considered this difference from the old law proposed by the research group undesirable. According to him, the effect of this proposal would be that the accused who states that he or she does not want to consent to extrajudicial disposal and is therefore summoned immediately would 'earn' an additional judicial process. It seems more desirable to the Minister to promote extrajudicial disposal by attaching 'advantages' to it.

---

[70] Art. 404 (2)(b) CCP sets a limit of € 50.

The third striking difference between the proposals of the Criminal Procedure 2001 research group and the Public Prosecution Service (Settlement) Act is the amount of the maximum fines that can be applied in the event of extrajudicial disposal. The research group proposes a distinction between natural and legal persons as well as between general and economic criminal cases. In economic criminal cases, legal persons could have a sixth-category fine imposed.[71] In general criminal cases, a maximum equal to that of the second category would apply to natural persons.[72] The Public Prosecution Service (Settlement) Act, on the other hand, barring a few exceptions,[73] does not set specific restrictions on a fine to be imposed in a punishment order but, with the obligation to examine the accused in the presence of legal counsel, introduces a guarantee tailored to high fines. In this context, the Minister remarked that a certain differentiation has been made in line with the proposals of the Criminal Procedure 2001 research group.[74] If the public prosecutor is granted the independent authority to impose a sanction which is binding in principle, it would be appropriate – it is possible to agree with the Minister to this extent – for the public prosecutor, as holds for all criminal cases, to have the possibility to include all aspects of the case in his decision, and to arrive at a decision accordingly that does justice to all relevant facts and circumstances of the case. In that perspective, it is not logical to bind the public prosecutor by a certain statutory maximum fine below the statutory maximum fine by which the criminal court would be bound in the same case. Such a restriction did not (and does not) apply under the settlement penalty either. On the other hand, the Public Prosecution Service (Settlement) Act relates to offences of a relatively minor gravity which are simple in nature. A link to a relatively low maximum fine seems logical for practical reasons. Such a link is explicitly made in Art. 257b CCP with respect to punishment orders issued by

[71] Pursuant to Art. 23 (4) CC a sixth-category fine amounts to € 740,000.

[72] Pursuant to Art. 23 (4) 4 CC a second-category fine amounts to € 3700.

[73] Art. 257b (2) CCP.

[74] Art. 257c (2) CCP, Art. 36 (2) Economic Offences Act and Art. 76 (3) General Tax Act. See also *Parliamentary Papers II* 2004/05, 29 849, no. 3, p. 66.

investigating officers. Such a link is also made with respect to community service and disqualification from driving motor vehicles.[75]

5. *IN CONCLUSION*

By introducing the Public Prosecution Service (Settlement) Act, the Dutch legislature provided for a completely new system of extrajudicial disposal of criminal cases. This system is characterised by the circumstance that, unlike before, offences can be disposed of extrajudicially by unilateral and, in principle, binding punishment by the Public Prosecution Service. The fact that this – unilateral, punishing – manner of extrajudicial disposal was chosen can be applauded because it enables the legal nature of criminal law to be expressed better than in the types of extrajudicial disposal based on consensus. Further, it can be considered a gain that the legislature has opened up a complete judicial process (in three instances) for the accused who does not agree with the punishment order issued against him or her. Conversely, it is not logical, as the legislature has done, to attach the consequence to the impossibility to enforce a sanction imposed by a punishment order that the accused still has to be summoned. This is hardly compatible with the final status of the punishment order. Partly for that reason, it is advisable to create a conversion procedure on this point.

[75] Art. 257a (2) (a) and (e) CCP: the community service imposed by a punishment order shall last 180 hours at most and disqualification from driving motor vehicles six months at most.

INTERNAL ACCESS IN THE PRELIMINARY INVESTIGATION

Dirk van der Landen[1]

1. *INTRODUCTION*

The title of this paper sounds complicated, while the subject-matter is actually simple. My paper is about the file. What should it contain? And: at what time is access granted (or even better: a copy provided) to the accused and his or her counsel? These are not trivial questions. The file is the basis of the examination in court. Moreover, the file is the trial judge's first acquaintance with the case. Viewed in this light, the file is the key to the trial. In this metaphor, the public prosecutor is the keeper of the key, as this officer determines which documents are included in the file. These are usually almost exclusively documents incriminating for the accused. As a lawyer, you must then have what it takes to adjust the picture these documents create of the accused and his or her trial.

As a lawyer, I have experience with the flaws in the prevailing legislation concerning the file. In the preliminary investigation, the lawyer does not have any idea of the composition of the file. He or she has no influence on the selection of the documents to be seized in a search and is not involved in the consultations between the public prosecutor and the investigation team on the selection of documents from the seizure with a view to the composition of the file. As the choices are not accounted for in writing, it is not possible for the defence to check them [the same holds for the (trial) judge]. This is all the more cogent, particularly in (major) fraud cases where – even more than in general cases – the accent is on paper documents. Furthermore, in such cases, the examination in court provides hardly any compensation for the very subordinate role of the defence

[1] Lawyer in Amsterdam. For this paper, I have gratefully made use of the input I received from many professional colleagues, in particular Bart Nooitgedagt, Enide Perez and Alexander de Swart.

in the preliminary investigation. In such cases, the point is usually not whether the accused 'did it', but whether the act charged is covered by a criminal provision. In such cases, an examination of (expert) witnesses is an exception. The act charged can be known only from the paper file. Although the immediacy principle – entailing that all facts and circumstances needed to judge the case must be presented before the court at trial – means that the judge must present all evidence to the accused, this is hardly ever done. The judge simply states that he or she *did* present the evidence, after which evidence can be taken from the entire file. This is understandable, because in such case, the file usually consists of dozens of folders, sometimes even more than a hundred, with tens of thousands of annexes. A lawyer who then has the nerve to ask for a separate discussion of each annex at trial is treated with unabashed hostility. You then hear the bench thinking "spanner in the works".

It is sometimes difficult to reach agreement on meeting the needs of accused persons and their counsel in major fraud cases. This surprises me somewhat, because wealthy suspects also have a right to a fair trial. In one respect they are even more vulnerable than the average accused person in a general case. A fraud case is usually already a lost cause for the accused if it comes to trial. This does, after all, ruin the reputation of the person concerned, regardless of the final outcome of the case. The defence strategy is therefore aimed mainly at avoiding a trial. This is possible only if the defence can have the substantiation of the suspicion at their disposal at an early stage. This hardly happens in practice. Files trickle in and accused persons 'dangle' calmly for about three years before they have a more or less complete file at their disposal. Please note: three years counting from the day of the action, i.e. the time they are informed of a criminal suspicion.

In general cases as well, the composition of the court file is at stake in many debates. The defence often seek information by which the reliability of the evidence and legitimacy of the collection of evidence can be assessed (and preferably challenged). Such information will be found in the file only by exception (one should perhaps say: only by mistake). Consequently, one must fight for it. In major (mega) criminal cases, the fight for information is often more intense than that to convince the court of the guilt or innocence of the accused. That fight already starts at the time of the preliminary investigation. In the absence of evidence showing for example how the suspicion arose, the defence (in the preliminary judicial inquiry or by applying to the examining magistrate for a so-called mini instruction), will request an examination of investigating officers etcetera in order to obtain the information needed. The examining magistrate may well require a specific indication of the interest of the defence in such an examination, but can usually not avoid examining a number of such witnesses (the leader of the investigation, the head of the Criminal Intelligence Unit). The results of those examinations are then used to formulate new applications, and with a bit of luck the Public Prosecution Service can be put substantially on the defensive. In that regard, it is remarkable that magistrates (both judges and representatives of the Public Prosecution Service) quite readily reproach the defence that the quest for the start of the investigation and the manner of obtaining evidence are a 'fishing expedition', while time after time it is evident that when this occurs, that expedition takes place in waters full of fish. I do not only mean sensational cases such as the recent Hells Angels case[2] but also drugs investigations, which are two a penny.

So it tallies that internal access in the preliminary investigation is far from ideal. There are still many more problems than I have mentioned above and which I only touch on here for the sake of conciseness.

Criminal tax cases are the result of a selection by the tripartite consultations (TPO) between the tax inspector, the Fiscal Intelligence and Investigation Service and Public Prosecution Service. This selection of means of criminal disposal centres on the question whether there is a suspicion of violation of Section 69 of the State Taxes Act (*Algemene wet inzake rijskbelastingen*) (AWR).[3] The TPO file is referred to quite frequently in the final criminal file. Public prosecutors are nonetheless of the opinion that in practice, TPO

[2] In Amsterdam District Court 20 December 2007, *LJN* BC0685, the Public Prosecution Service was barred from prosecution because for example, in conflict with the CCP, several discussions between the lawyers and accused persons had ended up in the file.

[3] Section 69 AWR criminalises deliberate failure to file a return provided by the Tax Administration, while the offence results in too little tax being levied.

documents are for internal use only. This also results in long witness examinations only about the time schedule of the TPO stage and other details, while that information could easily be taken from those documents if they were provided.

The standard practice at all investigation services is not to give people who are invited to examinations a single document. Instead of suspect status, these people are sometimes given 'merely' the status of cautioned witnesses. These people then tend to take a less firm attitude towards the documents. The underlying idea is apparently that truthful answers are obtained only by springing questions on people. This is of course a nonsensical idea, but one which is rather widespread in judicial circles.

Files in connected cases sometimes prove to be compiled very strategically. A colleague gave me the following example: 'In Piranha 1, the same Advocate General presided as in the Hofstad case. The Piranha file contained witness statements from the Hofstad file. Several of these witnesses had changed, qualified and challenged parts of their statements to the police in the Hofstad case in court during the hearing of the appeal. The Advocate General knew that, but did not add the available police reports of the court of appeal in the Hofstad case to the Piranha file'.

Nowadays, it is customary to impose 'every restriction' on people remanded in custody in major fraud cases. The staff of police stations and courts of appeal then assume that suspects may not have a single paper at their disposal. A lawyer who gives his client only a copy of his or her own arraignment report is often faced with agitated situations.

2. *THE STATUTORY RULES ON INTERNAL ACCESS TO THE PRELIMINARY INVESTIGATION*

All this misery in practice makes one curious about the statutory rules on internal access to the preliminary investigation. That statutory rules are surprisingly simple:

> Sec. 30(1) CCP:
> During the preliminary judicial inquiry, the examining magistrate, and during the preliminary investigation the Public Prosecution Service, shall allow the accused to examine the court documents.

Subsection 2 of Sec. 30 makes it possible 'in the interest of the investigation' not to allow the accused to read 'certain court documents', but that is an exception to the main rule that the accused has a right to examine the court documents. Corstens has clearly described the importance of internal access in the preliminary investigation as follows:

> In principle, the court documents are already internally accessible [Sec. 30(1)] during the investigation prior to prosecution, but also during the preliminary judicial inquiry. This rule expresses, for example, the (moderately) adversarial nature of the trial. The accused should be able to know the basis of the investigation launched into him or her. This is a humanitarian requirement. The tension under which people considered suspects are often put can be reduced if they are aware of the basis of the suspicion. Moreover, examining the court documents also gives accused persons the opportunity to give shape to their defence at an early stage. Those who are familiar with the incriminating material can endeavour to bring up any exculpatory material for discussion.[4]

I fully agree with Corstens, except that I rather tend to view Dutch trials as quite inquisitorial, but I ascribe that to my position as a defence counsel, who experiences from the accused's point of view how forbidding the daily practice of criminal procedure is. I assume that all criminal lawyers will endorse the importance of internal access. The alternative is, after all, a secret preliminary investigation, and that is hardly compatible with the starting points of our democratic state under the rule of law.

So much consensus arouses mistrust. The snake in the grass in this case can easily be traced. The accused has a right to examine the court documents. But the law does not specify what the court documents are. This gives the different actors in the trial the room to achieve their own objectives. Among public prosecutors, the opinion is generally held that the court documents which the accused may examine can be found in the case file, which is compiled under the direction of the public prosecutor. Not surprisingly, lawyers are mostly of the opinion that a broader definition is appropriate and should include all documents that could be important for a decision

---

[4] G.J.M. Corstens, *Het Nederlands strafprocesrecht*, sixth impression, Deventer: Kluwer 2008, p. 91.

to be taken by the court on the basis of Sections 348 and 350 CCP. With that, the lines have been drawn for an often heated legal battle.

One of the first cases in which the ECHR expressed itself on the right to court documents was the Edwards case.[5] After his conviction, it appeared that the police had failed to inform the defence of the fact that the neighbour's fingerprints had been found in the victim's house and that the victim had also looked at a rogues' gallery containing a photo of Edwards and did not recognise him. This information was not in the court documents. The ECHR ruled that the prosecuting authorities had to disclose all information, both incriminating and exculpatory, to the defence. That was not done in this case, which constituted a violation of Art. 6(1) ECHR.

The decision of the ECHR in the Edwards case resounds in the Dev Sol judgment of the Dutch Supreme Court (Hoge Raad). According to the Dutch Supreme Court, the court documents include "all documents which could reasonably be important for the accused in either an incriminating or exculpatory sense".[6] In the same judgment, the Supreme Court ruled (legal ground 5.11):

> A case could come up in which the defence challenges the reliability of some evidence or the lawfulness of the manner in which it was obtained. Such a defence should be investigated. The principles of due process entail that, as a rule, the defence may not be prevented from examining documents important for the assessment of such questions which are not included in the court documents. This does not mean that both counsel and the accused are automatically entitled to a copy of or to examine an aid such as that used by the police in this matter, or other documentation.

Under certain circumstances, therefore, the defence cannot be denied access to such documents, but that does not necessarily mean that such documents have to be added to the file (in this case, a rogues' gallery was concerned which was classified as a means of investigation, thus not as a court document).

This case law still applies. If I understand correctly, the public prosecutor is not required to add documents to the file by which the

---

5 ECHR 16 December 1992, Series A 247-B (Edwards v. UK).

6 HR 7 May 1996, *Nederlandse Jurisprudentie* 1996, 687 annot. Sch.

lawfulness of the collection of evidence can be tested. But if a specific defence is conducted in that case, the defence may not be prevented from examining the relevant documents. This also explains the fight for the documents in legal practice. Could things be different?

3. *CRIMINAL PROCEDURE 2001 (STRAFVORDERING 2001)*

In the second interim report by the Criminal Procedure 2001 research group, a proposal is made to lay down the criterion by law for the selection of documents to be included in the file. The research group opts for a very broad definition, namely 'all documents (in the broadest sense of the word) which are *relevant* to *any* court decision in the case'.[7] This broad definition is connected with the great importance the research group attaches to transparency in the preliminary investigation. The research group:

> The acts performed by the government in relation to the preliminary investigation should (at any rate in retrospect) be clear and verifiable. Transparency promotes the lawfulness of the actions and ultimately increases the reliability of the research results. Moreover, this serves the interests of non-criminal procedures as well, such as the monitoring of integrity.[8]

Important in addition is that the research group attaches importance to an 'adversarial structure of proceedings'. This means that more of an accent should be placed on interaction among the participants in the proceedings and optimisation of the rights of the defence. The research group observes that from this point of view, the rules on the preliminary investigation in the CCP fail seriously. The proposals by the research group are intended to change this. The thread is that the legal protection of citizens during the preliminary investigation should be enhanced, especially on points on which there is an actual need for such protection. Legal

---

[7] M.S. Groenhuijsen, *'Het vooronderzoek in strafzaken. Algemeen deel'*, in: M.S. Groenhuijsen & G. Knigge (ed.), *Het vooronderzoek in strafzaken. Tweede interimrapport onderzoeksproject Strafvordering 2001*, Deventer: Gouda Quint 2001, p. 43.

[8] Groenhuijsen 2001, p. 19.

protection therefore does not always need to be linked automatically to certain acts (intentional or not), but can usually be offered or activated if the defence or another interested party so wishes.

It is not all that easy to put this into practice First of all, the question is whether the positions of the accused and the State in the proceedings are so fundamentally unequal that equality between the parties cannot be taken as a starting point for new rules. This would, after all, ultimately result in less legal protection because the accused is not sufficiently able to invoke his or her rights, while protection by the judge carrying out the review ex officio is diminished. This would, in fact, work only if increasingly heavier requirements were set on the quality of counsel.[9]

In the second place, the question is whether current legal practice has got into such a rut that new legal rules would have no effect at all. I am thinking, for example of the penchant of investigation services to examine people without knowing the facts. I do not see this changing very quickly, not even if the law even more explicitly provides that people have a right to examine the documents. The same holds for the greater accent on interaction among the participants in the proceedings. If you write something like that, you should realise that the average public prosecutor is as good as inaccessible. I do not know whether this would change if more of an accent were placed in legislation on interaction with the bar, all the more so because the predictable consequence of such interaction is that the public prosecutor would have to do something.

4. *IN CONCLUSION*

These perhaps somewhat cynical observations may not conceal the fact that the proposals by the Criminal Procedure 2001 research group outline an alternative to the existing situation in which much (hearing) time is used for matters which do not primarily have to do with a fair trial of the accused. This is faced with sharp, fundamental criticism, while it is not certain that a change to the legal system on this point would also mean an improvement in practice.

---

[9] See A.A. Franken, 'Traditionele waarden van de advocatuur en schuivende verantwoordelijkheden voor de raadsman', *Delikt en Delinkwent* 2007, 27, pp. 360–369.

THE EXAMINATION IN COURT ACCORDING TO CRIMINAL PROCEDURE 2001 (*STRAFVORDERING 2001*), PARTLY AS A REFLECTION ON TRIAL BY JURY

Theo de Roos[1]

1. *INTRODUCTION*

In the first collection of the large research project Criminal Procedure 2001 (*Strafvordering 2001*), following an introduction in which the characteristics of the roles of the participants in Dutch criminal proceedings are described, the starting points are already formulated which should be met by qualitatively adequate and consistent and clearly regulated criminal proceedings.[2] It should not come as a surprise that the examination in court is given such a prominent place in the research report. This is, after all, the public part of the trial, where (in principle) all participants can put forward their points of view, interests and arguments before the authority called upon to decide on the various decisions to be taken. This does not only concern the so-called preliminary questions and main questions, laid down in Sections 348 and 350 CCP, but also numerous interim decisions, for example on the summoning of (further) witnesses and experts or the ex-officio decision of the court to summon the absent suspect, if necessary with a warrant to secure his or her presence. Further, it can also concern consultations between the Judge and the parties on the direction of the case, the so-called pre-trial review (to be dealt with further below), in other words: the (time) schedule of the hearing. It is pre-eminently this public stage in which criminal law acquires a 'face', and the dramatic and adversarial nature of the trial as a battle becomes visible to both the participants themselves and the public. The social importance of this can hardly be underestimated. This is not affected by the fact that

---

[1] Professor of Criminal Law, Department of Criminal Law, Tilburg University.

[2] M.S. Groenhuijsen & G. Knigge (ed.), *Het onderzoek ter zitting. Eerste interim-rapport onderzoeksproject Strafvordering 2001*, Deventer: Kluwer 2001.

the preliminary investigation is often 'decisive' and in the Dutch system, the file seems to take a more central place than the input of the parties and the judge him or herself at the hearing.[3] Compared to a top-rate jury trial according to the North American model, the Dutch trial can simply be called dull. This in itself is not a disqualification from the viewpoint of an objective and sincere pursuit of the truth. What one should realise, however, is that in comparing the – naturally – sharply accentuated American 'TV reality' with the Dutch day-to-day reality is that many American jury trials can also be very dull and not satisfy the ideal image of an O.J. Simpson trial. The interesting thing in this comparison, although it can be put in perspective, is that in essence a difference cannot be denied, entailing that in an American jury trial, much more is left to the parties than in a Dutch trial. In this context, it is striking that precisely now, one of the starting points of Criminal Procedure 2001 is that more should be left to the initiative of the parties to the trial. What I should like to undertake here is to give an impetus to the evaluation of the merits of the Dutch trial as evaluated by the Criminal Procedure 2001 research project and the results of this project itself in relation to this important part of the trial, mirrored by the jury trial including other models in which lay participation plays a part.

2. *THE JURY AS A MIRROR*

It requires some explanation, of course, why precisely trial by jury or – more broadly speaking – trials with lay participation are brought up in an evaluating discussion of the results of Criminal Procedure 2001. The researchers concerned did not, after all, want to introduce it under any circumstances, and one wonders if the theme lay participation is meaningful in this context. I am nevertheless of the opinion that this is the case. The circumstance alone that the Netherlands is an exception, certainly in Europe (together with Luxembourg) to the rule that laymen play a part in criminal procedure in one way or another makes one curious about the

[3] See also the contribution by Van der Landen to this collection.

motivations and assumptions on the basis of which all those other national legal systems made the choice to involve laymen in the criminal justice system. I have done a comparative and exploratory study into this elsewhere.[4] It emerged from this that the fundamental starting points of the trial quickly come up for discussions, also in particular the nature and function of the examination in court. What does Criminal Procedure 2001 (*Strafvordering 2001*) itself have to say about the intentional choice of the purely professional administration of criminal justice? In the third interim report, we find the following short passage on this subject:

> The project's (...) point of departure is the existing shortage of legislation. This entails that the research is aimed at finding solutions for the shortcomings that occur. That which functions smoothly needs no special attention, even if other solutions are theoretically conceivable, as evidenced by the law in other countries. For instance, the choice of professional judges – and therefore the rejection of jury trials – is undoubtedly one of the determining characteristics of the system of our code. This choice is still broadly endorsed. It is not a problem in any respect. So there is no reason to bring this 'fundamental' choice up for discussion.[5]

This passage deserves close reading. First of all, it is striking that it does not concern the position taken here in the Netherlands, but the actually biased position that jury systems do not perform as well as professional ones. Jury systems are rejected on pragmatic grounds, which one could represent by the familiar slogan: never change a winning horse. It is claimed further that the professional system is 'still' widely supported.

This position is still taken (in 2009), but when the researchers wrote these words, they could not have expected that, in the meantime, a debate would nevertheless be started over the desirability of lay participation. But in drawing up the final report (the fourth and last report), they already saw reason to deal more extensively with

---

[4] Th.A. de Roos, *Is de invoering van lekenrechtspraak in de Nederlandse strafrechtspleging gewenst?*, Tilburg: Tilburg University 2006.

[5] G. Knigge, 'Dwangmiddelen en rechtsmiddelen. Algemeen deel', in: M.S. Groenhuijsen & G. Knigge (ed.), *Dwangmiddelen en rechtsmiddelen. Derde interimrapport onderzoeksproject Strafvordering 2001*, Deventer: Kluwer 2002, p. 9.

the issue, as a result of ideas expressed in legal literature.[6] In the context of a reply to critics, they already explained in more detail why they maintained their position. The authors see several reasons "why, beforehand, it does not seem likely in the foreseeable future that any study could result in a recommendation for our country to allow any form of lay participation in the administration of justice". First of all, they point out cultural and historical reasons. In many countries which have a jury system as a constitutionally embedded right to trial by peers, this was a reaction to periods in which the administration of justice was experienced as an instrument of repression in the hands of the dominating power. In that case, the jury has traditionally been a bastion of freedom. The authors do not give any examples, but they are indeed easy to find: the United States, but also Spain and Russia. There is no such tradition or history in the Netherlands. Secondly, the authors mention the composition of the judiciary. Unlike in many countries where the jury is viewed as a guarantee against politicisation of the judiciary, in the Netherlands there is no real danger of political appointments on grounds other than quality. A third reason is social dissatisfaction with the administration of criminal justice. It cannot be denied that such dissatisfaction can indeed be detected in the Netherlands, but this holds firmly as well in no uncertain terms for the practical functioning of the jury in countries with jury systems. Lastly, the authors do not see much value in "exploring a totally alien new path" because there are good alternatives for the improvement of communication between the population and the judiciary, such as improvement of the substantiation culture.

For these reasons, it was not considered opportune at present to give priority to a comparative law study of forms of lay participation. We would see cause to broaden and deepen accountability for this choice only if the literature were to make somewhat worked out and reasoned proposals to amend the prevailing law on this point, say the researchers. But, as said, the debate over this material in the Netherlands started only after publication of the final report.

[6] M.S. Groenhuijsen & G. Knigge, 'Afronding en verantwoording. Algemeen deel', in: M.S. Groenhuijsen & G. Knigge (ed.), *Afronding en Verantwoording. Eindrapport onderzoeksproject Strafvordering 2001*, Deventer: Kluwer 2004, pp. 104–107.

This was due to the advance of 'Fortuynism' and the entry of the political party 'Lijst Pim Fortuyn' into Parliament. That is where the initiative came from to place the administration of justice by laymen on the political agenda.[7] At the end of 2005, the former Minister of Justice promised the Lower House that he would have research done into the desirability of lay participation in criminal procedure.[8] I issued advice at the Minister's request at the end of 2006,[9] entailing that, at present, no urgent reasons could be indicated for proceeding to make such a drastic reform, also taking into consideration that internationally, and certainly in Europe, the Netherlands is out of step on this issue. An opinion survey carried out on commission by the Minister of Justice pointed in the same direction.[10] But even if there no longer seems to be any urgent reason to pursue the theme, it has rather increased the significance of comparative law in this field. Of particular importance in this regard is a comparative strengths-weaknesses analysis for the purpose of mapping out where the weaknesses in an almost purely professional system can be pointed out in comparison with the systems having lay participation, albeit in very diverse forms. This would also help to facilitate reflection on the foundations of the Dutch system of the law of criminal procedure. In this way, new light could perhaps be shed on problems and tensions occurring within that system, such as tension between the pursuit of efficiency in criminal procedure (one of the points of view of Criminal Procedure 2001) and the thoroughness of the disposal of criminal cases; and also between the visibility and comprehensibility of such disposal for the public on the one hand, and the purely professional structure of the trial on the other, which sees to it that the man or woman in the public gallery soon loses track, and that debates between legal experts easily resemble private chats.

---

[7] Joost Eerdmans of the LPF was particularly active in this respect. The other political parties did not automatically reject this. The Netherlands Association for the Judiciary and the Council for the Judiciary wisely stayed in the background.

[8] *Parliamentary Papers II* 2005/06, 30 300 VI (and 29 279), no. 120.

[9] De Roos 2006.

[10] A. Klijn & M. Croes, 'Wil het volk ook meedoen? Burgers over hun bereidheid tot deelname aan de strafrechtspraak', in: *Rechtstreeks* 2007, pp. 81–102.

3. *STARTING POINTS OF CRIMINAL PROCEDURE 2001 AND THE EXAMINATION IN COURT*

According to Criminal Procedure 2001, an active, non-passive judge is a guarantee that the establishment of the facts (establishment of the 'substantive truth') is correct.[11] "It is assumed that the condition that the judge must be personally convinced that the facts are true reduces the chance of errors". This is no absolute guarantee; it can be exchanged for another (for example a confessing suspect). "The actual question is always what combination of guarantees provides a sufficient degree of certainty that the facts established are true." The researchers distinguish the following 'times for deliberation':

- The tension implied in the twofold objective of the trial: on the one hand, punishment of the guilty and, on the other, preventing punishment of the innocent. Although doubt must be to the accused's advantage, this does not yet relieve the tension completely. 'Unreasonable' acquittals should be avoided as well as questionable convictions, subject to the loss of social acceptance of criminal law.
- A reasonable proportion between the degree of legal protection of the accused and the costs of the trial.
- The interests of the accused should be weighed against the interests of certain third parties (for example witnesses).
- The importance of a fair hearing should be weighed against the importance of an efficient handling of the case.
- The more drastic the decision to be taken, the more guarantees are required for the accused.
- Facts which are disputed should be investigated more thoroughly than facts which are not in dispute.

As far as the procedure in court in 'major' cases is concerned, it should be noted that the researchers argue in favour of a greater role for the trial judge, expressed for example in the pre-trial review, where the course of the public, final investigation is coordinated. This element is in keeping with the goal of more input from the

---

[11] M.S. Groenhuijsen & G. Knigge, 'Algemeen deel', in: M.S. Groenhuijsen & G. Knigge (red.), *Het onderzoek ter zitting. Eerste interimrapport onderzoeksproject Strafvordering 2001*, Deventer: Kluwer 2001, p. 18 ff.

parties in giving shape to the proceedings.[12] It contributes to the adversarial nature of the proceedings, and also offers the Judge the opportunity to fulfil his or her leading, 'directive' role, for example by having witnesses or experts called up ex officio. Lastly, the pre-trial review helps to promote an effective use of the scarce hearing capacity and a timely disposal of the case.

4. THE PUBLIC EXAMINATION IN COURT AND THE ESTABLISHMENT OF THE TRUTH IN AN INTERNATIONAL PERSPECTIVE

In this context, I centre on the establishment of the truth, while taking a sidelong glance at jury systems (in a broad sense). The Dutch system highly values an efficient, timely settlement of the case. We also found this in the starting points of Criminal Procedure 2001. Although there are cases that take up many hearing days, these are exceptions. Serious cases as well (for example rape, murder and homicide) are often disposed of in a few hours, although by the three-judge section of the court or court of appeal. If the accused has confessed and persists in his or her confession, and no special problems with evidence occur, the debate will concentrate mainly on the severity of the sentence and the penal modality. On the other hand, for example the Belgian assizes procedure in which, in a manner of speaking, every stone is turned three times bears witness to a totally different approach.[13] The same holds for the jury in most North American states, but also for the German mixed courts, in which a professional judge decides on the evidence and penalty together with laymen. Those hearings last longer than the average Dutch hearing, because all evidence must be presented at the hearing (immediacy principle, 'Mündlichkeitsprinzip'). In his contribution to this collection, Weigend points out that the great trust placed in preliminary investigations in Dutch trials is possible only because lay judges are not employed. One may expect professional judges to

---

[12] Groenhuijsen & Knigge 2001, p. 44.

[13] L. van Almelo, *Dames en heren van de jury. Juryrechtspraak in Nederland*, Wormer: Inmerc 2007, and P.J.A. de Hert, 'Jury en leken in Nederland: een identiteitsonderzoek' *Nederlands Juristenblad* 2006, pp. 2226–2233.

be able to study and evaluate written documents properly, which cannot be required of laymen.[14] Another consequence of that choice is that everything dealt with at the hearing must be understandable to laymen, which facilitates understandability to the general public. The role of professional judges in American trials is different from that in the continental European systems; he or she is an arbitrator; establishing the truth is reserved for the parties to the trial, who exercise the right of examination and cross-examination in order to do so. Criminal Procedure 2001, on the other hand, emphasises the active role of the judge and his or her own responsibility for establishing the truth. If necessary, the judge can have experts and witnesses called up ex officio. If, after the investigation is closed, it proves in chambers that the investigation was not complete, it is possible that the case will be reopened, and further investigative acts can be ordered.[15]

In the Dutch system, the judge is *both* an investigator *and* an arbitrator, which is a difficult double role. In addition, he or she also takes final decisions. The trial court, particularly in the highest factual instance, bears a heavy responsibility resulting from that combination of tasks. One can best imagine this when serious cases are concerned with denying accused persons or accused persons who recant a previous statement containing a confession, partial or not, certainly when the evidence is problematic, i.e. the category in which, for example the Lucia de B., Ina Post, the Schiedam Park murder and Putten murder (and in the United Kingdom the Guildford Four and the Birmingham Six) cases belong. In such cases, the court's own responsibility for establishing the truth carry the most weight. Although the trial judge largely depends on the results of the preliminary investigation which are given to him or her by the Public Prosecution Service, the defence and – in recent years to a much

---

14 According to Weigend, Germany pays a high price for adhering to the immediacy principle, namely the disposal of increasingly more cases by plea bargaining (*Absprachen*).

15 See also Weigend in this collection: 'If we wish to still maintain the goal of reaching verdicts and sentences in accordance with 'substantive' truth – and I think that giving up that goal would seriously undermine the legitimacy of criminal justice as we know it – it is necessary that the court retain at least a residual authority to obtain information independently of the wishes of the parties.'

lesser extent because of the cutting down of the preliminary judicial inquiry to the bone – the examining magistrate. This should also demonstrate the added value of collegial decision-making. It is the counterpart of the of the multiple decision-making by twelve jurors in the Belgian courts of assizes and North American jury systems. A big difference between those systems and the Dutch one is that the decision-makers in the aforementioned system are completely dependent on information supplied by others (the parties or, in the Belgian assizes, also the judge). A Dutch trial judge, on the other hand, can exert considerable influence on the information passed on to him or her. In major criminal cases such as the abovementioned, the judge will under no circumstances be able to limit him or herself to 'verification' of the results of the preliminary investigation. If the defence is lacking in quality, the judge will have to be extra alert. In the project *Versterking Opsporing en Vervolging* (Addit ional Measures for the Investigation and Prosecution Authorities) which was started after the Schiedam Park murder case, among many other measures, provision was made for the designation of defence officers at the police and judicial authorities.[16] The three-judge panel in criminal cases must, as it were, organise their own defence.

5. *THE MEANING OF THE SUBSTANTIATION OF EVIDENCE*

An important aid in this respect is substantiation, which was also strongly emphasised by Criminal Procedure 2001. The recent legal developments have brought about major innovations on this very point: the toughening of the duty of substantiation through the addition of Art. 359 (2) CCP, and the so-called PROMIS project which was concluded in 2008, the results of which have now been implemented nationwide. I will deal briefly with both. But first of all, I will indicate why a careful substantiation practice can contribute towards reliable establishment of the truth by the criminal court. In doing so, I am in line with Gommer's considerations in his Tilburg University dissertation on the forming of opinions by the court in

[16] Report *Versterking opsporing en vevolging naar aanleiding van de Schiedammer parkmoord* (Public Prosecution Service/Police/Netherlands Forensic Institute 4 November 2005).

establishing the truth.[17] This author – referring to behavioural science literature – argues that judicial opinions are formed relatively quickly and intuitively, without it being possible to determine how the information is processed and weighed. This initial, intuitive phase is followed by an accountability phase in which, on the basis of the available information – the potential evidence – it must be demonstrated that rational reasoning can be formulated which is convincing and can be followed easily by third parties, which is conclusive for the judgment (acquittal or judicial finding of fact). All experienced judges will recognise this image: in chambers, the conviction which is established by the documents and the proceedings at trial (where the preliminary opinion formed can sometimes be overturned!) is supplemented by possible evidence taken from the documents and statements at trial. The charges then constitute the compulsory framework. It frequently happens that during the deliberations in chambers, holes appear which cannot be closed. In other words: there is no 'cover' for a finding of fact, even though all judges may be convinced, on whatever grounds. It frequently occurs as well, of course, that the defence has conducted meritorious defences, thereby outlining alternative scenarios. If such a meritorious defence is explicitly substantiated by arguments and results in a clear conclusion, any rejection by the court has to be substantiated. If the implausibility of the defence is not immediately clear, this may require some racking of brains and thus diligent substantiation work. This can only benefit the establishment of the truth. In addition to other functions substantiation has in criminal cases, such as the explanation function (explaining to parties and the public how the court reached its judgment), the 'reporting' function is very important here when it comes to the reliability of the judicial opinion regarding proof. In this light, the above-mentioned developments (the expansion of Art. 359 (2) CCP and PROMIS) can be hailed. The legislative amendments were drafted in a somewhat curious manner, namely during the debate over the Confessing Suspect Bill in the Lower House. The Members of Parliament Wolfsen [Partij van de Arbeid (Labour Party)] and Griffith [Volkspartij voor

[17] H. Gommer, *Onder de rechter* (diss. Tilburg), Nijmegen: Wolf Legal Publishers 2008, particularly Chapter 3.

Vrijheid en Democratie (People's Party for Freedom and Democracy)] announced that they would propose an amendment in which a duty of substantiation was imposed on the judge when he or she departed from the demand by the Public Prosecution Service.[18] After consultation with the Ministry of Justice, a well-considered formulation was chosen with a much broader scope, through which a duty of substantiation was created completely in the spirit of the proposals by Criminal Procedure 2001 for judges who depart from 'explicitly substantiated positions' of the parties to the trial.[19] The Dutch Supreme Court seized the first opportunity to develop a framework within which this expansion could take shape.[20] After some initial lack of clarity and debate, it can now be determined that there has indeed been an expansion of the duty of justification, although the requirement must be met that a meritorious defence by the defence counsel must be based on sufficient substantiation and that it must have an unambiguous point (the same holds for other positions taken by the Public Prosecution Service and the defence on the occasion of the examination in court).[21] After the PROMIS experiment, finalised in two phases, was concluded with a favourably disposed final report,[22] it is now (2008–2009) being implemented nationwide. My impression, based on discussions with judges, is that there has clearly been a change which in general has been evaluated positively by those concerned (also lawyers and members of the Public Prosecution Service). A warning note is appropriate here, namely that initial enthusiasm can dilute, resulting gradually in the creation of a routine which can remove a considerable part of the progress. This could be due in part to the heavy pressure on the

---

[18] About this curious course of affairs see M.S. Groenhuijsen, 'Over toeval in het wetgevingsdebat over strafprocesrecht: de uitbouw van een contradictoire gedingstructuur in strafzaken,' *Delikt en Delinkwent* 2005, 23, pp. 351–359.

[19] *Kamerstukken II* 2003/04, 29 255, nr. 8. See G.J.M. Corstens, *Het Nederlands strafprocesrecht*, sixth impression, Deventer: Kluwer 2008, pp. 722–725, and J.F. Nijboer, Strafrechtelijk bewijsrecht, fifth impression, Nijmegen: Ars Aequi Libri 2008, pp. 297–304.

[20] The PROMIS judgments HR 15 May 2007, *Nederlandse Jurisprudentie* 2007, 387 annot. Y. Buruma and HR 15 May 2007, *Nederlandse Jurisprudentie* 2007, 388.

[21] HR 15 May 2007, *Nederlandse Jurisprudentie* 2007, 374 annot. P.A.M. Mevis.

[22] *Eindrapport PROMIS II. Project motiveringsverbetering in strafvonnissen*, The Hague, Council for the Judiciary 2008.

criminal justice system, focused particularly on quantitative, easily measurable achievements ('end products'). Be that as it may, for the time being it can be considered a benefit of the expanded duty of substantiation in the amended paragraph 2 of Article 359 CCP together with the PROMIS practice that the judgments in cases in which there are serious differences of opinion between the parties to the trial are substantiated in a more readable and accessible manner (particularly through the narrative structure used), that the grounds are made available to the parties and the press at the time of the judgment – which means that the parties will be able to decide whether or not to use legal remedies much sooner than usual up to now – and, last but not least, that immediately after the session in chambers, it must be thoroughly examined whether the conviction formed, the scenario or the 'account' that will have to underpin the finding of fact, is actually supported sufficiently by evidence, every bit of which is convincing, reliable and conclusive. With that, something has been done about a point on which Dutch trials, strongly focused as they are on efficiency, showed a weakness compared with the trial culture in Germany and at the assizes in Belgium. In Germany, the thorough and extensive proceedings at the trial, combined with a strongly developed substantiation culture,[23] is a guarantee of a high quality establishment of the truth (which, by the way, does not mean that the German system is superior as a whole. One should bear in mind, for example, that, in principle, it does not have any possibility for appeal). The substantiation of the evidence and sentence is prepared by the chairman, a professional judge, and is subject to review by the Bundesgerichtshof. The assizes procedure, however, does not have a duty of substantiation. This was already a bone of contention in the political and legal debates over this procedure, but the critics have meanwhile received firm support from the European Court of Human Rights,[24] which ruled that the total absence of substantiation was in conflict with Art. 6 ECHR. The complainant had directed one of his grounds for appeal against a lack of substantiation by the Court of Assizes in Liege in answering

---

[23] W.H.B. Dreissen, *Bewijsmotivering in strafzaken* (diss. Maastricht), The Hague: Boom Juridische uitgevers 2007.

[24] ECHR 13 January 2009, Appl. no. 926/05 (Taxquet v. Belgium).

four questions which the chairman had posed to the jurors (the applicant was sentenced to 20 years imprisonment on 7 January 2004 for (among other offences) the murder of Minister André Cools). This complaint based on Article 6(1) ECHR was successful and therefore laid a mine under the Belgian system.[25] According to the Court of Human Rights, the laconic answers ('yes' or 'no') to vague and general questions could give the impression of an arbitrary and not very transparent administration of justice. It is important, according to the Court, to present the grounds which convinced the jury of the guilt or innocence of the accused, and to indicate specific reasons why each question was answered in the affirmative or the negative, in order to explain this to the accused but also to the public (the 'people' on whose behalf justice is administered).

6. *IN CONCLUSION*

In the foregoing, I have attempted to bring into perspective several important proposals of the Criminal Procedure 2001 project which have meanwhile been adopted in the law or legal practice by centring on the subject of lay participation in criminal procedure in the discussion thereof. The purpose was to use foreign systems which, unlike the Dutch law of criminal procedure, engage lay persons ('ordinary' citizens) in some way or another – strongly diverging amongst them – as just as many mirrors in order to detect weaknesses in our own system on the basis of a strengths-weaknesses analysis and to recognise what Criminal Procedure 2001 has done to strengthen those weaknesses. It was thus explicitly not my intention to answer the question whether the Dutch system scores better or worse than foreign systems, or whether for other reasons, for example the pursuit of democracy, (unlike the researchers of Criminal Procedure 2001 argue) a jury system or another system in which lay persons administer justice together with professionals should perhaps be introduced in the Netherlands nonetheless. It has been pointed out that at the time this paper was written, these questions were clearly not felt to be very urgent in broad political and social

[25] Based on the judgment, the High Council of Justice argued for abolishment of the courts of assizes.

circles. This does not alter the fact that knowledge of (elements) of such systems can sharpen one's eye for the flaws and points for improvement in our own system. It can be stated that the institution of pre-trial review and especially the improvement of substantiation practice, both suggested by Criminal Procedure 2001, have resulted in strengthening of the procedure. They confirm the adversarial nature of the trial without undermining its efficient nature (traditionally a strength of the trial in the Netherlands). Concerning the latter, however, there is also cause for some concern: the heavy pressure on the criminal justice system and the judgment of courts by quantitative results also puts the pursuit of quality under constant pressure.

THE LAW OF EVIDENCE AND SUBSTANTIATION OF EVIDENCE

Joep Simmelink[1]

1. *INTRODUCTION*

For several years, the legislation programme relating to the law of criminal procedure has centred on revision of the Code of Criminal Procedure (*Wetboek van Strafvordering*) (*Sv*). In the context of this revision programme, many amendments were made to the Code. A number of important bills are in different stages of preparation.[2] The term 'revision' entails more than making amendments to the Code. It also includes the clarification and adjustment of underlying assumptions and principles of the law of criminal procedure. The roots of this revision movement can be found in the research project '*Strafvordering 2001*' ('Criminal Procedure 2001'), the results of which are set out in four reports on '*Het onderzoek ter zitting*' ('The examination in court'), '*Het vooronderzoek in strafzaken*' (The preliminary investigation in criminal cases'), '*Dwangmiddelen en rechtsmiddelen*' ('Means of coercion and legal remedies') and '*Afronding en verantwoording*' ('Conclusion and information').

An important starting point for reform of the law of criminal procedure is to emphasise the nature of criminal proceedings as an adversarial process. Criminal proceedings should not focus only on applying substantive criminal law, but, in a broader perspective, should enable an adequate government response to presumably committed offences. Against the background of these starting points, the law of criminal procedure should be structured in such a way that justice is done to the concept 'adversarial'. Matters that are

---

[1] Advocate General at the Public Prosecutor's Office at the Leeuwarden Court of Appeal.

[2] A survey of legislative activities in the law of criminal procedure can be found in Parliamentary Papers (*Kamerstukken*) II, 29 271, *Algemeen kader herziening Wetboek van Strafvordering*.

'debated' between the participants in the trial then need special attention. Amendments to the Code which ensue from this idea are provisions relating to the phenomenon of 'pre-trial review'[3], the so-called 'confessing accused'[4], the introduction of Art. 359(2), second sentence, of the Code of Criminal Procedure (CCP)[5] and the structure of appeal based on the concept of 'progressive appeal'.[6]

Against the background of the Dutch practical style of conducting proceedings, emphasis on the adversarial nature of criminal proceedings cannot be considered a real, systematic turnaround. It can rather be said that the related legislative amendments are largely in line with a development that has taken place in practice. Those amendments are intended to provide a more appropriate procedural framework for that developed practice. An example of an amendment that can be considered a real revision of the original system of the Code is the acceptance of an independent sentencing authority for the Public Prosecution Service, with the introduction of the Public Prosecution Service (Settlement) Act (*Wet OM-afdoening*).[7] In this regard, reference can be made to the recognition of the

---

[3] Act of 10 November 2004, Bulletin of Acts and Decrees (*Stb.*) 2004, 579. A pre-trial review (*regiezitting*) is the first stage of the hearing of a criminal case in open court, intended to identify and list what additional investigation (such as examining witnesses, an investigation by experts or the drafting of a probation report) is still necessary before the substance of the case can be handled in court.

[4] Act of 10 November 2004, Bulletin of Acts and Decrees 2004, 580. The provisions entail that in the event of a 'confessing accused', under Art. 359(3) of the Dutch Code of Civil Procedure, the court may suffice with limited substantiation of the evidence: 'In so far as the accused has confessed to the proven charges, a statement of the articles of evidence may suffice, unless he subsequently makes a different statement or his counsel has argued for acquittal'.

[5] Act of 10 November 2004, Bulletin of Acts and Decrees 2004, 580. This sentence reads: 'If the decision departs from the positions explicitly substantiated by the accused or the public prosecutor, the judgment must in particular state the reasons resulting in such departure'.

[6] Act of 5 October 2006, Bulletin of Acts and Decrees 2006, 470. The 'progressive appeal' is no longer aimed at hearing the case again and completely on appeal (this was the original model), but at a hearing which centres on the objections of the defence and/or the Public Prosecution Service (*openbaar ministerie*) to the judgment in the first instance. See the paper by J.W. Fokkens in this collection.

[7] Act of 7 July 2006, Bulletin of Acts and Decrees 2006, 330. Regarding settlement by the Public Prosecution Service, see also the paper by T. Kooijmans in this collection.

independent place of a victim of an offence in the trial, as expressed in the legislation to strengthen the position of victims.[8]

The firmer embedment of the adversarial nature of criminal proceedings in the Code was achieved partly by amendments to evidentiary law and the rules relating to substantiation of the criminal judgment. The impetus for this legal development was set out in the first interim report on the examination in court and the sub-report included in it on evidentiary law and substantiation of evidence.[9] With the amendments made to date to the provisions on evidentiary law and substantiation of evidence, the legislature has only partially implemented the starting point formulated in the first interim report of rules of criminal procedure based on adversarial proceedings. A farther reaching legal development seems possible. In this paper, attention is devoted to possible reference points for such further development. For this purpose, it is important to give a brief description first of the starting points for the structuring of evidentiary law and substantiation of evidence referred to in the aforementioned sub-report (section 2). Next, the amendments made to the Code of Criminal Procedure on that basis are explained (section 3). The argument then focuses on ideas for further reform of the rules of evidentiary law and substantiation of criminal judgments (section 4).

2. *THE IMPETUS: THE SUB-REPORT ON 'EVIDENTIARY LAW AND SUBSTANTIATION OF EVIDENCE'*

In the sub-report on 'Evidentiary Law and Substantiation of Evidence' in the first interim report, several starting points were formulated for new legal rules on decisions on evidence and accountability for these decisions in court judgments.[10] Parts of these

---

[8] Act of 17 December 2009, Bulletin of Acts and Decrees 2010, 1 (Amendment of the Code of Criminal Procedure, the Criminal Code and the Criminal Injuries Compensation Fund Act to strengthen the position of victims in criminal proceedings).

[9] See the first interim report of the research project Criminal Procedure 2001 by M.S. Groenhuijsen & G. Knigge (eds.), *Het onderzoek ter zitting* (The examination in court), Groningen 1999, pp. 15–52 and 397–454.

[10] See Groenhuijsen & Knigge 1999, pp. 434–452. These starting points are only briefly touched on in the following. The aforementioned sub-report contains a more detailed explanation.

starting points are in line with the practice of the law of criminal procedure, as it has developed in the course of the years. Other parts propose adjusting evidentiary law to the model of criminal proceedings as adversarial proceedings. The recommendation to exchange the current evidentiary system in which one is innocent until proved guilty explicitly for a free evidentiary system is of the first category. The background of this recommendation is the fact that the current evidentiary system in which one is innocent until proved guilty actually functions already as a free evidentiary system. For this reason, it is argued that the law does not have to give a limitative list of admissible means of evidence, but should be based on the idea that evidence can be provided by all means.

The choice of a free evidentiary system does not imply that no rules need be set on separate means of evidence and the evaluation of evidence. Limitations are conceivable also in a free evidentiary system on the usability of evidence or on the possibility for the court to conclude that the charges have been proved. In this context, it is argued in the sub-report that the 'traditional' concept of minimum evidence now included in the Code (this concerns Art. 341(4)[11] and 342(2)[12] CCP, with the corresponding exception to the latter of official reports by investigating officers[13]), should be maintained.[14] In recognizing and accepting the limited meaning this minimum evidence has in evidentiary case law[15], one should consider them absolute minimum guarantees of the soundness and appropriateness of the decision on evidence.[16]

---

[11] This provision reads: 'Proof that the accused has committed the offence charged cannot be assumed by the court only on the basis of statements by the accused'.

[12] This provision reads: 'Proof that the accused has committed the offence charged cannot be assumed by the court only on the basis of a statement by one witness'.

[13] Even if the official report does not contain anything but a police officer's statement about observations concerning the offence, the court concludes on that basis that the charges have been proved.

[14] Regarding the other 'tradition' in Art. 344(1)(5) CCP, it is argued that this is not in keeping with a free evidentiary system.

[15] See Melai-Groenhuijsen, *Wetboek van Strafvordering*, Art. 341, note 10; Art. 342, notes 36 and 37 (D.M.H.R. Garé & A. Beier).

[16] See regarding Art. 342(2) CCP: HR 30 June 2009, LJN BH3704 and HR 30 June 2009, LJN BG7746.

Another limitation on the usability of evidence can be found in the current Article 341(3) CCP. Based on this rule, because of their alleged unreliability, the judge may not use statements made by co-accused.[17] Strictly speaking, this provision does not fit in very well with a free evidentiary system. In such a system, after all, it is left to the judge to decide what evidence he considers reliable and wants to use as a basis for the declaring the charges proved. Moreover, the consequences of Article 341(3) CCP can easily be avoided by the phenomenon of simultaneous but not joined hearings of criminal cases against co-accused.[18] Against this background, a proposal has been made to reformulate this traditional concept of minimum evidence, in the sense that only statements made at the hearing by co-accused being tried at the same time may not be used as evidence. In this proposal, it is not important whether the cases against the co-accused are joined or not. The underlying idea of this proposal is that this provision does not relate to the possible unreliability of such statements, but to guaranteeing due process at the trial.[19]

Regarding the 'modern' concept of minimum evidence in the present Article 344a CCP, a proposal has been made to arrive at different rules. In the present Article 344a CCP, against the background of the right of examination in Article 6 ECHR, issues that can be separated in the core are lumped together too much. With respect to 'anonymous witnesses', 'threatened witnesses', 'protected witnesses' and 'rewarded witnesses', the article contains rules on verification (particularly exercise of the right of examination) and the evaluation of evidence (support of the statements by other evidence). Because these issues concern diverse interests, I am of the opinion that such issues should also be dealt with diversely in the context of evidentiary law. Moreover, Art. 344a CCP only gives rules for limited categories of witnesses on the use of those witnesses' statements,

---

[17] The term 'co-accused' is construed fairly formally in the judicial system: a 'co-accused' is a person who stands trial at the same time *in the same case* as a co-accused.

[18] If cases are not joined, they are no longer the same case, but two or more different cases (depending on the number of co-accused), which are heard at the same time by coincidence.

[19] See also the conclusion of A-G Knigge in HR 2 December 2008, Dutch Law Reports (NJ) 2009, 10.

whereas, in practice, the criminal justice system shows that the right to examine witnesses is limited in many more situations and questions arise regarding the use of those statements and their support by other means of evidence which are necessary for a conviction. At present, the Code does not give rules for those cases which provide an impetus for an answer to the question whether a particular statement may be used as evidence and if so, under what conditions.

In so far as limitations are concerned on the usability of witness statements that relate to the right of examination under Art. 6 ECHR, it is argued in the sub-report that Art. 344a CCP as a minimum evidence provision can better be transformed into a general provision which prompts the court to weigh the interests in relation to the question of the use of a witness statement as evidence. The proposed provision comes down to the ability of the court to attach consequences to the impossibility to exercise the right to examine witnesses at trial, depending on a. the extent of violation of the right of examination, b. the possibility to examine the witness in the preliminary investigation, c. the existence of alternative possibilities to check the reliability of the witness and correctness of his or her statement, and d. support of the statement by other evidence. The advantages of this general provision are that it pertains to all cases in which exercise of the right to examine witnesses in court is under pressure[20] and that it enables the court to weigh all interests involved in the actual case.

An objection put forward against this amendment is that the current Art. 344a CCP gives judges relatively 'firm' rules for passing judgments. The proposed amendment would cause those 'firm' rules to be exchanged for an open provision that does not give judges much of a starting point for making their decisions. In my opinion, this objection is only relative. The scope of the firm rules of the current Art. 344a CCP is limited to quantitatively rarely occurring phenomena such as anonymous witnesses, threatened witnesses and rewarded witnesses. The Code does not provide for more everyday matters in which 'ordinary' witnesses cannot be examined for one reason or other, such as illness, reliance on a right not to give

[20] And thus not only applicable to anonymous witnesses, threatened witnesses and protected witnesses.

evidence or inability to trace him or her. In these cases, judges have to fall back on the case law of the ECHR and Dutch Supreme Court (Hoge Raad) to answer the question of the usability of witness statements as evidence, and weigh all interests involved in the particular case. The advantage of the proposed provision is that precisely this 'general model' would be taken as a starting point in the Code.

In addition to statutory limitations on the use of evidence or the evaluation of evidence, the free evidentiary system does not prevent further 'refining' in evidentiary case law. It is assumed in the case law for instance that statements by the counsel for the accused or by the public prosecutor charged with handling the case[21] cannot be used as evidence.[22] The legal basis of this 'exclusion of evidence' is connected with the position of the persons involved in the trial and the context in which the statements are made. A lawyer should not be limited in the context of his defence of the accused by the risk that his comments will be used as evidence against his client. Exercise of the right of prosecution and the duties of the public prosecutor at the trial prevents statements by the public prosecutor from being used as a basis for declaring the charges proved. Nor can statements made by an accused be used as evidence under current evidentiary case law. This applies for example to statements the accused makes to an expert (such as a staff member of the probation service or a forensic psychiatrist) who is charged with preparing a social inquiry report about the accused. In the context of the assistance relationship between the reporting expert and the accused, for the purposes of a sound social inquiry report, the accused should be able to tell his or her story uninhibitedly. If it were possible to use the accused person's statement as evidence, there would be a risk that accused persons will be less willing to cooperate in the drafting of social inquiry reports, which would have a negative effect on the information the judge needs for sentencing.[23] The foregoing limitations in case law

---

[21] Statements by counsel or the public prosecutor are perceived by the judge in court, so these statements, as the judge's 'own perceptions', could be considered legal evidence.

[22] Cf. HR 15 September 1980, Dutch Law Reports 1981, 13; HR 17 February 1981, Dutch Law Reports 1981, 536; HR 19 December 1995, Dutch Law Reports 1996, 249.

[23] See HR 18 September 2007, Dutch Law Reports 2008, 192, annotated by Y. Buruma, LJN BA5632. See also HR 2 October 2007, Dutch Law Reports 2008, 374,

on the use of sources of information also have an independent right to exist in a legally free evidentiary system.

Against the background of the functions of judges' duty to provide grounds for their judgments, a recommendation is included in the sub-report to take the adversarial nature of criminal proceedings as a guideline in this statutory provision. The main idea in the research project Criminal Procedure 2001 was that criminal proceedings are aimed at hearing the arguments on both sides and that and that significance should be given in the statutory provision to dialogue among all those involved in the criminal proceedings. Directed at evidentiary law and substantiation of evidence, this starting point means that the arguments put forth on both sides should take a central place in substantiating the judgment. Of the functions of the duty to provide grounds, namely self-review, explanation and review of the judgment by a higher court, the accent is on the explanatory function. Against the background of the debate in court, the judge should explain the decisions he took to the parties to the proceedings in his judgment.

Although this starting point does not sound very spectacular, its legal development nevertheless results in a break with the model of judicial obligations to provide grounds, as was laid down in the Code of Criminal Procedure. This model was rather formal in nature and specified which decisions had to be included and substantiated.[24] The idea of adversarial proceedings played only a limited role particularly in the latter respect. The judge had to render account for his or her decision only if he or she rejected a certain type of defence put forward by the defence counsel.[25] Regarding the main decisions

---

annotated by J. Leegemate, LJN BA3610, which concerned a recorded telephone conversation between the accused and a doctor. It follows from Art. 126aa CCP that the recording of the telephone conversation should have been destroyed. As this was erroneously not done, the judge should not have been allowed to use this telephone conversation as evidence.

[24] Extensively about this: G. Knigge, *Beslissen en motiveren, de artt. 348, 350, 358 en 359 CCP*, H.D. Tjeenk Willink: Alphen aan den Rijn 1980; Melai-Groenhuijsen, *Wetboek van Strafvordering*, Art. 358–359, note 3 (C.M. Pelser).

[25] These are defences relating to so-called 'preliminary questions' (concerning the validity of the summons, jurisdiction of the court, whether or not the Public Prosecution Service is barred from prosecuting and reasons for staying the prosecution) or relating to the classification of the offences declared proved or the punishability of the offender; see Arts. 358(3) and 359(2) CCP.

in the judgment, namely declaring the charges proved and the sentencing, the Code did not provide for special substantiation rules in relation to defences put forward. The legal system did not attach further importance to positions taken in court by the Public Prosecution Service. In addition to the statutory provisions, the Dutch Supreme Court has developed case law in the course of the years, particularly relating to additional requirements for substantiation. These additional requirements further to a specific defence by the defence counsel[26] were nevertheless rather fragmentary in nature and did not essentially alter the formal character of the substantiation model of the Code.

Taking the adversarial nature of criminal proceedings as a starting point in modelling the judicial duty to provide grounds emphasises the relationship between the course of affairs in court and the contents of the criminal judgment. The judge must, after all, account for his or her decision in the judgment on the basis of the positions taken by the defence and Public Prosecution Service at the hearing. Consistent development of this principle would entail the following. Should there prove to be no difference of opinion during the hearing on decisions to be taken by the judge, justification of those decisions in the judgment could remain brief. If, for example, the accused confesses to the offence charged and puts forward a specific argument regarding the sentencing, the judge may suffice with a concise indication of the evidence with respect to the decision on that evidence, but in providing grounds for the sentence, the judge must show that he or she has taken the defence's arguments into consideration. If, on the other hand, there is an extensive debate between the Public Prosecution Service and the defence over the evidence or over the use of certain evidence, the judge would have to justify his or her decision in detail in the judgment, in the event of acquittal as well as in the event the charges are declared proved, including the selection and evaluation of evidence.

The second consequence of a duty to provide grounds which is structured on the basis of adversarial proceedings is that the court

---

[26] For a survey, see: W.H.B. Dreissen, *Bewijsmotivering in strafzaken*, BJu: The Hague 2007, p. 240 et seq.

must not only pay attention to positions of the defence, but to those of the Public Prosecution Service as well. If the public prosecutor has argued specifically in his or her demand that the offence charged can be declared proved, the judge must explain a decision to acquit in the judgment and may not suffice by merely stating that the offence cannot be proved legally and convincingly. The judge will have to account in more detail for a decision departing from the position of the public prosecutor.

3. LEGAL DEVELOPMENT AFTER 'CRIMINAL PROCEDURE 2001'

The recommendations briefly summarised above for a new model of the legal system with respect to the law of evidence and the substantiation of evidence did not bring about a cohesive reform of the statutory provisions on this material. Parts of the proposals were reflected in the Code only in two scattered amendments.

The legislature substantiated a limited amendment to the statutory provisions on documents that may be used as evidence (Art. 344 CCP) on the basis of the free evidentiary system. This concerns an amendment to Art. 344(1)(3°) CCP which was made on the occasion of the adoption of statutory provisions on the examination of protected witnesses.[27] As a result of this amendment, documents drafted by domestic or foreign intelligence and security services can be used as evidence by the criminal court. The legislature was of the opinion that the previously existing limitation that these documents could be used as evidence only in connection with the contents of other means of evidence was no longer appropriate. Nor did the requirement have to be set that if these documents were to be used as evidence in criminal proceedings, they had to be 'intended to serve as evidence of some fact or circumstance'. In modern criminal proceedings, sufficient arguments would have to be given for such limitations on the usability of reliable information as evidence. And

[27] Now Art. 226m-226s CCP; see the Act of 28 September 2006, Bulletin of Acts and Decrees 2006, 460 and Parliamentary Papers (*Kamerstukken*) 29 743.

there was no such reasoning for the documents referred to at present in Art. 344(1)(3°) CCP, according to the legislature.[28]

In the Act of 10 November 2004, Bulletin of Acts and Decrees 2004, 580 (Act amending the Code of Civil Procedure for the purpose of adjusting the requirements for providing grounds for a declaration that the charges have been proved in the event of a confessing suspect) amendments were made to Art. 359 CCP which were intended to do justice to the adversarial nature of criminal proceedings. In the second paragraph of Art. 359(2) CCP a special obligation for the judge to provide grounds was included for decisions departing from an explicitly substantiated position taken by the accused or by the public prosecutor.[29] In the third paragraph, a power for the judge was included with respect to the grounds for admitting evidence to suffice with a mere list of evidence if the accused has confessed to the offence declared proved.[30]

The provisions relating to limited grounds for admitting evidence in the event of a confessing accused was explained thoroughly by the legislature in the Parliamentary Papers. For instance, they indicated when the accused's attitude towards the trial may be understood as a confession and how the court can give shape to the 'list' of evidence.[31] Against the background of the relative simplicity of the provisions and the explanation of them given by the legislature, it is remarkable that in several judgments, the Dutch Supreme Court had to draw the judge's attention to the conditions under which grounds for admitting evidence need not be given and a list of evidence may suffice.[32]

The situation is very different regarding the special grounds required further to explicitly substantiated positions of the public prosecutor or the accused. This provision ended up in the Bulletin of Acts and Decrees (*Staatsblad*) in the course of the parliamentary debate over the proposed legislation on the confessing accused by

---

28 Parliamentary Papers II 29 743, no. 3 (Explanatory Memorandum), pp. 13–14.

29 See note 5 for the text of this provision.

30 See note 4 for the text of this provision.

31 Parliamentary Papers 29 225.

32 Cf. HR 18 April 2006, Dutch Law Reports 2006, 645; HR 19 June 2007, Dutch Law Reports 2007, 507 and HR 13 January 2009, Dutch Law Reports 2009, 57.

way of an amendment[33] and without proper explanation by the legislature. Such explanation would have been very desirable, because it was rather unclear how the special obligation to provide grounds should be placed in the statutory framework of the whole of the rules on decisions and grounds in Articles 358 and 359 CCP on the one hand, and, on the other, the case law of the Supreme Court on special obligations to provide grounds further to meritorious defences of the accused.[34] It was certainly not clear either what the consequences were of the expansion of judicial obligations to provide grounds in the event of explicitly substantiated positions of the public prosecutor. It is therefore not surprising that after the special obligation to provide grounds was introduced in Art. 359(2) CCP, diverse legal questions arose to which an answer had to be given in case law and literature. Some of these questions were:

- When does an 'explicitly substantiated position' exist?
- Is the new obligation to provide grounds anything more than a codification of the case law of the Supreme Court on requirements that must be set on grounds for admitting evidence as a response to a specific type of meritorious defence?
- How does the new rule relate to the defences referred to in Art. 358(3) CCP (with the statutory defences as the most important category), on which the judge has to decide with substantiation?
- What meaning does the new rule have for the grounds for the sentence?
- What consequences does the new obligation to provide grounds have for the review of decisions of the court deciding questions of fact, particularly in relation to acquittals?

After a debate in the literature, in which diverse answers were given to the legal questions brought up,[35] contours have meanwhile been

33 Parliamentary Papers II 29255, no. 8.

34 Cf. M.S. Groenhuijsen, 'Over toeval in het wetgevingsdebat over strafprocesrecht: de uitbouw van een contradictoire gedingstructuur in strafzaken' *DD 2005, 23*.

35 See e.g.: M.J. Borgers & F.G.H. Kristen, 'Verweren en responderen', *DD 2005, 39*; Y. Buruma, 'Motiveren: waarom?', in: *Systeem in ontwikkeling. Liber Amicorum G. Knigge*, WLP: Nijmegen 2005, pp. 71–87; in the same collection: J.W. Fokkens, 'De

drawn in the case law of the Supreme Court. In three judgments of the Supreme Court, by way of 'Considerations preceding the judgments on the appeals,' various aspects of the obligation to provide grounds in Art. 359 (2) CCP were dealt with in more detail.[36] The Supreme Court stated that the purpose of Art. 359(2) CCP was not limited to a mere codification of the judgments passed up to that time on obligations to provide grounds further to special meritorious defences. Besides this case law and the already existing statutory obligations to provide grounds under Art. 358(3) in conjunction with 359(2) CCP, according to the Supreme Court, the new rule does indeed have added value. With respect to the accused's defences, these are generally defences relating to the evidence and the sentencing. With respect to the public prosecutor, these are all explicitly substantiated positions concerning the decisions on the issues of Arts. 348 and 350 CCP which the judge has to take at the end of the hearing. The Supreme Court also defines in more detail the positions that count as 'explicitly substantiated'. The judge is required to give further grounds for a decision if the position is 'clearly supported by arguments and provided with an unequivocal conclusion before the judge deciding questions of fact', and preferably put forward in writing. The Supreme Court also gives some points of view that are important for interpretation of the extent of the obligation to provide grounds to which the judge is subject. In this context, the Supreme Court states first of all that Art. 359(2) CCP does not impair the freedom of the judge deciding questions of fact to select and evaluate the available evidence or to choose and weigh the factors

---

wijziging van art. 359 lid 2 CCP: een stap op weg naar een contradictoir strafproces', pp. 139–149; P. Vegter, 'Strafprocessen niet of nauwelijks te volgen? Iets over eisen aan de motivering van het strafvonnis in het bijzonder in verband met uitdrukkelijk onderbouwde standpunten', in: *Praktisch strafrecht. Liber amicorum J.M. Reijntjes*, WLP: Nijmegen 2005, pp. 577–589; W.H.B. Dreissen, *Bewijsmotivering in* strafzaken, BJu: Den Haag 2007, pp. 259–279; C.B. Veldman & E.F. Stamhuis, 'De verweren in de zin van ... Een tussenstand in de ontwikkeling van het responderen op verweren', *DD 2008, 49*.

[36] HR 11 April 2006, Dutch Law Reports 2006, 393, annotated by Y. Buruma; HR 18 April 2006, Dutch Law Reports 2006, 395 and HR 16 May 2006, LJN AU8266. Remarkable and at the same time interesting is that these judgments were preceded by three conclusions of Advocates General at the Supreme Court (Hoge Raad), who have somewhat different viewpoints on the meaning of Art. 359(2) CCP.

that are important for sentencing. The new rule only has the consequence that under certain circumstances, the judge will have to give more detailed grounds for his or her decisions on these matters. In general, there is not much to say about the requirements to be set on the desired provision of grounds: 'In that context, significance will be given, for example to the nature of the matter at issue and the contents and invasiveness of the arguments put forward', as the Supreme Court held. Moreover, grounds will not have to be provided for every minor point of difference between explicitly substantiated positions and decisions by the judge. More detailed grounds are appropriate only if there is an essential difference, in which case the judge will not have to deal with every detail of the arguments of the public prosecutor or the accused.

After these pickets hammered in by the Supreme Court, in a short time rather a lot of case law has been passed on the meaning of the new obligation to provide grounds under Art. 359(2) CCP. This partly concerns casuistic decisions on the question whether or not there was a defence in a certain case which the judge should have considered a 'substantiated position' and whether the judge had indeed provided sufficient grounds for departing from such a position in the particular case. Decisions are more interesting that show the added value of the new obligation to provide grounds compared to the old system. In this context, regarding evidence and the grounds for admitting evidence, HR 16 December 2008, Dutch Law Reports 2009, 29 can be cited. This judgment related to defences by the defence counsel in which the reliability of the witness statements is challenged. Prior to introduction of the new obligation to provide grounds under Art. 359(2) CCP, it was accepted by the judicial system as the principal rule that, if a judge did not accept such a defence, the judge did not have to account for using the challenged witness statement as evidence in his or her judgment. Things are different now. If the challenge of the reliability and concomitant inability to use the statement as evidence is reflected in an 'explicitly substantiated position', the judge must account for the use of the statement as evidence in the judgment by indicating why the statement, unlike the defence has argued, can indeed be considered reliable. In relation to sentencing and grounds for the sentence, HR 9 December 2009, Dutch Law Reports 2009, 226, annotated by

Y. Buruma, is in line with this. After an explicitly substantiated position directed against the imposition of a non-suspended prison sentence, to which no special obligation to provide grounds applied in the event of departure, under Art. 359(2) CCP, the judge must now give special grounds for imposing the non-suspended prison sentence.

The additional meaning for the defence of the new rule in Art. 359(2) CCP on providing grounds with respect to the previously applicable model of decision-making and providing grounds is evident from the foregoing. It has meanwhile become clear as well that the new rule, particularly the requirement that positions must be 'explicitly substantiated', has no consequences for the defences which were traditionally supposed to result in a reasoned decision pursuant to Articles 358(3) and 359(2) CCP and the case law of the Supreme Court. The requirement of 'explicitly substantiated' applies only to positions of the defence in relation to the evidence and sentencing, which were outside the framework of the original model. No higher requirements should be set on the contents of defences which were previously supposed to result in the provision of special grounds. Nor has the new rule raised the requirements set on court decisions on such defences.[37]

In accordance with the legislature's intention and the text of the provision, it is evident from the case law that court decisions that depart from 'explicitly substantiated positions' taken at the hearing by the Public Prosecution Service have to be specially reasoned pursuant to the new obligation to provide grounds. The case law published to date relates to positions of the Public Prosecution Service concerning evidence[38] and sentencing.[39]

---

[37] Cf. HR 13 January 2009, Dutch Law Reports 2009, 60 on the relationship between Art. 359(2) 2nd sentence CCP and defences within the meaning of Art. 358.3; HR 12 February 2008, Dutch Law Reports 2008, 117, HR 8 April 2008, Dutch Law Reports 2008, 231, HR 24 March 2009, Dutch Law Reports 2009, 170 and HR 24 March 2009, Dutch Law Reports 2009, 171: on the relationship between Art. 359(2) 2nd sentence CCP and the meritorious defences recognized in the case law).

[38] Cf. HR 5 February 2008, Dutch Law Reports 2008, 422, HR 19 February 2008, Dutch Law Reports 2008, 423 and HR 19 February 2008, Dutch Law Reports 2008, 425.

[39] Cf. HR 16 December 2008, Dutch Law Reports 2009, 227.

As the Supreme Court stated in its three important judgments about the meaning of Article 359(2) CCP, if an explicitly substantiated position is departed from, little is said in general about the requirements that should be set on providing grounds for court decisions. In this respect, the obligation to provide grounds to which judges are subject depends too much on the matter at issue and the way in which the position is substantiated. Assessment of the question whether the grounds can be considered sufficient in a given case therefore seems to focus on a casuistic review. Nevertheless, there seems to be a difference in the case law in this respect between review of the grounds given in response to a position of the defence and review of the grounds given in response to a position of the Public Prosecution Service. When a position of the defence is departed from, the grounds given seem to be reviewed more intensively than in a review further to a position of the Public Prosecution Service. Especially striking in this context is HR 19 February 2008, NJ 2008, 425, in which the accused was prosecuted for attempted murder. At the trial, the representative of the Public Prosecution Service argued extensively that attempted murder, particularly acting with 'premeditation', could be considered legally and convincingly proved. The Court of Appeal, however, acquitted the accused and gave as grounds for this that the contents of the evidence did not convince the Court of Appeal that the accused was guilty of attempted murder. More specific grounds in which the position of the Public Prosecution Service was dealt with were absent. The Supreme Court nevertheless ruled that the Court of Appeal, against the background of the freedom of the court deciding questions of fact to select and evaluate the evidence, was not required to give further grounds for its ruling. The very general sounding ruling of the Court of Appeal thus proved to be an adequate response to the detailed argument of the Public Prosecution Service that the offence as charged, and specifically the premeditation, could indeed be proved.[40]

---

[40] In line with this, see also HR 19 February 2008, Dutch Law Reports 2008, 423, annotated by Y. Buruma.

In view of the legislative history and the rationale of the rule on providing grounds in Art. 359(2) CCP, no immediate justification can be given for this difference in review of the adequacy of the grounds further to positions of the defence and of the Public Prosecution Service. An explanation of this difference can perhaps be found in the fact that the judge's freedom of judgment regarding the reliability of evidence, particularly in the event of inadequately persuasive evidence and acquittal on that basis, seems only susceptible to a limited degree of being captured in rationally tinted and specific grounds. Moreover, review of the court's grounds further to positions of the Public Prosecution Service usually involves an assessment of statements which have turned out to be favourable for the accused as the end result of proceedings in two factual instances (usually acquittal). If such a decision is quashed owing to insufficient grounds, new criminal proceedings will follow which will perhaps have a favourable end for the accused once again. Because of the onerous nature of a new trial for the accused, such a scenario should be considered undesirable.

4. *REFERENCE POINTS FOR FURTHER LEGAL DEVELOPMENT*

The preceding sections focused on the past. After the description of the recommendations made by the research project Criminal Procedure 2001 on the issue of evidentiary law and substantiation of evidence (sec. 2) and of the amendments the legislature made to the Code of Criminal Procedure (sec. 3), attention is now focused on the future. The development of law did not, of course, come to a standstill even after the recommendations were partially worked out in legislation. The question is thus how the law of evidence and the substantiation of evidence could or should develop further.

4.1. Firmer Embedment of the 'First Track'

In this context, I want to focus my attention first of all on the further embedment of the adversarial nature of criminal proceedings in the Code. The law of evidence and the substantiation of evidence should not be considered as stand-alone matters, but as the conclusion of the debate in court between the participants in the criminal proceedings. In an adversarial case, which requirements should be set on the evidence and its substantiation in a specific case is determined by the attitudes the defence, the Public Prosecution Service and the insights of the judges take during the proceedings. In this connection, the starting point may be taken that the attitudes of the defence and Public Prosecution during the proceedings are important indications of the manner of hearing the case in court.

In relation to the gravity of the offence, the research project Criminal Procedure 2001 developed the 'Three-track Model' for the organisation of the examination in court. This model is based on the idea that the procedure to be followed in disposing of offences should be in proportion to the interests at stake for the accused and for society in a specific case. In this model it is understandable that the procedure to be followed in disposing of minor offences is simpler than the procedure for a serious offence for which the accused runs the risk of being sentenced to a long term of imprisonment. In this line of reasoning, the research project maintained a three-way division. For minor offences, which are usually disposed of by a fine, a simple, out-of-court procedure is indicated, with the possibility for the accused to appeal to the court. The middle category of offences for which prison sentences not exceeding six months can be imposed can be disposed of by a single judge. More serious offences should be tried by panel of three judges.[41] Because of the drastic nature of the penalties that can be imposed for serious offences (longer terms of imprisonment) and to promote adversarial proceedings, the research project argued that the procedure prescribed for these offences should contain more guarantees than the Code now provides. Especially the immediacy principle should be given a stronger effect in rules of positive law. In cases where the accused predominantly or completely denies the charges against him or her, the starting point should be that the most important evidence must be produced in court. Witnesses who are essential to the evidence should be examined in court as far as possible. In this way, because of the accused's denial of all or most of the charges, the judge will be better able to form his or her own opinion on the correctness of statements made

---

[41] Groenhuijsen & Knigge 1999, pp. 41–42.

by witnesses. This will enhance the function of the trial in finding the truth.

In relation to the 'Three-track Model', however, the legislature made room in the Code for the out-of-court settlement of more minor offences.[42] The legislature, however, worked out the procedure for more serious offences only in a fragmentary fashion. In this regard, the arrangement of several powers of the president of the court can be pointed out to take decisions on the order of the trial during the run-up to the trial.[43] The rules on calling up and examining witnesses in court have been adjusted as well, in order to facilitate that witnesses who made statements of essential importance to the evidence, and whose examination in court is considered important by the public prosecutor, defence or judge, are also examined in court.[44] This limited elaboration of the 'First Track' did not result in any essential adjustment to the trial culture in the Netherlands. All too often, witnesses whose statements are challenged by the defence are not examined in court, but outside open court by the examining magistrate. To assess the reliability of the statements made, the trial judge has to rely on the records made of the examinations. It would be good for the adversarial structure, and with that the quality of criminal proceedings, if the legislature consistently elaborated on the model for trying more serious offences which was developed during the research project.

4.2. Accountability for the Selection and Evaluation of Evidence

Following on from the foregoing, I arrive at the issue concerning the selection and evaluation of the evidence by the judge. A criminal file

---

[42] See the Ac of 7 July 2006, Bulletin of Acts and Decrees (*Stb.*) 2006, 330 (Public Prosecution Service (Settlement) Act) (*Wet OM-afdoening*). In the 'Second Track' - the procedure middle-category offences – proceedings for a single police judge were already adequately provided for.

[43] See Articles 258(5) and 263(4) CCP: the president may decide that the accused has to appear in person and may order him or her to be brought to court. The president may also order the public prosecutor to have certain witnesses to be called up and possibly issue a warrant to have witnesses who were called up brought before the court. The president can also instruct the public prosecutor to conduct further investigation or to have documents or pieces of evidence submitted.

[44] See Articles 287 and 288 CCP.

provides the judge with a quantity of evidence. In forming his opinion on the charges against the accused, the judge should disregard the unreliable evidence and base his decision on material he considers reliable and in accordance with the truth. As stated in section 3 above, it is settled case law regarding such selection and evaluation of evidence that

> it is reserved for the fact-finding judge to use the evidence that appears reliable enough to be useful in finding those facts, and to disregard what he considers of no value to the evidence. Except in special cases, this decision on the selection and evaluation of evidence needs no substantiation.[45]

According to this 'main rule', the judge does not have to account for his choice of the evidence on the basis of which he decides in his judgment that the accused has committed the offences charged. In this line of reasoning, see e.g. HR 1 December 2009, LJN BJ8686. In this case, the defence had pointed out inconsistencies in the statements made by various witnesses. Based on these inconsistencies, the defence were of the opinion that the evidence of the offences with which the accused was charged was inadequate. In the convicting judgment, the judge had not paid any attention to the defence put forward by the defence counsel. According to the Dutch Supreme Court, the judge was not obliged to do so either:

> The Court of Appeal was at liberty to use the statements in question as evidence and to disregard the statements on which the defence had relied. Art. 359(2) CCP does not compel the Court of Appeal to give further reasons. This provision, after all, did not alter the freedom of the fact-finding judge to select and evaluate the available evidence.

A further ruling on evidence is required only in 'special cases'. If one takes a look at the case law, it appears that 'special' means that the defence has argued in an explicitly substantiated viewpoint that for specific reasons (legal, factual or methodological), an individual piece of evidence cannot be used.[46] If the judge, departing from

---

[45] HR 2 February 2010, LJN BJ7266; about this main rule: G.J.M. Corstens, *Het Nederlandse strafprocesrecht*, 6th impression, Kluwer: Deventer 2009, p. 719.

[46] About these special cases, see the annotation of A.C. 't Hart under Supreme Court (HR) 30 March 1999, NJ 1999, 451; see also 'Het onderzoek ter zitting', pp. 410–411.

such a specific defence, nevertheless uses the challenged piece of evidence for proof, he must indeed account for this decision in the judgment.[47]

Apart from the fact that the difference between meritorious defences of the defence counsel which do or do not belong to the category of 'special cases' – and therefore do or do not compel an individual ruling on evidence in the judgment – is rather subtle, making that difference is not logical in the adversarial model. In this model the leading idea is precisely that adversarial proceedings should result in a reasoned response from the judge. If certain matters are not up for discussion at the trial on which the judge has to decide, the judicial substantiation of such decision may remain brief. If, however, different positions are taken on a decision to be made, the judicial task does not only entail that the judge has to decide, but that he should also explain the reasons that caused him to form his opinion. Against this background, I consider a development desirable in which the judge is required, against the background of the positions taken on this at the trial by the Public Prosecution Service and the defence, to provide insight into his train of thought regarding the selection and evaluation of the evidence.[48] Such a development is in keeping with an attitude towards the judicial task in line with the adversarial model and with the explanatory function of court judgments.[49]

---

[47] Such an account can be very brief and not focused very much on the defence conducted, as HR 1 December 2009, LJN BJ8686 make clear.

[48] In this sense, see also: J.D. den Hartog, 'De selectie en waardering van het bewijsmateriaal', in: A.E. Harteveld et al. (ed.), *Systeem min ontwikkeling. Liber amicorum G. Knigge*, WLP: Nijmegen 20065, pp. 217–230; M.S. Groenhuijsen, 'Bewijsrecht als toetssteen voor de systematiek van een Wetboek van Strafvordering', in: A.H. Klip et al. (ed.), *Kri*Ties, Kluwer: Deventer 2004, pp. 147–158.

[49] The Supreme Court's judgment of 2 February 2010, LJN BJ2766 can be interpreted as an initial impetus for a development in this direction. This judgment may well have been one of the 'special cases' that result in an obligation to substantiate the selection and evaluation of evidence, but it is remarkable that it concerned a detail that had never been brought up before in the judicial system. The accused presented an alternative scenario as the cause of the offences at the trial. The judge disregarded this alternative scenario, without rendering account for this in his judgment. The Supreme Court decided that the substantiation of evidence was inadequate.

4.3. Towards an exhaustive evaluation and substantiation of evidence?

In Dreissen's opinion, the above-mentioned development I consider desirable does not go far enough. Against the background of her research into the requirements set by the German law of criminal procedure on the evaluation and substantiation of evidence, she argues in favour of farther-reaching reform of the Dutch law of criminal procedure. In relation to the function of criminal proceedings in finding the truth, she proposes requiring the judge to give an exhaustive evaluation of the evidence in his judgment. According to Dreissen, the judge may also be required to 'formulate his judgment in such a way that the decision can be brought up for discussion and, in so far as that is done, that it can also be reviewed on substantive grounds. Only in this way can it be guaranteed that the judge has taken all relevant facts and circumstances – incriminating and exculpatory – into consideration'. For her, this requirement applies regardless of the attitudes of the parties to the proceedings and the viewpoints put forward at the trial. For the substantiation of evidence, this means that the judge must always account in his judgment for his considerations of the usability or unusability of the evidence at his disposal and its power of persuasion.

According to Driessen, the judge's obligation to account for his selection and evaluation of evidence in all cases has consequences for the review of the opinion on the evidence in cassation. In this regard, the Supreme Court should not suffice with a review of the comprehensibility of the substantiation, but should consider the substance of such substantiation of evidence:

> The Supreme Court (...) should compel judges deciding on questions of fact to give reasons for their opinions on evidence that can support those opinions. This requires the Supreme Court also to conduct a substantive review of those reasons by not only reviewing the contents for comprehensibility, but also (...) for whether they are in accordance with general empirical rules and scientific insights.[50]

Groenhuijsen supports the development of law advocated by Dreissen. In his view, a toughening of the requirements that should

50 Dreissen 2007, pp. 406–408.

be set on the substantiation of evidence would reduce the chance of erroneous decisions by the courts.[51]

Driessen's proposal is legally and practically radical. For instance, the requirements to be set on the substantiation of evidence, as in the current system, no longer focus on the adversarial nature of criminal proceedings, but on 'establishing the material truth'. In that case, the requirements actually to be set on such substantiation will no longer be related to the viewpoints taken by the parties to the proceedings at the trial, but will apply to all cases. Even to cases where, for example, the accused fully confesses to the offences with which he is charged, the judge would be required to account for the evaluation and selection of evidence. In that account, the judge would have to state why the accused's confession can be considered correct. The advocated toughening of the review of the substantiation of evidence in cassation would result in a substantive change to the cassation system. The Supreme Court would have to involve itself deeply in a great many cases with the actual evaluation and substantiation of the evidence. To date, this has been a matter which the Supreme Court has not taken upon itself, but considers at the discretion of the judge deciding questions of fact to select and evaluate. It is clear as well that the extensive obligation of the judge deciding questions of fact to provide grounds and the related attitude of the Supreme Court towards its task, as advocated by Dreissen, would have major consequences for the workload of the judiciary.

The observation that Driessen's proposal is rather far-reaching leads to the question of the desirability of introducing the obligation to provide grounds in the Dutch law of criminal procedure. In my opinion, this question should be answered in the negative. The considerations that led me to this viewpoint are the following.

An ex officio obligation to provide grounds, also in cases where the defence and Public Prosecution Service have no difficulty with the judge's declaring the charges proved, as evidenced by the viewpoints taken at the trial, would give rise to practices sparing work experienced as 'superfluous'. In this connection, a revival of the

---

[51] M.S. Groenhuijsen, 'Deskundigen in de aanval. Het strafrecht in de verdediging?', in *Delikt en Delinkwent* 2008, pp. 933–934.

previous practice of head-tail judgments[52] is not inconceivable. The essence of this practice was that the judge did not work out his substantiation of the evidence until one of the parties had instituted a legal remedy. If the accused and Public Prosecution Service acquiesced in the judgment, the judgment was not completed. In this context of 'escape routes', it is appropriate to point out examples from the practice of the German law of criminal procedure, which show that the 'Aufklärungspflicht' applicable to German criminal courts and the obligation to evaluate evidence prompt concessions, to prevent the criminal judges from collapsing under their workload. The obligation to make an exhaustive evaluation of evidence applies only to the 'Hauptverfahren', the trying of offences in open court. This manner of settlement is considered for the more serious offences. The more minor categories of offences can be settled out of court in the 'Strafbefehlsverfahren'.[53] In the German law of criminal procedure, this type of settlement by way of a 'Strafbefehl' has expanded enormously. As is customary for out-of-court settlement, the procedure leading to imposition of a 'Strafbefehl' is very simple. There is no provision for a comprehensive evaluation of evidence and the intervention of the court with the procedure is minimal, if only because of the large numbers. To the extent offences cannot be settled otherwise than by the criminal court in open court because of their gravity, the sharp edges are removed by a practice, extralegal until recently, of agreements during the criminal proceedings.[54] In this practice, all parties to the criminal proceedings, both the defence and the Public Prosecution Service, make agreements on how the case is to be handled in court. The confession of the offence by the accused plays an essential part in this. If a case is settled on the basis of agreements, no comprehensive substantiation of evidence is necessary, if only because the parties to the proceedings will not institute legal remedies.

---

52 This was a customary practice for years, in which the judge only fully worked out his judgment after a legal remedy had been instituted. In giving his judgment, he sufficed with a judgment containing only the major decisions. See P.A.M. Mevis, *Ingekort en weggelaten*, Gouda Quint: Arnhem 1992.

53 § 407 et seq. StPO.

54 The agreements in criminal proceedings are now based on the StPO; see *Bundesgesetzblatt 2009, Teil I*, no. 49, 3. August 2009, 2353.

The fact that obligations to give grounds for decisions which are not up for discussion will give rise to a practice of cliché grounds also argues against Driessen's proposal. Judges would then base their decisions on 'sacred' formulas which have passed the review of a higher court, but are essentially meaningless. The history of various rules in Art. 359 CCP on sentencing grounds can serve as an example. This history shows that decisions which are very obvious, such as imposing a prison sentence on an accused who is found guilty of manslaughter,[55] cannot be substantiated by anything but clichés.[56] The same will hold for the grounds for example for a decision that the accused had made a confession in complete freedom and maintained it in all instances or that an unchallenged witness statement can be considered reliable and can be used as evidence. Nobody wants grounds which are included only in the judgment simply because this is required by law, but are in reality nothing but phraseology.

In conclusion, I am of the opinion that, in order to deal carefully with scarce judicial capacity, the legislature will have to set priorities on the work to be required from judges.[57] In that case it would not be a strange idea for criminal proceedings to be in line with the essence of judicial work: settling disputes. From this point of view, the efforts of judges should be aimed at matters which are up for discussion in the criminal proceedings and keep the 'parties' divided. This not only holds for the need to examine witnesses or carry out investigative acts, but also for the requirements that may be set on the grounds for a judgment. The decisions to be included in a judgment on which no difference of opinion proves to exist between the Public Prosecution Service, defence and judge may then be substantiated briefly. Decisions on which totally different ideas exist need a comprehensive account in the judgment. In essence, these are the basic ideas of trials as adversarial proceedings.

---

55 According to Art. 359(6) CCP, the judge must in particular give the reasons for this decision in the judgment which made him choose this type of punishment. More than the statement entailing that the choice of prison sentence was inspired by the gravity of the offence is not considered in most cases.

56 Cf. G. Knigge, 'Een wetboek van elastiek', *Delikt en Delinkwent* 2000, p. 224.

57 Cf. Groenhuijsen & Knigge 1999, pp. 18–22; 24–27.

REFORM PROPOSALS ON DUTCH CRIMINAL PROCEDURE – A GERMAN PERSPECTIVE

Thomas Weigend[1]

1. *INTRODUCTION: THE PLEASURES OF COMPARING LAW*

Preparing for this contribution has reacquainted me with the pleasures of comparative law. In trying to get at least a vague idea of the structure and the perceived problems of Dutch criminal procedure I felt like a man in a foreign land who, while trying to find his way around, keeps meeting old acquaintances – some of them good friends, some of them acquaintances he had hoped not to see again abroad. And reading about a foreign, but not totally strange legal system is always enlightening in that it opens new perspectives on one's own way of thinking about the issues, often showing simple practical solutions to problems that one has been led to believe – particularly in Germany – to resist resolution short of a longwinded philosophical disquisition.

The fact that one meets many old acquaintances when one crosses the Dutch-German border has to do, of course, with our common heritage dating back to the German-Roman empire and, more importantly, to the strong influence of Napoléon's *Code d'instruction criminelle*. The Netherlands has perhaps remained a little more faithful to that French model, whereas Germany has in the 19th century opened up to influences from the British island, especially with respect to the participation of lay persons in criminal trials. Although the practical relevance of lay participation on verdicts is today very limited in Germany, the fact that lay judges with full voting rights participate at the criminal trial has had a significant impact on the structure of the process. I will return to this shortly.

Another remarkable difference between the two systems is the much greater confidence that the Dutch seem to place in the wise use of discretion granted to judges, prosecutors and even police.

---

[1] Professor of Criminal Law, University of Cologne.

The recognition of a broad opportunity principle with respect to the filing of charges and even to initiating an investigation is but one example of that attitude. Another example of trusting the wisdom of judges rather than establishing complicated rules is the way Dutch law treats the reaction to procedural faults before trial. If I understand art. 359a of the Dutch Code of Criminal Procedure (hereinafter: CCP) correctly, it leaves it to the court to decide what consequence should follow a violation of procedural norms before trial, with possibilities reaching from a permanent stay of proceedings to a mere verbal recognition of the fault in the written judgment. An enormous amount of ink has been spilt on this issue in German doctrine and jurisprudence, dozens of theories have been proposed and refuted[2] – all that eventually leading to very much the same practical result as in the Netherlands, namely, a broad discretion on the part of judges to deal with violations of procedural law that occurred in the investigative stage of the criminal process.[3]

After these general observations, I will concentrate on some issues that have concerned the authors of the great and impressive project *Strafvordering* 2001.

2. *ASPECTS OF* STRAFVORDERING 2001: *GENERAL ISSUES*

I will set out with three general characteristics of the project's proposals before I turn to a few more specific questions.

2.1. Reliance on the Pretrial Process

One feature that is typical of the Dutch criminal process is its strong reliance on the pretrial process and its treatment of the trial as a "verification meeting" rather than a locus where the critical evidence is, for the first time, being presented in full. This specialty

---

[2] For overviews, see Eisenberg, *Beweisrecht der StPO. Spezialkommentar*, 6th ed., 2008, notes 356 et seq.; Gössel, in: Löwe/Rosenberg, *Die Strafprozessordnung und das Gerichtsverfassungsgesetz. Großkommentar*, 26th ed., vol. 1, 2006, Einleitung L.

[3] See for example Bundesverfassungsgericht, *Neue Juristische Wochenschrift* 2007, 499; Bundesgerichtshof, *Entscheidungen des Bundesgerichtshofes in Strafsachen* (BGHSt) 51, 285 (2007).

certainly has to do with the inquisitorial heritage that our systems have in common; but the reduction of the relevance of the trial has been made possible, I think, only by the fact that the Dutch system dispenses with lay justices. Professional judges can be expected to study and properly evaluate written documents; lay persons cannot. When lay persons are to co-determine the outcome of the process (or when they, in a jury system, are the sole fact-finders) the evidence must be presented "live" before them and cannot just be referred to by citing from a dossier.

The Dutch system, being devoid of lay influence – and I say this with a certain measure of envy – has greater freedom in allocating fact-finding between the pretrial and trial stages. German theory, on the other hand, clings to a substantive interpretation of the principle of immediacy,[4] thereby trying to shield the trial phase from too much spill-over from the pretrial investigation. The main instrument of limiting the relevant fact-finding to the trial itself is the prohibition of introducing certain documentary evidence, especially protocols of prior interrogations, in lieu of a witness's live testimony at the trial.[5] But the honorable intentions behind this rule have long given way to pragmatic considerations. On a first level, the Code of Criminal Procedure itself contains a lengthy list of exceptions to the "live witness testimony" rule. For example, a witness's testimony can be replaced by reading a protocol whenever the witness is not easily available or when all parties, including the defense lawyer, agree to waive his presence.[6] Secondly, the courts have further contributed to eroding the principle of immediacy by permitting a practice of reading to a witness the protocol of his prior interrogation by the police or a magistrate, asking the witness to confirm or comment on his earlier statement. When the presiding judge reads the protocol to the witness, the contents of the protocol itself becomes court evidence that can later be used for the judgment.[7] On a third level, when the requirements of "immediate" presentation of all necessary

[4] For a brief account of the 'rule of immediacy under German law, see Kühne, *Strafprozessrecht*, 7th ed.', 2007, notes 914 et seq.

[5] See § 250 Code of Criminal Procedure (CCP).

[6] For details, see § 251 CCCP.

[7] BGHSt 3, 199 at 201 (1952). For a critical analysis of this practice, see Eisenberg 2008, notes 868 et seq.

evidence before the trial court threaten to prolong the trial, the German version of plea bargaining is employed to dispense with the regular trial process altogether. A practice of *Absprachen* has flourished and continuously expanded in Germany for the last 30 years.[8] In the German version of plea negotiations, the defense deals directly with the court (that is, the professional judges), offering a total or partial confession of the defendant in exchange for an agreed-upon sentence to be handed down by the court. It is open to debate whether that practice actually benefits the defense or whether it has become a system where the prosecution and the court exert pressure on defendants to confess for fear of a much heavier sentence if they should demand full proof of their guilt. Whatever its benefits to either side, there can be no doubt that plea bargaining undermines the criminal process as a whole and deprives the court's judgment of its foundation in truth and justice.

Germany is thus paying a high price for its official adherence to a substantive version of the principle of immediacy. I think that there is much to commend the Dutch alternative of conducting a reliable and open fact-finding process at the investigation stage and to base the judgment on the results of this process, barring special circumstances or a particular need to hear additional evidence which may have been neglected during the pretrial stage.

The critical issue then is to make certain that the investigation before (or perhaps, instead of) trial is conducted such that it produces reliable findings of fact in a way acceptable to all parties involved, including the defendant. The Dutch system may have profited in this regard from two aspects: first, the continuing existence of a judicial pretrial investigation, even though it may have lost much of its practical relevance; and second, the recognized position of the public prosecutor as a neutral, non-partisan magistrate. If one chooses to abolish the option of a judicial investigation, as the *Strafvordering* 2001 project proposes, one of these support structures

[8] For an English language account of plea bargaining in Germany, see Weigend, 'The Decay of the Inquisitorial Ideal: Plea Bargaining Invades German Criminal Procedure', in: Jackson, Langer and Tillers (eds.), *Crime, Procedure and Evidence in a Comparative and International Context. Essays in Honour of Professor Mirjan Damaška*, Oxford 2008, p. 39.

would fall. As far as prosecutorial neutrality is concerned, I am not certain to what extent that ideal is honored in practice, and what defense lawyers would have to say about it. In the German experience at least, prosecutors are interested in exonerating evidence to the extent that they don't wish to make fools of themselves by bringing charges that turn out to be clearly untenable in court; but once the police and the prosecution have made up their minds that a case has been "resolved" and that there is enough evidence to show the suspect's guilt, it would demand very high ethical standards indeed for them to keep searching for evidence that might contradict their conclusion.

A more persuasive approach than placing one's trust in the impartiality of the prosecutor might be to strengthen the position of the defense in the pretrial phase. The introduction of the judicial *mini instructie* in Art. 36a–36d Dutch CCP appears to me as an innovative and useful step in that direction. If the investigative stage is to produce findings that all parties involved can accept as trustworthy and close to reality, then it is important that the defense have the option of challenging the version developed by the prosecution and also of introducing its own version of the facts. Recent German debate has centered around reform proposals for a "participatory investigation."[9] Under various versions of this model, the defense would have the right to be present at investigatory acts and especially to question witnesses at their first interview; on the other hand, the defense would be able to request the investigatory judge to take evidence on its behalf, much as in the Dutch *mini instructie*. So far, such proposals have not been successful in Germany. Criticism has come from both sides of the spectrum. Prosecutors and police have objected to defense involvement in the very early stages of an investigation, arguing that it is necessary for the police to first catch up with the offender's better knowledge of relevant facts.[10] Defense lawyers have likewise been skeptical. They fear that they might be compelled to

---

[9] For an overview, see Satzger, *Chancen und Risiken einer Reform des strafrechtlichen Ermittlungsverfahrens.* Gutachten C zum 65, Deutschen Juristentag, 2004, pp. C 32 et seq.

[10] Senge, ‚Gesetzliche Erweiterungen des Anwesenheitsrechtes der Verteidigung bei Vernehmungen im Ermittlungsverfahren?', in: Jung, Luxenburger and Wahle (eds.), *Festschrift für Egon Müller*, Baden-Baden 2008, p. 693.

actively cooperate in the investigation and might forfeit their right to challenge incriminating evidence if they choose not do so (or are unable to do so) at the very first opportunity.[11]

I think that it should be possible to devise a workable compromise solution that permits (but does not force) the defense to contribute to the investigation without unreasonably restricting the tactical and strategic options of the defense lawyer.[12] An acceptable "participatory" pretrial investigation would go a long way toward laying the foundation for a provisional judgment at the end of the investigation stage. Such a judgment could be offered to the parties in the hope that they accept it rather than seeking a public trial.[13] A similar model has been adopted in Italy, where it goes by the name of *giudizio abbreviato*. In the Italian system, a sentence reduction by one third gives a further incentive to the defendant to accept the provisional judgment issued by the investigatory judge.[14]

2.2. Strengthening of Party Control

The idea of introducing a "participatory" investigation raises another general issue that the authors of *Strafvordering* 2001 have embraced, namely the strengthening of party control in the criminal process. This reflects a general trend worldwide, and it comports with the procedural model underlying art. 6 sec. 3 of the European Convention on Human Rights. Increased party control of the process not only promises to give autonomy to citizens rather than subjecting them to a one-sided state inquisition. Party control is also said to enhance the efficiency of the process since it saves time and effort by dealing only with those issues as to which the parties differ.

A great number of criminal procedural systems function on the basis of complete party control: in the so-called adversarial system, it is the parties that determine the issues to be raised and the evidence to be presented, and the role of the court is to make sure that

---

11 Salditt, *Eckpunkte – Streitfragen des partizipatorischen Strafprozesses*, Strafverteidiger 2001, 311 at 312.

12 For a proposal in this direction see Satzger 2004 at C 43 et seq.

13 For a more detailed proposal see Weigend, 'Die Reform des Strafverfahrens', *Zeitschrift für die gesamte Strafrechtswissenschaft* 104 (1992), pp. 486, 506 et seq.

14 Arts. 438 et seq. Italian Code of Criminal Procedure.

the proceedings are conducted according to the rules and to eventually render the verdict. Whether or not this system provides the parties with more autonomy is an open question, however. The answer depends not so much on the amount of *formal* control a participant has but on the *actual* balance of power among the parties and the court. In many systems, the defendant and his counsel, in spite of their being parties in the same formal sense as the public prosecutor, lack the means, the resources and the legal authority to genuinely influence the process; the defendant neither autonomously engages in the criminal process nor can he autonomously co-determine its outcome.

More importantly, party control over the initiation and contents of the criminal process is at odds with the goal of basing the judgment on "the truth", of linking the outcome to what actually happened. Parties often have an interest in withholding information or of shaping it in their favor, and they may agree to keep certain facts from the court because they deem them irrelevant or, for different reasons, detrimental to their cause. The court's verdict then necessarily refers to the reality as shaped and presented by the parties, not to "real" reality. If we wish to still maintain the goal of reaching verdicts and sentences in accordance with 'substantive' truth – and I think that giving up that goal would seriously undermine the legitimacy of criminal justice as we know it – it is necessary that the court retain at least a residual authority to obtain information independently of the wishes of the parties. The court should thus have the power to question witnesses and to call for additional evidence even if none of the parties is ready to offer it. Only if the court controls, in the last resort, the information base of the judgment can it render a verdict and sentence based on based on its own independent and honest search for that elusive thing that we call the truth.

The principle of court control should be respected even if the defendant confesses to the crime charged. To be sure, a credible confession that provides detail about all objective and subjective elements of the offense can relieve the court of the need to hear additional evidence. But the court should make certain that the defendant has spoken the truth and may want to back up his statement by additional testimony or documents. The Dutch rule on the need for corroboration, old-fashioned as it may appear, is based on wisdom and century-long experience, which counsel caution rather than blind trust in the truth of self-incriminating statements.

2.3. Procedures for Organized Crime and Terrorism Offenses

A third general characteristic of today's (and perhaps tomorrow's) Dutch criminal process seems to be a distinction between procedures for "normal" crime and those for organized crime and terrorism offenses. The Dutch prosecutor seems to have far-reaching authority to permit the infiltration of criminal organisations by police even before a concrete suspicion of criminal wrongdoing exists, and special rules apply to the detention of terrorism suspects, which is authorized for much longer periods than for other suspects.

Combatting criminal organisations and their activities typically lies in a gray area between investigation of past crime and prevention of future crime. The contours of that area are also shaped by the substantive criminal law, which can turn even the attempt to form a criminal organisation into a criminal offense,[15] thus opening up avenues for investigative police work long before the members of a group have set out to actually commit crimes. In the German system, the police can also rely on their independent powers to prevent crime in dealing with criminal organisations,[16] and it seems that they have settled quite comfortably in that "gray area", changing from their coats of investigators into those of crime preventers and back as needed.

It should thus be possible to resolve the practical problems of early police involvement in dangerous groups even without special powers in the context of criminal procedure. This makes me a bit hesitant to support the trend – by no means limited to our two countries – of singling out some forms of crime for special treatment under the procedure code. Criminological fashions come and go, but each of them tends to leave its trace in legislation. Crime fashions have in common that they lend popular support to the expansion

---

[15] See § 129a German Penal Code.

[16] See, for example, §§ 16 et seq. *Polizeigesetz des Landes Nordrhein-Westfalen* (permitting, *inter alia*, the use of hidden cameras and microphones as well as undercover agents).

both of criminal law and of investigative measures, in the name of meeting a challenge unforeseen when the "regular" laws were made. For example, organized crime, the buzz word of the 1990s, has in the Netherlands as well as in Germany led to a series of laws designed specifically to combat the perceived special dangers posed by that phenomenon – which, by the way, still defies clear definition and seems since to have receded somewhat to the background of the political debate. The same may well happen with terrorism, and indeed I very much hope that the wave of terrorist attacks that evolved with and after the atrocities of September 11, 2001 may soon become a phenomenon that we can leave to the care of historians. We might therefore be well advised to think twice before granting special powers to criminal justice agencies in the "war against terrorism". Of course, investigating clandestine and especially heinous crime typically planned and committed by foreigners presents special problems of policing. But we should not forget that in the criminal process suspects are presumed to be innocent until found guilty, so that any special measures have to be justified by a mere *suspicion,* not by the *fact* that someone is a terrorist. And special powers, once written into the law books and found to be useful by the police, have the tendency to seep into other areas for which they were not originally designed, on the argument that what has proved effective for fighting terrorists may be doubly effective when used against suspected rapists or drug dealers. We should beware of giving up standards of fair criminal justice *propter enormitatem criminis*. Such dangerous policy decisions could easily infect the whole system of criminal justice.

3. *ASPECTS* OF STRAFVORDERING 2001: *SPECIFIC ISSUES*

3.1. Pretrial Investigation

With respect to the pretrial investigation, the *Strafvordering* 2001 project has recommended the abolition of the judicial investigation and would retain the *rechter-commissaris* only as an agent of control over invasive investigative measures and an official who can perform interrogations at the prosecutor's request. Germany has taken this step in 1975, and there have since been very few nostalgic calls for a return of the ancient *Untersuchungsrichter*. Yet, in the present system the judge in the investigation phase lacks a coherent mission. He is, on one hand, only a helper of the prosecutor who, in the German system, cannot even deny a prosecutor's request to hear a witness or to take another act of investigation as long as that act is legally permissible.[17] The judge is, on the other hand, a control organ to whom the prosecutor must turn if he wishes to conduct a search, to arrest or detain a suspect, or to seize contraband. What complicates matters further is the fact that the judge's involvement in an investigation lacks continuity: he is called upon to authorize an arrest today and to decide on a search three weeks later, and may be requested to interrogate a witness in the same proceeding a few months after that. The judge thus never sees the whole forest but must decide on felling individual trees, normally on the basis of information only from one side, namely the police. It is not surprising, then, that according to empirical studies conducted in Germany the instances where a judge denies a prosecutorial request for an invasive measure are as frequent as snow in September.[18]

The old-style *juge d'instruction*, by contrast, can develop and pursue his own theory of any case referred to him. His decision-making certainly is more independent of prosecutorial influence and may be closer to the ideal of neutrality. The investigating judge could thus add a genuine element of independent control to the criminal process. His position would, moreover, be perfectly suited to a "participatory" model of the investigation, as I have sketched it before. A judge responsible for his own investigation of the case could be trusted by the defense to follow up on clues for additional evidence to be considered – more so, in any event, than the public prosecutor.

The main argument, at least in Germany, for the abolition of the *Untersuchungsrichter* was one of economy. It was regarded as too

---

[17] See § 162 sec. 2 CCP.

[18] See Albrecht, Dorsch & Krüpe, *Rechtswirklichkeit und Effizienz der Überwachung der Telekommunikation nach den §§ 100a, 100b StPO und anderer verdeckter Ermittlungsmaßnahmen*, Freiburg i.Br. 2003; Backes & Gusy, *Wer kontrolliert die Telefonüberwachung? Eine empirische Untersuchung zum Richtervorbehalt bei der Telefonüberwachung*, Frankfurt 2003.

expensive and too cumbersome to have two investigations of the same matter occurring side by side, and the effort to streamline the procedure had led to a gradual reduction of the judge's caseload until he was eventually regarded as dispensible altogether. Our times may be such that arguments of economy trump any other consideration. But I would think twice before throwing overboard an institution that the Netherlands have had for such a long time and that may well be worth retaining at least for instances of a *mini instructie*. It may be necessary to integrate the judicial investigation into the general investigation conducted under the auspices of the public prosecutor, but it might be useful to leave the judge the role of an independent investigator beyond carrying out on-the-spot requests of the prosecutor.

Traditionally, the pretrial investigation was shrouded in secrecy. These times have long passed, and in both Germany and the Netherlands the defense has, in principle, access to the prosecutor's file even before an indictment has been filed. In Germany, the defense is also entitled to participating in all judicial acts of investigation and in some prosecutorial acts as well.[19] Still, many German defense lawyers complain that they are cut off from crucial information during the investigation phase. For example, it took decisions of the highest courts to make sure that a judge cannot impose pretrial detention on a suspect based on information to which the defense had never had access.[20] And while the Code of Criminal Procedure guarantees the defense lawyer the right to inspect the prosecution file at any time,[21] that principle is in practice often swallowed by the exception, namely that the prosecutor can keep the file closed when doing otherwise would jeopardize the purpose of the investigation.[22] The defense lawyer can also be excluded from a prosecutor's

---

[19] §§ 168c, 163a sec. 3 CCP.

[20] ECtHR, cases of Garcia Alva (23541/94), Lietzow (24479/94) and Schöps (25116/94) v. Germany, judgments of Feb. 13, 2001; Bundesverfassungsgericht NStZ 1994, 551.

[21] § 147 sec. 1 CCP.

[22] § 147 sec. 2 CCP. Only under limited circumstances can the defense obtain a judicial review of the prosecutor's decision to keep significant parts of the file secret until the end of the investigation (§ 147 sec. 5 CCP).

interrogation of a witness or expert witness[23] as well as from any investigatory act performed by the police, including an interrogation of the lawyer's own client.[24] These rules are more reminiscent of the secret inquisition of the *ancien régime* than of modern "participatory" pretrial proceedings.

It cannot be denied, however, that total openness of the investigation would not be a responsible strategy in all cases, given the fact that the suspect or his friends might well abuse any information they can glean from the file for undermining the process, in particular for intimidating adverse witnesses. It is thus necessary to strike a viable compromise between trust and secrecy, between sharing and withholding information. One possibility might be to presume openness and to allow restrictions only when the prosecution cites individualized grounds for believing that information would be abused by the suspect or on his behalf. Given the importance of early information on the case for any defense effort, any restriction of openness should be subject to immediate judicial review.

3.2. Trial Stage

One of the critical issues at the trial is the question of who is primarily responsible for presenting evidence, the parties or the judge. Germany has traditionally followed the French model, in which the presiding judge is the dominating figure, but has accorded the parties extensive rights of questioning witnesses and expert witnesses. These rights are not subject to discretionary limitation by the judge but can be restricted only when a line of questioning violates the law or is clearly irrelevant.[25] Scholars have at various times suggested a reversal of roles, making the parties the initial presenters of evidence and relegating judges to the role of supplementary

---

[23] According to §§ 163a sec. 3, 168c sec. 1 CCP, only a prosecutorial interrogation of the *suspect* is open to the defense lawyer.

[24] This result is derived from the fact that § 163a sec. 4 and 5 CCP, which deal with police interrogations, make no reference to § 168c CCP. The suspect can, however, rely on his right to remain silent and refuse to make a statement unless his lawyer is permitted to attend the interrogation.

[25] See §§ 240 sec. 2, 241 sec. 2 CCP.

interrogators.[26] If the court retains the ultimate control over the intake of evidence – as has been suggested above – then the question of who interrogates witnesses first becomes a rather technical issue.

It is more important to decide whether the court, or at least the presiding judge, should be familiar with the prosecution dossier before the trial begins. In Germany, that is the case. Critics have argued that knowing the file in advance jeopardizes the judge's impartiality and neutrality.[27] But on the other hand, a judge who does not know the basic facts of the case is not in a position to ask intelligent questions of witnesses and experts, and he is even less in a position to pursue lines of inquiry that the parties have neglected or chosen not to bring out at trial. If the court is ultimately responsible for establishing "the truth" about the case and is to base its judgment on reliable fact-finding, it is hardly possible to keep the judges ignorant of the facts until they have been revealed by the parties at the trial.[28] The German experience has shown that professional judges, by and large, manage to perform the difficult balancing act between knowing in advance and being open for new information.

A crucial element of the trial is the ability of the defense to challenge adverse evidence and to introduce its own evidence in order to contradict the version presented by the prosecution in its dossier. The German system provides several possibilities for the defense to do so. The defense have the right to extensively question any witness and expert witness in court.[29] They can also nominate witnesses of their own and oblige them to appear in court.[30] Finally, the defense as well as the prosecution can request the court to hear additional evidence, and the court can deny such a request only on very limited grounds, mainly for clear irrelevance or redundance.[31] The parties,

---

[26] See, e.g. J. Herrmann, *Die Reform der deutschen Hauptverhandlung nach dem Vorbild des anglo-amerikanischen Strafverfahrens*, 1971; V. Haas, *Strafbegriff, Staatsverständnis und Prozessstruktur*, 2008, pp. 365 et seq.

[27] See Schünemann & Bandilla, 'Perseverance in Courtroom Decisions', in: Wegner, Lösel & Haisch (eds.), *Criminal Behaviour and the Justice System*, 1989, p. 181.

[28] See also Kühne 2007, note 116.

[29] § 240 sec. 2 CCP.

[30] § 220 CCP.

[31] § 244 sec. 3 CCP.

although not formally in charge of presenting the evidence at trial, can thus substantively influence the flow of information to the decision maker.

Germany like the Netherlands adheres to the principle that the court is free in evaluating the evidence, according to its conscientious appreciation.[32] German courts can thus convict on the defendant's confession alone, or on the statement of a co-defendant, and they can, on the other hand, acquit just on the defendant's word even if there have been several witnesses testifying that the defendant is guilty. The German CCP goes even further than the Dutch Code in protecting to the court's freedom. Unlike the Netherlands, Germany does not recognize any formal requirement of corroboration of a confession or of any other item of evidence. The courts have, however, declared that certain "suspect" evidence, such as the testimony of a crown witness or of an anonymous witness, cannot be the sole basis of a finding of guilt,[33] thus recognizing a corroboration requirement at least for certain situations.

Two important restrictions on the "free flow" of evidence should be noted. First, for matters of conviction and sentence, German law recognizes only four types of evidence, namely witnesses, expert witnesses, documents and real evidence. And, more importantly, the court must explain in the written judgment what weight it has given to each piece of evidence and how it has arrived at its factual conclusions.[34] The reasoning of the court in that respect is subject to review on appeal.[35] The requirement of giving reasons is meant to strike a balance between the court's freedom in evaluating the evidence and the necessity of having a rational basis for each judgment.

3.3. Victims and Witnesses

The victim has traditionally played a marginal role in the criminal process. The worldwide victims' movement, which started in the

---

[32] Cf. § 260 CCP.

[33] BVerfGE 57, 250 at 292–293 (1981); BGHSt 17, 382 at 385 (1962), 33, 178 at 181 (1985).

[34] § 267 sec. 1 CCP.

[35] See cases cited in Meyer-Goßner, *Strafprozessordnung. Kommentar*, 51st ed. 2008, § 267 notes 12, 12a.

1970s, has brought gradual change to this state of affairs. Under the German CCP, victims have a broad range of rights, including the possibility of bringing a private prosecution for some offenses,[36] the right to file suit against the public prosecutor's dismissal of a case for lack of sufficient evidence,[37] and the right to present a claim for monetary compensation at the criminal trial.[38] But many of these rights are neglected in practice. The right of the victim to challenge the prosecutor's decision not to bring charges has proven to be rather ineffective because appeals courts are reluctant to order a prosecutor to file an accusation against his will, and joining civil claims with the criminal case is an option disfavored by judges and lawyers alike.

The most important means for the victim to have an impact on the criminal process is to join the public prosecution as an auxiliary prosecutor (*Nebenklage*).[39] This possibility is however limited to the victims of certain offenses against the person.[40] If a victim joins the prosecution he has much the same rights as the public prosecutor; in particular, he can ask questions of witnesses at the trial[41] and can file an appeal against an acquittal even if the public prosecutor acquiesces in the judgment.[42] There has been some criticism of the institution of *Nebenklage* because it gives too many rights to some victims and leaves all others without the possibility of appearing at the trial except as witnesses. Although practitioners have accepted this incongruity it might be better to extend to all victims the right to be informed regularly about the progress of the criminal process and to address the court in person or through a lawyer rather than granting full party rights to just some selected victims.[43]

As is the case in the Netherlands, witnesses in Germany seem to have a long list of duties but no rights. In recent years, greater

---

36 §§ 374 et seq. CCP.

37 § 172 CCP.

38 §§ 403 et seq. CCP.

39 §§ 395 et seq. CCP.

40 Nebenklage is available, for example for survivors of a murder victim and for victims of sexual offenses, intentional assault and abduction (§ 395 CCP).

41 § 397 CCP.

42 § 400 CCP.

43 For a more extensive argument in this regard see Weigend, *Deliktsopfer und Strafverfahren*, Berlin 1989, pp. 509 et seq.

sensitivity for the plight of witnesses, especially young and sensitive witnesses, has evolved and has led to some legal reforms. For example, a witness can bring a lawyer or can have a lawyer assigned to him during the trial if it is likely that the witness might face a situation where he needs legal advice immediately.[44] Witnesses who are at risk of being harassed by the defendant or his friends in connection with their testimony can withhold their name and address.[45] When a witness is seriously troubled by the situation of having to testify in open court with the defendant present, the court can protect the witness's health by either sending the defendant to another room[46] or by interrogating the witness through a video link.[47] Under narrow conditions, it is also possible to use a videotape of an earlier interrogation – for example, by the police or the investigating judge – in lieu of the witness's live testimony at the trial.[48] Some of these protective measures raise the problem of interfering with the confrontation rights of the defense: the witness's gain in protection of privacy and health may well come at the cost of curtailing the defendant's right to challenge the witness's testimony. In recent years, the balance in Germany has been struck more in favor of witnesses.

3.4. Sanctions without Trial

One of the recent reforms in Dutch procedural law has been the transformation of the contract-like *transactie* into a form of unilateral prosecutorial sanctioning. In Germany, both types of dealing with less serious crime without a trial exist side by side. Under § 153a of the Code of Criminal Procedure, the prosecutor can dismiss any crime with a legal miminum punishment of less than one year in exchange for a payment or some other service offered by the suspect. This disposition is also possible after the case has been brought to court, but in that case it is the judge who imposes the conditions

---

44 § 68b CCP.
45 § 68 sec. 3 CCP.
46 § 247 CCP.
47 § 247a CCP.
48 § 255a CCP.

of dismissal, with the consent of the prosecutor.[49] Because conditional dismissal leaves the presumption of innocence intact and does not presuppose a confession, this disposition is sought after by many suspects and their lawyers. Contrary to what the legislature had intended when this possibility was introduced in 1975, conditional dismissal is being used not only for petty offenses but also for serious economic crime, with "penance payments" reaching millions of Euros. Often prosecutors demand a higher payment than the fine to be expected after conviction in court, adding a bonus payment for the discrete, non-public way of resolving the matter.

The alternative way of sanctioning without trial is the penal order,[50] which resembles the new form of prosecutorial sentencing introduced in the Netherlands. Due to the judicial monopoly on convicting a person of a crime,[51] a penal order, which contains a finding of guilt as well as a sentence, must be signed by a judge. It is the prosecutor, however, who fills out the form to be signed, and judges tend to sign it without examining in detail the prerequisites of the disposition proposed. The defendant is not usually asked for his consent in advance, but if he files a protest against the penal order that document loses its force and a regular trial in the local court will be held.[52] The penal order procedure is also being used, rather frequently, when a defendant does not appear for trial in the local court. In that case, the court can issue a penal order on the basis of the prosecutor's dossier,[53] thus shifting to the defendant the burden of protesting against the disposition. If he does not react within two weeks, the penal order becomes final and can be executed. The normal sentence in a penal order is a fine, but if the defendant has a lawyer the court can also impose a suspended prison sentence of one year or less.[54] It should be noted that the German police have no sanctioning authority for criminal offenses.

---

49 § 153a sec. 2 CCP.

50 §§ 407 et seq. CCP.

51 According to Art. 97 Basic Law, judges have a monopoly on 'jurisprudence' (*Rechtsprechung*), and imposing criminal punishment has been interpreted as belonging to the core of 'jurisprudence'.

52 § 411 CP.

53 § 408a CCP.

54 § 407 sec. 2 CCP. A penal order cannot be issued in cases of *Verbrechen* (offenses with a legal minimum sentence of one year imprisonment).

To give a rough idea of the frequency with which informal sanctioning mechanisms are being used in Germany: of all cases with a known suspect that were dismissed or prosecuted, in about 6% the conditional dismissal option was used in 2007. More than half of the cases that were not dismissed (that is about 15% of all cases with known suspects) were resolved by penal order.[55]

3.5. Appeals

With respect to the appeals system, Germany does not have to offer much to other countries by way of positive example. The German appeals system is in fact not very rational and suffers from similar defects as the Dutch system. The German system offers a choice between two extremes: a full re-trial, meaning that the first trial loses all effect if one party files a one-liner containing the word "*Berufung*";[56] and a very limited appeal for questions of law only (*Revision*),[57] by which the fact-finding of the lower court cannot be challenged even if the facts stated in the judgment are clearly at variance with what had been said in court. Although the court on *Revision* is precluded from taking evidence on the substance of the case, high courts have managed to find ways to review the fact-finding in extreme cases,[58] but the system remains awkward and unbalanced. In Germany, there have been similar proposals as those made by the authors of *Strafvordering* 2001, namely to require the appealing party in the case of *Berufung* to name the issues it wishes to raise and to thus limit the scope of the re-trial; but so far the legislature has not reacted to these suggestions. It seems that practitioners as well as courts have learned to live well with the quirks of the appeals system and are reluctant to make changes.

---

[55] About one third of all cases were dismissed for lack of sufficient evidence and another 27% were dismissed without any consequence because of their insignificance. Only 14% of all cases were brought to trial. Source: Statistisches Bundesamt: Rechtspflege Staatsanwaltschaften, 2007 (online).

[56] §§ 312 et seq. CCP. The appellant can, however, limit the appeal to part of the judgment, for example, to the sentence only (§ 318 CCP).

[57] §§ 333 et seq. CCP.

[58] The Federal Court of Appeals reverses a judgment when it finds that the evaluation of the evidence by the lower court, as documented in the written judgment, is self-contradictory or incomplete or contradicts common experience; for case law, see Meyer-Goßner 2008, § 337 notes 26–32.

4. CONCLUSION

This terminates my brief *tour d'horizon*. It is difficult to state general conclusions beyond those mentioned at the outset about the slightly different styles of criminal justice in our countries. On the whole, the similarities seem to be greater than the differences, and there appears to be a common trend toward emphasizing the functionality and economy of the process at the cost of the traditional ideal of searching for the truth. We will have to accept as a fact that criminal justice cannot escape the general tendency of public administration to cut costs and to cut edges. The 19th century ideal of a careful and slow investigation of a criminal case, followed by a full public trial where all relevant information is produced in open court, may well be a luxury of the past. But I think that it is worthwhile to try to retain, as the *Strafvordering* 2001 project does, the general spirit of an honest search for truth and justice, albeit in a more efficient way and with the use of modern technology which allows the faithful reproduction of words and images. Germans can learn from their Dutch neighbors about modernizing the process without giving up its core, especially without resorting to open-ended bargaining instead of making the effort of finding the facts.

A REVIEW OF THE CRIMINAL COURTS OF ENGLAND AND WALES BY THE RIGHT HONOURABLE LORD JUSTICE AULD

September 2001

RECOMMENDATIONS

CHAPTER ONE INTRODUCTION

Codification (*paras 35–36*)

1. A Code of criminal law should be produced and maintained in four sections:

   - criminal offences;
   - criminal procedure;
   - criminal evidence; and
   - sentencing.

CHAPTER FOUR MAGISTRATES

Introduction (*paras 1–14*)

2. Magistrates and District Judges should continue to exercise summary jurisdiction.

Present working patterns (*para 18*)

3. Whilst magistrates should continue to be appointed to one commission area, there should be a ready mechanism for enabling them, when required, to sit in adjoining areas.

The extent of summary jurisdiction (*para 20*)

4. There should be no general change in the level of summary jurisdiction as it is presently defined, of District Judges or magistrates; though the matter may need review in the light of the Halliday recommendations for the introduction of a new sentencing framework, including combined custody and community sentence orders.

Deployment and allocation of work (*paras 21–49*)

5. In the exercise of their summary jurisdiction:
   5.1 District Judges and magistrates should not routinely sit as mixed tribunals to deal with the general range or any particular type of case or form of proceeding, though there may be training and local 'cultural' advantages in their doing so from time to time depending on their respective availability and case loads;
   5.2 subject to changing workloads resulting from implementation of any of my recommendations or otherwise, there should be no significant change in the balance of numbers of District Judges and magistrates, or in the relative volumes or nature of summary work assigned to each of them; and
   5.3 summary work should continue to be allocated between District Judges and magistrates in accordance with the recommendations of the Venne Committee, namely that each, normally sitting separately, should be available to deal with the whole range, but that District Judges should concentrate on case allocation and management, cases of legal or factual complexity, cases of priority, such as those involving young offenders or offences of a sexual nature, and long cases.

Justices' Clerks (*paras 50–58*)

6. District Judges should normally sit without a legal adviser.
7. There should be no extension of justices' clerks' case management jurisdiction.

Composition of the bench

Selection and appointment of magistrates (*paras 80–86*)

8. Steps should be taken to provide benches of magistrates that reflect more broadly than at present the communities they serve by:
   8.1 reviewing the number, role and support given to them, including, in the event of the establishment of a unified Criminal Court, the present division of responsibility for them between the Lord Chancellor's Department and the Duchy of Lancaster;

8.2 passing responsibility for determining the number of magistrates required for each commission area from local Advisory Committees to court staff in consultation with the chairman of each bench, the justices' clerks and, in the event of the establishment of a unified Criminal Court, also the Resident Judge;

8.3 reviewing the community relations and educational initiatives of benches with a view better to inform the public of their work and to attract more suitable candidates for appointment;

8.4 in support of the local Advisory Committees, establishing a properly resourced National Recruitment Strategy aimed, not only at candidates for the magistracy, but also at their employers;

8.5 equipping local Advisory Committees with the information to enable them to submit for consideration for appointment, candidates that will produce and maintain benches broadly reflective of the communities they serve, including the establishment and maintenance of national and local data-bases of information on the make-up of the local community and on the composition of the local magistracy;

8.6 instituting a review of the ways in which the role and terms of service of a magistrate might be made more attractive and manageable to a wider range of the community than is presently the case; and

8.7 persisting with the current search for occupational and/or social groupings as a substitute for political affiliations as a measure of local balance.

9. The Lord Chancellor should continue with - but keep under careful review - his present policy of not normally appointing certain persons who are close to the criminal justice system or who, by the nature of their occupation, could not commit themselves to sitting regularly, or whose character or association would make them undesirable for appointment.

District Judges (paras 87–90)

10. The Lord Chancellor should be more ready to take the initiative to assign a District Judge to an area where, having consulted

as appropriate, he is of the view that local justice in the area requires it.

Training (paras 91–100)

11. The Judicial Studies Board should be made responsible, and be adequately resourced, for devising and securing the content and manner of training of all magistrates.
12. Such training should, in the main, be provided at local level through trainers, ideally justices' clerks and/or legal advisers, appropriately trained for the purpose by the Board.
13. District Judges should also be involved in the training of magistrates in the area or at the court centre at which they are normally based.
14. The Magistrates' National Training Initiative scheme should be refined in order to provide a less complex, weighted set of competences for magistrates, supported by clear national standards.
15. The Judicial Studies Board should establish systems to ensure that appraisal of magistrates takes place in a timely and effective manner across the country and that training programmes take account of the training needs identified during that process.

Chapter Five Juries

Composition of the jury

Size of the jury (paras 17–20)

16. A system should be introduced for enabling judges in long cases, where they consider it appropriate, to swear alternate or reserve jurors to meet the contingency of a jury otherwise being reduced in number by discharge for illness or any other reason of necessity.

Qualification for jury service (paras 21–24)

17. There should be no change in the present statutory criteria for qualification for jury service, save as to registration, as distinct from entitlement to registration, on an electoral roll.
18. The law should be amended to substitute for the condition of registration on an electoral roll, inclusion in such a roll and/or

on any one or more of a number of other specified publicly maintained lists or directories, but excluding anyone listed who, on investigation at the summons stage, is found not to be entitled to registration as an elector.

Enforcement of jury service (*paras 25–26*)

19. There should be rigorous and well publicised enforcement of the obligation to undertake jury service when required, and consideration should be given to doing so by way of a system of fixed penalties subject to a right of appeal to the magistrates.

Ineligibility (*paras 27–34*)

20. Everyone should be eligible for jury service, save for the mentally ill, and the law should be amended accordingly.
21. There should be no change to the categories of those disqualified from jury service.

Excusals as of right and discretionary excusal (*paras 35–40*)

22. Save for those who have recently undertaken, or have been excused by a court from, jury service, no-one should be excusable from jury service as of right, only on showing good reason for excusal.
23. The Central Summoning Bureau or the court, in examining a claim for discretionary excusal, should consider its power of deferral first.
24. The Bureau should treat all subsequent applications for deferral and all applications for excusal against clear criteria identified in the jury summons.

Random selection

Ethnic minority representation on juries (*paras 52–62*)

25. A scheme should be devised, along the lines that I have outlined in Chapter 5, paragraphs 60 and 61, for cases in which the court considers that race is likely to be relevant to an issue of importance in the case, for the selection of a jury consisting of, say, up to three people from any ethnic minority group.

Verdicts

Jury research (paras 76–87)

26. There should be no amendment of section 8 of the Contempt of Court Act 1981 to enable research into individual juries' deliberations.
27. Careful consideration should be given to existing research material throughout the common law world on jury trial in criminal cases, with a view to identifying and responding appropriately to all available information about how juries arrive at their verdicts.
28. If and to the extent that such research material is insufficient, consideration should be given to jury research of a general nature that does not violate the 1981 Act.

The unreasoned verdict (paras 88–98)

29. Section 8 of the Contempt of Court Act 1981 should be amended to permit, where appropriate, enquiry by the trial judge and/or the Court of Appeal (Criminal Division) into alleged impropriety by a jury, whether in the course of its deliberations or otherwise.

Perverse verdicts (paras 99–108)

30. The law should be declared, by statute, if need be, that juries have no right to acquit defendants in defiance of the law or in disregard of the evidence, and that judges and advocates should conduct criminal cases accordingly.

Trial of cases on indictment without a jury

Defendant's option for trial by judge alone (paras 110–118)

31. Defendants, with the consent of the court, after hearing representations from both sides, should be able to opt for trial by judge alone in all cases tried on indictment (whether, as now, in the Crown Court or, if my recommendations in Chapter 7 for a new unified Criminal Court are adopted, in the Crown or District Divisions).

'Either-way offences' (paras 119–172)

32. In all 'either-way' cases, magistrates' courts, not defendants, should determine venue after representation from the parties.
33. In the event of a dispute on the issue, a District Judge should decide.
34. The defence and the prosecution should have a right of appeal on paper from any mode of trial decision on which they were at issue to a Circuit Judge nominated for the purpose, and provision should be made for the speedy hearing of such appeals.
35. The procedure of committal of 'either-way' cases to the Crown Court for trial should be abolished and, pending the introduction of a system of allocation as part of my recommendations in Chapter 7 for a new unified Criminal Court, such cases should be "sent" to the Crown Court in the same way as indictable-only cases.
36. The procedure of committal for sentence should be abolished.

Fraud and other complex cases (paras 173–206)

37. As an alternative to trial by judge and jury in serious and complex fraud cases, the nominated trial judge should be empowered to direct trial by himself sitting with lay members or, where the defendant has opted for trial by judge alone, by himself alone.
38. The category of cases to which such a direction might apply should, in the first instance, be frauds of seriousness or complexity within sections 4 and 7 of the Criminal Justice Act 1987.
39. The overriding criterion for directing trial without jury should be the interests of justice.
40. Either party should have a right of appeal against such decision to the Court of Appeal (Criminal Division).
41. Judges trying such cases, by whatever form of procedure, should be specially nominated for the purpose as now, and provided with a thorough, structured and continuing training for it.
42. There should be a panel of experts, established and maintained by the Lord Chancellor in consultation with professional and other bodies, from which lay members may be selected for trials.

43. The nominated trial judge should select the lay members after affording the parties an opportunity to make written representations as to their suitability.
44. Lay members should be paid appropriately for their service.
45. In a court consisting of a judge and lay members, the judge should be the sole judge of law, procedure, admissibility of evidence and as to sentence; as to conviction, all three should be the judges of fact.
46. The decision of a court so constituted should wherever possible be unanimous, but a majority of any two could suffice for a conviction.
47. The judge should give the court's decision by a public and fully reasoned judgment.

Young defendants (*paras 207–211*)

48. All cases involving young defendants who are presently committed to the Crown Court for trial or for sentence should in future be put before the youth court consisting, as appropriate, of a High Court Judge, Circuit Judge or Recorder sitting with at least two experienced magistrates and exercising the full jurisdiction of the present Crown Court for this purpose.
49. The only possible exception should be those cases in which the young defendant is charged jointly with an adult and it is considered necessary in the interests of justice for them to be tried together.
50. The youth court so constituted should be entitled, save where it considers that public interest demands otherwise, to hear such cases in private, as in the youth court exercising its present jurisdiction.

Fitness to plead (*paras 212–213*)

51. Legislation should be introduced to require a judge, not a jury, to determine the issue of fitness to plead.

Information for and treatment of jurors

Information (*paras 217–220*)

52. The essential parts of the jury summons and explanatory documents issued by the Central Summoning Bureau should be

expressed in several languages, and over-all, the documentation should be more informative and couched in a more informal and friendly tone than at present.

53. The Court Service should review the adequacy of the information courts provide to potential jurors against the best provided by other jurisdictions.

Length and frequency of service (paras 221–224)

54. There should be an urgent review of the machinery, as between the Central Summoning Bureau and the courts, for summoning jurors who may be called upon to serve on long case.
55. There should be an examination and piloting of options for shortening the length of jury service by introducing as an aim a one day or one trial system or a variation of it.
56. Consideration should be given to lengthening the cycle over which it is possible to claim excusal by reason of previous jury service.

Facilities (para 225)

57. The Court Service should press on with its present programme to improve court facilities for jurors and jurors in waiting, including those who are disabled.
58. As a matter of urgency, it should also institute a programme of provision at all courts of adequate working facilities and other means to enable jurors in waiting to conduct their own affairs.

Compensation (para 226)

59. There should be a review of the amounts of allowances payable to jurors for their attendance at court.
60. Consideration should be given to an additional allowance to cover the cost to potential jurors who, but for it, could justifiably claim excusal because of caring responsibilities.

CHAPTER SIX THE JUDICIARY

The judicial hierarchy

Recorders (paras 14–16)

61. It should be a condition of a Recorder's appointment to sit for a minimum of three weeks a year in one continuous block, unless

for exceptional reasons a Presiding Judge permits him to sit in more than one block.

62. The Judicial Group in the Lord Chancellor's Department should, in consultation with the Presiding Judges, liaise closely with the Court Service to ensure that a minimum of three weeks' annual sitting is provided for each Recorder.

Matching judges to cases

'Ticketing' (paras 20–25)

63. Most of the rigidities of the present 'ticketing' system should be removed and replaced by the conferment on Resident Judges wide responsibility, subject to general oversight of the Presiding Judges, for allocation of judicial work at their court centres, but coupled with:
    - 63.1 regular and systematic appraisal enabling Resident Judges and Presiding Judges to determine the experience and interests of the judges; and
    - 63.2 the undertaking by judges of such training by the Judicial Studies Board as may be required as a pre-condition for the trial of particular categories of work.

Circuit listing *(paras 26–43)*

64. Consideration should be given to reducing the formal legal vacation periods for High Court Judges sitting in the Crown Court, in particular, to confining the summer vacation to the month of August.

65. This should be achieved by greater staggering of the existing sitting commitments of the High Court Bench, not by increasing them.

66. The systems of appointment and assignment of judges should be reviewed with a view to achieving a more efficient system than now obtains to ensure a planned and prompt succession of Resident Judges and appropriately experienced judges at court centres and, for this purpose, the Presiding Judges, Resident Judges, and Circuit Administrators should be consulted regularly.

67. The Lord Chancellor's Department should agree targets with the Presiding Judges within which vacancies for Resident,

Circuit and District Judges should be filled after it has received notification of projected or actual vacancy.

Better matching of judges to cases (*paras 44–56*)

68. There should be a formal and significant shift in the balance of heavy circuit work from High Court Judges to the more experienced Circuit Judges, coupled with greater flexibility in the system of allocating work between them, along the following lines:
    68.1 all work within the jurisdiction of the Crown Court should be triable by a Circuit Judge unless, on referral to a Presiding Judge, he specially reserves it for trial by a High Court Judge;
    68.2 the listing officer should draw to the attention of the Resident Judge any case which in accordance with criteria set by the Lord Chief Justice may be appropriate for reservation to a High Court Judge, for the Resident Judge, if he agrees, to refer it to one of the Presiding Judges for his decision; and
    68.3 the overriding criterion for reservation for trial by a High Court Judge should be whether "the case is one of special complexity and/or seriousness and/or public importance requiring trial by a High Court Judge".
69. The formal 'tiering' of court centres for the trial of certain classes of cases should be abolished and replaced by a more flexible system, overseen by the Presiding Judges, for the assignment of cases, adapted to the needs of each circuit and the work, and having regard to the physical constraints and convenience of location of different courts.
70. Save for the Presiding Judges, the present regular pattern of circuiteering by High Court Judges should be replaced by one under which the Presiding Judges decide, in consultation with their Circuit Administrators, where and when cases specifically reserved to High Court Judges should be tried.

Judicial administration (*paras 57–59*)

71. Adequate time should be given to:
    71.1 judges to enable them to manage and prepare cases assigned to them; and

71.2 judges with additional administrative responsibilities to enable them to fulfil those responsibilities.

72. In each case suitable provision should be made in secretarial, administrative or clerical help, as may be appropriate, to meet those needs.

Judges' lodgings (*paras 60–64*)

73. Future use of judges' lodgings should depend on the future volume and pattern of distribution of High Court Judge work on each circuit, not the other way round.
74. In assessing the future volume and pattern of circuit High Court Judge work, allowance should also be made for present and projected needs of civil and family work and the development of intermittent provincial administrative law and appellate jurisdictions.
75. If my recommendations are adopted for confining High Court Judge work on circuit to the gravest cases and for greater flexibility as to where and when they should be tried:

    75.1 lodgings that are reasonable value for money, taking into account among other things their convenience to major court centres and the number of judges they normally accommodate and for how long, should be retained or obtained; and

    75.2 in other cases consideration should be given to suitable alternative accommodation appropriate to length of sitting and type of case[s], for example, hotels, guest houses of the Wolsey Lodge variety and rented and serviced accommodation.

Composition of the judiciary

Appointment to judicial office (*paras 68–87*)

76. The risk of indirect discrimination in those cases where the candidates for judicial appointment may not have had much exposure in the consultation process, notably women, ethnic minorities and solicitors is the most constantly raised and anxious concern of those who feel that the appointments system is unfair to them. It is not enough to wait for the professions to present the Lord Chancellor's Department with suitably 'visible'

as well as qualified candidates for appointment. He should vigorously pursue his declared policy of consulting as widely as possible in all cases.

77. If the assessment centre pilot proposed by the Lord Chancellor proves to be successful, consideration should be given to extending its use to other full and part-time judicial appointment procedures.

Disability (para 88)

78. The Lord Chancellor's Department should establish and publish clear guidelines on the appointment of disabled persons to judicial office.

Training and appraisal

Training (paras 89–97)

79. The Judicial Studies Board should be adequately resourced to meet the increasing training needs of the judiciary, including those in respect of special jurisdictions, case management, information technology and judicial administration.

Appraisal (paras 98–104)

80. An appraisal scheme should be introduced for all part-time judicial post-holders, and reinforced by a system of regular self-appraisal.
81. The assessments produced should be available to those advising the Lord Chancellor on full-time judicial appointments.
82. Consideration should be given, following wide consultation among the judiciary and others, to a system of appraisal for full-time judges; the results of such assessments should, however, only exceptionally be made available to anyone other than the Presiding Judges or the relevant Head of Division.

Chapter Seven a Unified Criminal Court

A unified Criminal Court *(paras 2–35)*

83. A unified Criminal Court should be established.
84. There should be three levels of jurisdiction within the unified Criminal Court consisting of: the Crown Division to exercise

jurisdiction over all indictable-only matters and such 'either-way' cases as are allocated to it; the District Division to exercise jurisdiction over such 'either-way' matters as are allocated to it; and the Magistrates' Division to exercise jurisdiction over all summary-only matters and such 'either-way' cases as are allocated to it.

85. The Crown and Magistrates' Divisions should be constituted as are the Crown Court and magistrates' courts respectively, and the District Division should consist of a judge, in the main a District Judge, and at least two experienced magistrates (or if a defendant with the consent of the court so opts, of a judge alone).
86. The District Division's jurisdiction over 'either-way' offences should be limited to those within a likely maximum sentence in the circumstances of the case viewed at its worst (as distinct from the legal maximum for a case or cases of that category) of, say, two years custody, a maximum financial penalty to be determined and/or a maximum of community, or combination of custody and community, sentences to be determined in the light of future reforms of the sentencing framework.
87. The District Division, sitting as a youth court, should also try grave cases against young defendants presently dealt with in the Crown Court; see recommendation 48.

The allocation of cases (*paras 36–40*)

88. All cases should have an allocation hearing in the Magistrates' Division at which pleas should be taken.
89. All cases triable only summarily should remain in the Magistrates' Division and all cases triable only on indictment should be sent to the Crown Division.
90. The court should allocate all 'either-way' cases according to the seriousness of the alleged offence and the circumstances of the defendant in accordance with statutory and broadly drawn criteria, looking at the case at its worst from the point of view of the defendant and bearing in mind the jurisdiction of each division.
91. Where there is no dispute or uncertainty as to venue, magistrates should allocate the case; otherwise a District Judge should do so after hearing representations on the matter from both parties.

92. The Government should ensure, as a matter of urgency, routine provision, through an integrated system of information technology or otherwise, of complete and accurate information of a defendant's criminal record at all allocation hearings.
93. Where there are linked charges and/or defendants, all should normally be allocated to the division with jurisdiction to hear the most serious of the charges.
94. The defence and the prosecution should have a right of appeal on paper from a contested allocation decision to a Circuit Judge nominated for the purpose, and provision should be made for speedy hearing of such appeals.
95. The defence and the prosecution should be able, up to a specified point before trial, to seek re-allocation in the light of any material change in the circumstances of the alleged offence(s) and/or of the defendant between allocation and trial.

The circuits (*paras 41–49*)

96. For the foreseeable future circuit boundaries and administrations should remain broadly as they are.
97. Each circuit should continue to have Presiding Judges, Chancery Supervisory and Family Liaison Judges and a Circuit Administrator undertaking their present respective functions, so that the Circuit Administrator continues to act as the focal point of contact for them.
98. Whatever changes are contemplated for the administrative organisation of the circuits, a decision should first be made whether to replace the present dual system of courts with a unified Criminal Court paying close attention to the needs of the civil and family jurisdictions outside London as well as to those of crime.
99. There should be a review from time to time of the appropriateness of the South Eastern Circuit remaining one circuit, taking into account, among other things, its size and the special needs of Greater London.

A new management structure (*paras 50–73*)

100. A single centrally funded executive agency, as part of Lord Chancellor's Department, should be responsible for the

administration of all courts, civil, criminal and family (save for the Appellate Committee of the House of Lords), replacing the Court Service and Magistrates' Courts Committees.

101. The agency should be headed by a national board and chief executive.
102. Within each circuit the criminal courts should, if consistent with the efficient and effective operation of civil and family courts, be organised managerially on the basis of the 42 criminal justice areas.
103. Implementation of national policy and management at local level for all three jurisdictions should be the responsibility of local managers working in close liaison with local judges and magistrates, much as the Circuit Administrators and Presiding Judges, Chancery Supervisory and Family Liaison Judges do at circuit level.

The future role of the justices' clerk (para 74)

104. In a unified Criminal Court:
    104.1 justices' clerks should continue to be responsible for the legal advice provided to magistrates;
    104.2 arrangements should be made to ensure that, in the absence of the justices' clerk, magistrates at each courthouse have ready access to a senior legal adviser; and
    104.3 justices' clerks should not normally exercise administrative responsibilities unrelated to their role as legal adviser to the magistrates.

Judicial management *(paras 75–83)*

105. In a unified Criminal Court:
    105.1 Resident Judges should be responsible, under the oversight of the Presiding Judges, for judicial management of court centres;
    105.2 in relation to the District Bench and magistracy, these responsibilities should include oversight of: listing; membership of panels; case allocation; training and development; and appraisal;
    105.3 Resident Judges should be provided with the necessary time out of court and degree of administrative and other support to carry out these additional responsibilities;

105.4 there should be consequential reviews of the number and location of Resident Judges, and also of their remuneration; and

105.5 the future organisation and structure of the District Bench should be reviewed in the light of these changes.

Court accommodation (*paras 84–90*)

106. If my recommendations in Chapter 8 for a national Criminal Justice Board and local Criminal Justice Boards are accepted, decisions as to the provision and closure of court centres should become the responsibility of local Boards, subject to oversight and guidance of the national Board.

107. Decisions should be made in the interests of all involved in the criminal justice process in their areas, and with the benefit of a cost/benefit exercise taking the public interest in its widest sense into account.

108. There should be a review of all accommodation of the courts and criminal justice agencies to enable a joint assessment of the most efficient use for the system as a whole of available accommodation and planning for future needs.

109. In the planning and provision of court accommodation, proper allowance should be made for the fact that a just and efficient criminal justice system does not require all courtrooms to be in use full-time.

110. In the planning and provision of court accommodation, a significant tolerance should be allowed for the high volatility of demands on court time and the uncertainties of future criminal justice policy initiatives (that is, "an adequate tolerance over assumed full capacity").

111. A new Criminal Court Design Guide should be prepared as a standard to which, over time, court buildings should conform.

Information technology (*paras 91–102*)

112. A single information technology system should be developed for the unified Criminal Court, combining the best design elements of all the systems currently under development in the magistrates' courts and Crown Court and taking into account corresponding developments in the civil and family jurisdictions.

113. The management of the implementation of information technology for a unified Criminal Court should be under the supervision of a Board upon which the judiciary are represented, and should be undertaken in close consultation with the Judicial Technology Group.
114. Planning and implementation of procedural reforms should go hand in hand with development and introduction of the necessary supporting information technology.

Security (*paras 103–116*)

115. The Lord Chancellor should, as a matter of urgency, take direct responsibility for and control of security of courts of all levels and jurisdictions.
116. Those invested with a duty of providing security should have the same powers in all criminal courts.
117. Consideration should be given to requiring the police to resume provision of security in all criminal courts, or to the establishment of a uniformed Sheriff Officer Service which would be fully trained, have police powers and would operate under the general oversight of the local judiciary.
118. There should be a review of the necessary provision, in terms of accommodation, technology and otherwise, to protect vulnerable witnesses and others at court, and to enable the former where appropriate and necessary to give their evidence by video-link away from the court.
119. In the event of my recommendations in Chapter 8 being adopted, the extent of and financial responsibility for security provided in the Criminal Court should become a joint criminal justice responsibility exercised by the Criminal Justice Board on behalf of Ministers.

Inspection (*para 117, page 314*)

120. If, in accordance with my recommendations, a unified Criminal Court and single supporting administrative agency are established, there should be created an independent Inspectorate of that agency, which should report to the Lord Chancellor.

CHAPTER EIGHT THE CRIMINAL JUSTICE SYSTEM

Managing criminal justice (*paras 43–77*)

121. A Criminal Justice Board should replace the Strategic Planning Group, the national Trials Issues Group and its sub-groups, and take over such responsibilities of the Criminal Justice Consultative Council as may be operational.
122. The Criminal Justice Board should be responsible for over-all direction of the criminal justice system, with a remit including, but not limited to:

    - planning and setting criminal justice system objectives;
    - budgeting and the allocation of funds;
    - securing the national and local achievement of its objectives;
    - the development and implementation of an integrated system of information technology;
    - research and development; and
    - combating inequality and discrimination throughout the criminal justice system.

123. The Board should be chaired by an independent chairman and its membership should include senior civil servants from the three main criminal justice departments and the Treasury, the Chairman of the Youth Justice Board, Chief Officers of the Criminal Case Management Agency, the unified Criminal Court, Police, Prison and Probation Services and a small number of non-executive members.
124. The Board should not include a judge, but should consult regularly with the Lord Chief Justice and other senior judiciary.
125. The Board should be supported by a secretariat and a national administrative structure accountable to it and be responsible for developing a system of information technology for the whole criminal justice system.
126. Local Criminal Justice Boards should replace the Area Strategy Committees, local TIGs, Chief Officer Groups and, where they exist, informally constituted local Criminal Justice Boards, and should draw on their memberships.

127. Local Criminal Justice Boards should be responsible for giving effect at local level to the national Criminal Justice Board's directions and objectives and for management of the criminal justice system in their areas.
128. Membership of the local Boards should include: local managers of the Criminal Court, the Prison Service and the National Health Service; the local Chief Constable; the local Chief Crown Prosecutor; the local Chief Probation Officer; representatives from the Youth Offenders Team, Victim Support, possibly representatives of the local Bar and solicitors and at least two non-executive members.
129. Each local Board should be provided with a dedicated and properly resourced secretariat accountable to the national secretariat, be provided with a joint local budget and should select its own chairman.

Advising on criminal justice (*paras 78–88*)

130. The Criminal Justice Consultative Committee should be replaced with a Criminal Justice Council with a statutory power and duty, and suitably equipped:

    - to keep the criminal justice system under review;
    - to advise the Government on the form and manner of implementation of all proposed criminal justice reforms and to make proposals to it for reform;
    - to provide general oversight of the programme and structures for introduction and maintenance of codification of substantive criminal law, procedure, evidence and sentencing that I recommend in Chapter 1;
    - to advise the Government on the framing and implementation of a communication and education strategy for the criminal justice system; and
    - for any of those purposes, to consult and/or commission programmes of research.

131. Before initiating key proposals for reform of the criminal justice system, the Government should be statutorily obliged to refer them to the Council for advice and to take account of any

proposals or advice tendered by it in response to such reference or of its own accord.

132. The Council should be chaired by the Lord Chief Justice or a senior Lord Justice of Appeal and composed of judges of all levels, magistrates, criminal practitioners,representatives of the key agencies and organisations involved in the criminal justice process and one or more distinguished legal academics specialising in the field (none of whom should be members of the Criminal Justice Board).
133. The Council should be provided with a properly resourced secretariat and research staff.
134. Such of the Criminal Justice Consultative Council's functions as relate to the development and improvement of inter-agency co-ordination, through the Area Strategy Committees and otherwise, of national policies and objectives should become the responsibility of the Criminal Justice Board and its administrative support structure.
135. The Area Strategy Committees should cease to exist.

Joint inspection (*paras 89–91*)

136. A Joint Inspection Unit should be formally established under the collective control of the Criminal Justice Chief Inspectors and be given sufficient resources to instigate and co-ordinate a programme of cross-agency inspection.

Information technology (*paras 92–114*)

137. The Criminal Justice Board should discontinue the IBIS project of linking up the six main information technology systems in the criminal justice system, and should instead, within a set timescale, produce an implementation plan for an integrated information technology system for the whole of the criminal justice system based upon a common language and common electronic case files.
138. The implementation of an integrated system of information technology should be organised in six projects, to run either in parallel or sequentially, namely:

   - case tracking;
   - management information;

- unification of data;
- extending the categories of user;
- case management; and
- unification of enabling technologies.

139. A Criminal Case Management Agency should be established, to be accountable to the Criminal Justice Board for managing the implementation of the integrated system and, when implemented, managing those elements of the system that require central management, namely:

- production of system protocols and quality assurance of system data;
- management and monitoring of case progression;
- data standards for system management information;
- standards and protocols for access by victims, witnesses, defendants and their representatives;
- storage and maintenance of data;
- data security and control of access to data; and
- case management at the system level.

Chapter Nine Decriminalisation and Alternatives to Conventional Trial

Summary prosecutions

Television licence evasion (paras 10–13)

140. The use of a television without a licence should remain a criminal offence, but should be dealt with in the first instance by a fixed penalty notice discounted for prompt purchase of a licence and payment of penalty, and subject to the defendant's right to dispute guilt in court.

Other summary matters (20–25)

141. Fixed penalty notices should be used in respect of all offences provided for in the Road Traffic Offenders Act 1988, Part III and Schedule 3, unless there are special circumstances requiring the offender to attend court.

142. There should be a systematic review leading to similar fixed penalty and/or notice-to-correct schemes for a wider range of infringements that are presently the subject of criminal prosecution.

Alternative procedures

'Caution-plus' (*paras 41–47*)

143. Consideration should be given to the introduction of a conditional cautioning scheme over a wide range of minor offences, enabling the prosecutor with the consent of the offender and, where appropriate, with the approval of the court:
    - to caution him subject to his compliance with specified conditions; and
    - to bring the conditionally cautioned offender before the court in the event of his failure to comply with the conditions.

144. In considering the introduction of such a scheme, regard should be had to its place alongside existing provisions for avoiding or modifying the criminal process and future developments in the form of 'restorative justice', with a view to over-all rationalisation into a single scheme.

Regulatory enforcement (*paras 48–51*)

145. Once the Financial Services Authority has assumed full responsibility for supervision in the financial services field, consideration should be given to transferring appropriate financial and market infringements from the criminal justice process to its regulatory and disciplinary control.

Parallel proceedings (*paras 52–55*)

146. Consideration should be given, for appropriate cases of parallel proceedings, to combining the criminal justice and regulatory processes, with a judge as the common president, and with lay members or expert assessors for the second and regulatory part.

147. In cases of fraud and other financial offences courts should, wherever possible and appropriate, exercise their existing powers of a regulatory nature as part of their sentencing disposal.
148. Consideration should be given, in appropriate offences, to enlarging or extending the courts' conventional sentencing powers in this respect.
149. In the exercise of such powers courts should be assisted by counsel on behalf of the parties, properly instructed for the purpose.

Restorative justice (*paras 58–69*)

150. A national strategy should be developed and implemented to ensure consistent, appropriate and effective use of restorative justice techniques across England and Wales.

Enforcement of civil debts (*paras 70–77*)

151. Preparatory work should be undertaken with a view to the removal, in due course, of all civil debt enforcement from courts exercising a criminal jurisdiction.

Chapter Ten Preparing for Trial

Essentials

A strong and independent prosecutor (*para 12*)

152. The Crown Prosecution Service should be given greater legal powers, in particular the power to determine the initial charge, and sufficient resources to enable it to take full and effective control of cases from the charge or pre-charge stage, as appropriate.

Efficient and properly paid defence lawyers (*paras 13–27*)

153. Urgent consideration should be given to changing the structure of public funding of defence fees in the criminal courts so as properly to reward and encourage adequate and timely preparation of cases for disposal on pleas of guilty or by trial, rather than discourage such preparation as it perversely does at present.

Identifying the issues

The charge (paras 35–45)

154. The Crown Prosecution Service should determine the charge in all but minor, routine offences or where, because of the circumstances, there is a need for a holding charge before seeking the advice of the Service.
155. In minor, routine cases in which the police charge without first having sought the advice of the Service, they should apply the same evidential test as that governing the Service in the Code for Crown Prosecutors.
156. Where the police have preferred a holding charge, and in other than minor, routine offences, a prosecutor should review and, if necessary, reformulate the charge at the earliest possible opportunity.
157. 'Minor' or 'routine' offences for this purpose should be identified in the Criminal Procedure Code that I have recommended or in other primary or subsidiary legislation.

Private prosecutions (paras 46–50)

158. The right of private prosecution should continue, subject to the power of the Director of Public Prosecutions, on learning of a private prosecution, to take it over and discontinue it.
159. Any court before which a private prosecution is initiated should be under a duty forthwith to notify the Director of it in writing.
160. The Director, in deciding whether to discontinue a private prosecution that he has taken over, should apply the public interest test as well as the evidential test set out in the Code for Crown Prosecutors.

Consent to the charge (paras 51–52)

161. The Law Commission's recommendation to remove the requirement for the Attorney General's or Director of Public Prosecution's consent to prosecution should be adopted, save in those categories of case where its retention clearly protects the public interest.

Mechanics of charging (paras 53–63)

162. All public prosecutions should take the form of a charge, issued without reference to the courts, which should remain the basis of the accusation against the defendant throughout all stages of the case, irrespective of the level of court in which it is tried.
163. The charge may be oral or in writing, a written copy or original, as the case may be, being served manually or by postal service.
164. In either case, under arrangements with the court's administration, the charge should specify the date of first attendance at court on pain of arrest on warrant.
165. The present procedure for application for a warrant, by swearing an oath as to service of process, in summary offences should be abolished and replaced by paper application considered and determined in open court.
166. The same regime for commencing proceedings should apply to private prosecutions, save that: 1) the charge should only be administered in writing; 2) it should be subject to the prior permission of the court; 3) the permission should be endorsed on the charge sheet by an officer of the court; and 4) the court, before listing the matter, should notify the Director of Public Prosecutions.
167. The voluntary bill of indictment should be abolished and, to the extent necessary under new procedures of allocation of work in a unified Criminal Court, safeguards should be introduced to secure the interests of justice by Criminal Procedure Rules.
168. The form of charge should be common to summary and indictable offences.
169. The prosecution should be entitled to amend the charge up to the pre-trial assessment date (or in a summary trial without such an assessment, up to a date to be specified), but thereafter only with the permission of the trial court.
170. The procedure for issue of warrants should be simplified.

Dropping the prosecution (*paras 64–68*)

171. The law should be amended to provide a form of procedure common to all courts to enable a prosecutor, without the

consent of the defendant or the approval of the court, to discontinue proceedings at any stage before close of the prosecution case on trial.

172. In the event of the prosecution discontinuing at any time before pre-trial assessment or, where there is no pre-trial assessment, before a stage to be specified, the prosecution should be entitled to reinstate the prosecution, subject to the court's power to stay it as an abuse of process.
173. In the event of the prosecution discontinuing after that stage, the defendant should be entitled to an acquittal, save where the court for good reason permits the prosecution to 'lie on the file'.
174. There should be common provision for all courts, subject to their approval and the agreement of the parties, to give formal effect to such discontinuance and, where appropriate, acquittal in the absence of the parties.

Bail (*paras 69–82*)

175. Magistrates and judges in all courts should take more time to consider matters of bail.
176. Listing practices should reflect the necessity to devote due time to bail applications and allow the flexibility required for all parties to gather sufficient information for the court to make an appropriate decision.
177. Courts, the police, prosecutors and defence representatives should be provided with better information for the task than they are at present, in particular, complete and up to date information of the defendant's record held on the Police National Computer, relevant probation or other social service records, if any, verified information about home living conditions and employment, if any, and sufficient information about the alleged offence and its relationship, if any, to his record so as to indicate whether there is a pattern of offending.
178. Courts and all relevant agencies should be equipped with a common system of information technology, as recommended in Chapter 8, to facilitate the ready availability to all who need it of the above information.

179. There should be appropriate training for magistrates and judges in the making of bail decisions, with Article 5 ECHR and risk assessment particularly in mind, as the Law Commission has proposed.
180. All courts should be provided with an efficient bail information and support scheme.
181. Bail notices should be couched in plain English, printed and given to the defendant as a formal court order when the bail decision is made, so that he understands exactly what is required of him and appreciates the seriousness of the grant of bail and of any attached conditions.
182. All courts should be diligent in adopting the Law Commission's proposals for the recording of bail decisions in such a way as to indicate clearly how they have been reached.

Appeals against bail decisions (paras 83–90)

183. The right of application to a High Court Judge for bail after determination by any criminal court exercising its original or appellate jurisdiction should be removed, and there should be substituted therefor a right of appeal from the District Division or Crown Division (Crown Court) on a point of law only.
184. Defendants should have a right of appeal against conditional grants of bail in the Magistrates' Division (magistrates' courts) to the Crown Division (Crown Court) in respect of conditions imposed as to their residence away from home and/or to the provision of a surety or sureties or the giving of security.
185. The prosecution should have a right of appeal to the Crown Division against the grant of bail by the Magistrates' Division (magistrates' courts) in respect of all offences that would, on conviction, be punishable by a custodial, or partly custodial sentence.

Advance indication of sentence (*paras 91–114*)

186. There should be introduced, by way of a judicial sentencing guideline for later incorporation in a Sentencing Code, a system of sentencing discounts graduated so that the earlier the tender of plea of guilty the higher the discount for it, coupled

with a system of advance indication of sentence for a defendant considering pleading guilty.

187. On the request of a defendant, through his advocate, the judge should be entitled formally to indicate the maximum sentence in the event of a plea of guilty at that stage and the possible sentence on conviction following a trial.
188. The request to the judge and all related subsequent proceedings should be in court, in the presence of the prosecution, the defendant and his advisers and a court reporter, but otherwise in private, and should be fully recorded.
189. The judge should enquire, by canvassing the matter with both advocates, as to the mental competence and emotional state of the defendant and as to whether he might be under any pressure falsely to admit guilt.
190. The prosecution and defence should be equipped to put before the judge all relevant information about the offence(s) and the defendant, including any pre-sentence or other reports and any victim impact statement, to enable the judge to give an indication.
191. The judge should only give an indication if and when he is satisfied that he has sufficient information and if he considers it appropriate to do so.
192. Where, as a result of such an indication, a defendant's advocate indicates to the judge that he wishes to plead guilty, the judge should, by questioning the defendant direct, satisfy himself that the defendant understands the effect of his proposed plea, that it would be true and that it would be voluntary.
193. The judge should be bound by his indication, as should any other judge before whom the defendant may appear for sentence, on the consequent plea of guilty.

Disclosure

Advance disclosure by the prosecution (paras 117–120)

194. There should be a single set of statutory rules imposing on the prosecution in all cases a duty to provide its proposed evidence in sufficient time to enable the defence adequately to prepare for trial, the precise timescale to be prescribed by rules.

Disclosure of unused material and defence statement (paras 121–184)

195. The Criminal Procedure and Investigations Act 1996 scheme of material disclosure should be retained, in particular, two stages of prosecution disclosure under which the second stage is informed by and conditional on a defence statement indicating the issues that the defendant proposes to take at trial.
196. The present mix of primary and subsidiary legislation, Code, Guidelines and Instructions should be replaced by a single and simply expressed instrument setting out clearly the duties and rights of all parties involved.
197. There should be the same test of disclosability for both stages of prosecution disclosure providing in substance and, for example, for the disclosure of "material which, in the prosecutor's opinion, might reasonably affect the determination of any issue in the case of which he knows or should reasonably expect" or, more simply but tautologically, "material which in the prosecutor's opinion might weaken the prosecution case or assist that of the defence".
198. In addition, there should be automatic primary disclosure in all or certain types of cases of certain common categories of documents and/or of documents by reference to certain subject matters.
199. The police should retain responsibility for retaining, collating and recording any material gathered or inspected in the course of the investigation; police officers should be better trained for what, in many cases, may be an extensive and difficult exercise regardless of issues of disclosability, and subject, in their exercise of it to statutory guidelines and a rigorous system of 'spot' audits by H.M. Inspectorates of Constabulary and/or of the Crown Prosecution Service.
200. Such responsibility as the police have for identifying and considering all potentially disclosable material should be removed to the prosecutor.
201. The prosecutor should retain ultimate responsibility for the completeness of the material recorded by the police and assume sole responsibility for primary and all subsequent disclosure.

202. The requirements of a defence statement should remain as at present, as should the requirements for particulars where the defence is alibi and/or the defence propose to adduce expert evidence.
203. More effective use of defence statements should be facilitated by the general improvements to the system for preparation for trial that I have recommended, and encouraged through professional conduct rules, training and, in the rare cases where it might be appropriate, discipline, to inculcate in criminal defence practitioners the propriety of and need for compliance with the requirements.
204. There should be a clearly defined timetable for each level of jurisdiction for all stages of mutual disclosure unless the court in any individual case orders otherwise.
205. The Prison Service should introduce national standards for access to due process for remand prisoners that ensure they experience no greater difficulty than bailed defendants in preparing for their trials.

Third party disclosure (paras 185–190)

206. There should be consideration of a new statutory scheme for third party disclosure, including its cost implications to all concerned, to operate alongside and more consistently with the general provisions for disclosure of unused material.

Public interest immunity (paras 191–197)

207. A scheme should be introduced for instruction by the court of special independent counsel to represent the interests of the defendant in those cases at first instance and on appeal where the court now considers prosecution applications in the absence of the defence in respect of the non-disclosure of sensitive material.

Case management

Case allocation (paras 200–202)

208. Under the present system of criminal courts, a single, simple form of procedure for movement of all cases from magistrates'

courts to the Crown Court should be substituted for the present mix of procedures of committal, voluntary bill, transfer and sending.

209. If my recommendations for a unified Criminal Court are adopted, a similar, single procedure should govern the movement of all cases from the Magistrates' Division to the District or Crown Divisions.

Pre-trial hearings and pre-trial assessments (paras 204–235)

210. In the preparation for trial in all criminal courts, there should be a move away from plea and direction hearings and other forms of pre-trial hearings to co-operation between the parties according to standard or adapted time-tables, wherever necessary seeking written directions from the court.
211. There should be national standard timetables and lists of key actions for preparation for trial in each of the three divisions of the new unified Criminal Court, with suitable variations to meet categories of case of different nature and complexity.
212. The Magistrates' Division, when allocating cases to the Crown or District Divisions and, where appropriate, in summary cases at an early administrative hearing, should issue the parties with the appropriate standard timetable and list, including dates for mutual disclosure and a date within a short period after secondary disclosure for 'pre-trial assessment'.
213. The parties, by agreement or on notice to each other, should be at liberty to seek in writing leave from the trial court to vary the standard timetable.
214. The parties should endeavour to prepare for trial in accordance with the timetable and list of key actions appropriate to the case and to resolve between themselves any issues of law, procedure or evidence that may shape and/or affect the length of the trial and when it can start.
215. The timetable in each case should set a date for the 'pre-trial assessment', that is, an assessment by the parties and the court as to the state of readiness for trial.
216. By the pre-trial assessment date the parties should complete and send to the trial court a check-list showing progress in

preparation and as to readiness for trial, and seeking, if appropriate, written directions.

217. Only if the court or the parties consider it is necessary for the timely and otherwise efficient preparation for, and conduct of, the trial should there be a pre-trial hearing, for example where one or other of the parties cannot comply with the timetable, or where there are unresolved issues affecting the efficient preparation for or conduct of the trial, or when the case is sufficiently serious or complex to require the guidance of the court.

218. Where there is a pre-trial hearing, and the defendant is in custody and consents, he should not be brought to court, but should participate in it to the extent necessary by video-link with the prison in which he is housed.

219. A judge or magistrates conducting an oral pre-trial hearing should be empowered to give binding directions or rulings subject to subsequent variation or discharge if justice requires it.

220. Where a pre-trial hearing is necessitated by one or other or both parties' failure without good cause to comply with the time-table or other directions of the court, or to resolve issues of procedure, law or fact between them, the court should have power:

    220.1 to make such order as to payment of a publicly funded defence advocate for his attendance at the hearing as may be appropriate in the circumstances; and/or publicly to reprimand either party's advocate or those instructing them as appropriate; any such public reprimand to be communicated to and taken into account by the professional body of the person reprimanded and, where the person is franchised for publicly funded defence work, by the Legal Services Commission; and/or

    220.2 to make such order of costs against one or other or both sides as may be appropriate.

221. All interlocutory court rulings, orders or directions in criminal courts as presently structured or in a new unified Criminal Court should be expressed in writing as a formal document

of the court and served forthwith or shortly afterwards on all parties.

Listing and docketing (*paras 236–238*)

222. There should be a move to greater use of fixed trial dates in cases of substance.
223. There should be a corresponding move to early allocation of such cases to a judge for case management and trial.

Information technology (*paras 256–261*)

224. The present provision for the use of video-link with prisons in pre-trial hearings in magistrates' courts should be extended to all such hearings in all criminal courts; and as technology develops, consideration should be given to the use of web technologies for them.

Time limits (*paras 262–270*)

225. The present maximum custody periods should continue, save that, in the event of abolition of committal proceedings for 'either-way' offences and/or of the establishment of a unified Criminal Court, the periods should be 56 days for cases tried summarily (whether summary only or 'either-way') and 182 for those tried otherwise.
226. Section 22 of the Prosecution of Offences Act 1985 should be amended to enable a court to consider and grant an extension of the custody time limit after its expiry, but only if such power is closely circumscribed, including a provision that the court should only grant an extension where it is satisfied that there is a compelling public interest in doing so.
227. An effective right of appeal should be provided outside the custody time limit period against the refusal of an extension within the period.

A code of criminal procedure (*paras 271–280*)

228. The law of criminal procedure should be codified, but in two stages:
    228.1 first, the Law Commission should be requested to draft legislation consolidating existing primary and secondary

legislation coupled, possibly, with some codification of the more important and uncontroversial common law rules; and

228.2 second, a statutory Criminal Procedure Rules Committee should be established to draft a single procedural code for a unified Criminal Court, restating and reforming as necessary statute and common law, custom, judicial practice directions and other guidance.

229. The code, which should be expressed concisely and in simple English and Welsh, should provide, so far as practicable, a common set of rules for all levels of jurisdiction, and different rules only to the extent that they are necessary for different forensic processes.

230. The draft code should be enacted in primary and subsidiary legislation, and the Committee should, thereafter maintain it, proposing amendments where necessary for the Lord Chancellor's approval and initiation of amendment by secondary legislation subject to negative or positive resolution as may be appropriate.

231. In all its activities, the Committee should be under the general oversight of the Criminal Justice Council.

232. The Government should be under a statutory duty to refer to the Committee all proposals for amendment of the law of criminal procedure.

233. The Criminal Procedure Rules Committee should be chaired by the Lord Chief Justice and its membership should include: the Vice-President of the Court of Appeal (Criminal Division), the Senior Presiding Judge, at least two High Court Judges and two Circuit Judges sitting in crime, together with an appropriate number of District Judges, magistrates and justices' clerks, a number of experienced criminal practitioners from both branches of the profession and at least one academic specialising in the field, together with appropriate representatives of voluntary organisations with a direct interest in the work of the criminal courts.

234. The Committee should be supported by a full-time staff of lawyers and administrators experienced in the work of the criminal courts.

Chapter Eleven the Trial: Procedures and Evidence

The start of a jury trial (paras 15–24)

235. In all cases tried by judge and jury:
   235.1 each juror should be provided at the start of the trial with a copy of the charge or charges;
   235.2 the judge at the start of the trial should address the jury, introducing them generally to their task as jurors and giving them an objective outline of the case and the questions they are there to decide;
   235.3 the judge should supplement his opening address with, and provide a copy to each juror of, a written case and issues summary prepared by the parties' advocates and approved by him;
   235.4 The judge, in the course of his introductory address, and the case and issues summary, should identify:

- the nature of the charges;
- *as part of a brief narrative*, the evidence agreed, reflecting the admissions of either side at the appropriate point in the story;
- *also as part of the narrative*, the matters of fact in issue; and
- with no, or minimal, reference to the law, a list of likely questions for their decision.

236. If and to the extent that the issues narrow or widen in the course of the trial, the case and issues summary should be amended and fresh copies provided to the judge and jury.

Time estimates (paras 25–26)

237. Advocates should regard it as of the highest importance to attempt accurate estimates of the likely length of their principal witnesses' evidence, including a review of them as the issues become clearer in the course of preparation for trial.

Opening speeches (paras 27–28)

238. I endorse the Runciman Royal Commission's recommendation that a defence advocate should be entitled to make a short opening speech to the jury immediately after that of the prosecution advocate, but normally of no more than a few minutes.

Evidence in chief (paras 29–33)

239. Screens and projection equipment should be more widely available to enable electronic presentation of evidence in appropriate cases.

The defence case (para 35)

240. A defence advocate who makes a short opening speech after the prosecution opening should not, thereby, forfeit his right to make an opening speech at the beginning of the defence case.
241. A defence advocate's entitlement to make an opening speech at the start of the defence case should no longer depend on whether he intends to call a witness as to fact other than the defendant.

Taking stock (paras 37–39)

242. At the close of evidence and before speeches, the judge and advocates, in the absence of the jury, should finally review the case and issues summary and, if necessary, amend it for the jury.
243. Such a procedure, along with those already established by the Court of Appeal for review of evidential and legal issues at this stage of a trial, should be considered for express inclusion in the Criminal Procedure Code that I have recommended and, in the meantime, by the Lord Chief Justice for a special practice direction.
244. If, and to the extent that, the law and professional codes of conduct do not require a defending, as well as a prosecuting, advocate to seek to correct a judge's error of law or of material fact of which he becomes aware, both the law and the codes should be changed to require it.

Judges' directions on law and summing up (paras 41–55)

245. Consideration should be given to including in the Code of Criminal Procedure that I have recommended and, in the meantime in a practice direction of the Lord Chief Justice, a requirement that a judge should use a case and issues summary and any other written or visual aid provided to a jury, as

an integral part of his summing-up, referring to the points in them, one by one, as he deals with them orally.

246. Courts should equip judges with, and in cases meriting it they should consider using, other visual aids to their summings-up, such as PowerPoint and evolving forms of presentational software.

247. So far as possible, the judge should not direct the jury on the law, save by implication in the questions of fact that he puts to them for decision.

248. The judge should continue to remind the jury of the issues and, save in the most simple cases, the evidence relevant to them, and should always give the jury an adequate account of the defence; but he should do it in more summary form than is now common.

249. The judge should devise and put to the jury a series of written factual questions, the answers to which could logically lead only to a verdict of guilty or not guilty; the questions should correspond with those in the updated case and issues summary, supplemented as necessary in a separate written list prepared for the purpose; and each question should be tailored to the law as the judge knows it to be and to the issues and evidence in the case.

250. The judge, where he considers it appropriate, should be permitted to require a jury to answer publicly each of his questions and to declare a verdict in accordance with those answers.

Trial by judge and magistrates in the District Division (*paras 57–60*)

251. In the District Division:

251.1 the judge should be the sole judge of law;

251.2 the judge and the magistrates should together be the judges of facts, each having an equal vote;

251.3 the judge should normally conduct any pre-trial hearings on his own;

251.4 the judge should be empowered to make binding pre-trial rulings as would a Crown Division judge;

251.5 the judge should rule on matters of law, procedure and the admissibility of evidence in the absence of the magistrates whenever he considers it would be potentially unfairly prejudicial to the defendant to do so in their presence;

251.6 the same order of speeches and structure of trial should apply as in the Crown Division;

251.7 the judge should not sum up the case to the magistrates, but, after retiring with them to consider the court's decision, should give a publicly reasoned judgment of the court; and

251.8 the judge should be solely responsible for sentence.

Trial in the Magistrates' Division (*paras 62–64*)

252. The structure and procedures of trial in the Magistrates' Division of a new unified Criminal Court should broadly follow those of the present magistrates' courts.

Abbreviated procedures (paras 65–67)

253. All prosecuting authorities should use the provisions of section 12 of the Magistrates' Courts Act 1980, as amended, for disposal of cases on pleas of guilty or on proof of guilt in the absence of the defendant.

Evidence

General principles (paras 76–78)

254. The English law of criminal evidence should, in general, move away from technical rules of inadmissibility to trusting judicial and lay fact-finders to give relevant evidence the weight it deserves.

Refreshing memory/witness statements (paras 81–85)

255. As a first step and/or failing adoption of the following recommendation for use of prior witness statements as evidence, consideration should be given to making the only condition for a witness's use of a written statement for refreshing memory that there is good reason to believe that he would have been significantly better able to recall the events in question when he made or verified it than at the time of giving evidence.

Prior witness statements as evidence (paras 86–94)

256. Consideration should be given to amending the law as to admissibility of witness statements so that:
    256.1 where a witness has made a prior statement, in written or recorded form, it should be admissible as evidence of any matter stated in it of which his direct oral evidence in the proceedings would be admissible provided that he authenticates it as his statement;
    256.2 an integral part of the new rule should be that a defendant's previous statement should in principle be admissible whether it supports or damages his case and the fact that it may appear to be self-serving should go only to weight; and
    256.3 the witness should be permitted, where appropriate, to adopt the statement in the witness box as his evidence in chief.
257. There should be consideration in the long term of extending the present provisions for the use of video-recorded evidence to the evidence of all critical witnesses in cases of serious crime, coupled with provision where required of a record and/or transcripts or summaries of such evidence and also of that in cross-examination and re-examination.

Hearsay (paras 95–104)

258. There should be further consideration of reform of the rule against hearsay, in particular with a view to making hearsay generally admissible subject to the principle of best evidence, rather than generally inadmissible subject to specified exceptions as proposed by the Law Commission.
259. In this respect, as with evidence in criminal cases generally, there should be a move away from rules of inadmissibility to trusting fact finders to assess the weight of the evidence.

Unfair evidence (paras 105–111)

260. As part of the over-all reform of the law of criminal evidence that I have recommended, consideration should be given to rationalising and simplifying the various forms of statutory

and common law rules for exclusion of evidence because of its unfairness and that of staying a prosecution for abuse of process on account of improperly obtained evidence.

Previous misconduct of a defendant/Similar fact evidence (paras 112–120)

261. There should be consideration of the Law Commission's imminent final report on evidence in criminal proceedings of a defendant's misconduct in the context of a wider review of the law of criminal evidence, having regard, in particular, to the illogicality, ineffectiveness and complexity of any rule, whatever its form, directed to keeping a defendant's previous convictions from lay, but not professional, fact finders.

Expert evidence (paras 129–151)

262. Consideration should be given to concentrating in one self-governing professional body within England and Wales the role of setting, or overseeing the setting, of standards and of conduct for forensic scientists of all disciplines, the maintenance of a register of accreditation for them and the regulation of their compliance with its conditions of accreditation.
263. For those purposes, the several existing expert witness bodies providing for all or most forensic science disciplines should consider amalgamation with, or concentration of their resources in, the Council for the Registration of Forensic Practitioners.
264. The new Criminal Procedure Rules that I recommend should contain a rule in the same or similar terms to that in Part 35.3 of the Civil Procedure Rules that an expert witness's overriding duty is to the court.
265. Any witness statement or report prepared by an expert witness for the assistance of the court should contain at its head a signed declaration to that effect.
266. Criminal courts' power to control the admission of experts' evidence should be formalised in the new Criminal Procedure Rules that I have recommended, and put on a similar footing to that for the Civil Courts as set out in the Civil Procedure Rules, Part 35, 1 and 4, namely by imposing upon them a duty, and

declaring their power, to restrict expert evidence to that which is reasonably required to resolve any issue of importance in the proceedings.

267. Judges and magistrates should rigorously apply the test governing that power and duty, and the Court of Appeal should support them.
268. In publicly funded defence cases, where a judge or magistrates' court has directed that it would be justifiable to call a defence expert, that direction should constitute authorisation for the expenditure of public money on an expert at a specified rate.
269. Where there is an issue on a matter of importance on which expert evidence is required, the court should not have a power to appoint or select an expert, whether or not it excludes either party from calling its own expert evidence.
270. Where there is no issue, or one in which the parties are content that the matter should be resolved by a single expert, they should be encouraged to deal with it in that way, agreeing his report or a summary of it as part of the evidence in the case.
271. The prosecution and defence should normally arrange for their experts to discuss and jointly to identify at the earliest possible stage before the trial those issues on which they agree and those on which they do not agree, and to prepare a joint statement for use in evidence indicating the measure of their agreement and a summary of the reasons for their disagreement.
272. Failing such arrangement, the court should have power to direct such a discussion and identification of issues and preparation of a joint statement for use in evidence and to make any consequential directions as may be appropriate in each case.
273. Close attention should be given in any further and general review of the rule against hearsay to the increasing reliance of forensic science laboratories and of many experts in certain disciplines on electronic recording, analysis and transmission of data.
274. There should be greater use by legal practitioners of video-conferencing and other developing new technology for communicating and conferring with experts in preparation for trial.

275. The law and the provision of national facilities should be developed to enable experts to give evidence by video-link or other new technologies in appropriate cases.

Interpreters (*paras 155–162*)

276. The Government should continue to encourage the concentration in the two national Registers as appropriate of the role of oversight of national training, accreditation and monitoring of the performance of interpreters, with a view to providing an adequate national and local coverage of suitably qualified interpreters.
277. Training and accreditation of all interpreters should include coverage of the basics of criminal investigation and court procedures, and should provide for changing and different geographic demands for linguists.
278. The Government should consider central funding of further education establishments to equip them, where necessary, to provide courses in lesser known languages for the Diploma in Public Service Interpreting.
279. The Government should undertake a national publicity campaign in further education establishments and other colleges in support of the two national Registers.
280. There should be a review of the levels of payment to interpreters with a view to encouraging more and the best qualified to undertake this work and to establishing a national scale of pay.
281. Interpreters should be provided with facilities appropriate to an officer of the court when attending court to provide their services.
282. The standard check-list for agreement or directions leading to the pre-trial assessment should require all parties to indicate to the court in good time before the trial date the need for an interpreter, identifying the party or witness for whom he is required and the language.
283. The check list should also require the parties to agree or, failing agreement, to seek the court's directions for making available to the interpreter in good time before trial, any documents likely to assist him in his task at court.

284. An engaged interpreter should be entitled to apply direct to the Court for such access.
285. In all cases where an interpreter is provided with or given access to such documents, it should be in circumstances under which he undertakes to preserve their confidentiality until trial or otherwise in conditions of security directed by the court.
286. Standards of best practice in the design of new court buildings should be developed and equipment adapted in existing courtrooms for the provision of adequate accommodation and facilities to interpreters.

Information about the court (*paras 163–168*)

287. Early progress should be made to equip each court centre or group of court centres, as appropriate, with:
   287.1 its own website containing information of cases listed for future hearing and their fixed or estimated hearing dates, daily listings of cases and information as to their progress; and general information about the court centre, travel to it and local facilities; and
   287.2 an automated telephone information system giving like information.
288. Early progress should also be made to equip each court centre with:
   288.1 electronic bulletin boards indicating the progress of cases listed each day; and
   288.2 diagrams of the layout of courtrooms in waiting areas and corresponding signs inside each courtroom.

Sitting times (*paras 169–178*)

289. There should be thorough examination of the need for and the costs/benefits of extending court working hours, including the use of evening, night and weekend courts, whether as a general provision or for areas with a concentration of serious and/or minor crime.
290. Out-of-hours provision should be made for administrative assistance to court users through the medium of help-desks, the telephone and electronic means for obtaining advice or information, paying fines, obtaining forms etc.

Court dress (*paras 179–184*)

291. The Higher Judiciary, in consultation with all levels of the judiciary, the legal professions and any other appropriate bodies, should consider and advise the Lord Chancellor on what, if any, formal court dress judges, barristers and solicitors should wear in future in the Supreme Court of Justice and the County Court.

Forms of address (*paras 185–187*)

292. The Higher Judiciary, in consultation with all levels of the judiciary, the magistracy, the legal professions and any other appropriate bodies, should consider and advise the Lord Chancellor on future forms of address in all courts.

Court language (*paras 188–189*)

293. A Criminal Procedure Rules Committee should examine all court procedures, forms and terms with a view simplifying their language and content.

Oaths and affirmations (*paras 190–196*)

294. The witness's oath and affirmation should be replaced by a solemn promise to tell the truth.
295. The juror's oath and affirmation should be replaced with a promise in the following or similar form: "I promise to try the defendant and to decide on the evidence whether he is guilty or not".

Sentencing (*paras 197–226, pages 600–610*)

296. There should be early establishment of an online sentencing information service for all full- and part-time judges. The system should include:
    - 296.1 a statistical record of sentences imposed in the criminal courts at all levels, analysed according to key case features;
    - 296.2 a statement of sentencing principles and the text of judgments in key cases via an online sentencing textbook; and
    - 296.3 online and up-to-date information about the availability of sentencing and related facilities.

297. The sentencing information system should be available online to members of the public and the media and should be designed with their needs also in mind.
298. Consideration should be given to charging the Judicial Studies Board with the responsibility for establishing and administering a sentencing information system, resourcing it sufficiently for the purpose.
299. I support the recommendation in the Halliday Sentencing Review Report for the creation of a sentence review jurisdiction for the criminal courts, provided that resource and practical difficulties can be overcome.

Chapter Twelve Appeals

The appellate tests (*paras 5–11*)

300. There should be the same tests for appeal against conviction and sentence respectively at all levels of appeal below the Appellate Committee of the House of Lords, namely those applicable to the Court of Appeal.
301. Consideration should be given to amendment of the statutory test of unsafety as the ground for quashing a conviction so as to clarify whether and to what extent it is to apply to convictions that would be regarded as safe in the ordinary sense, but that follow want of due process before or during trial.

Appeals from magistrates' courts (*paras 14–35*)

302. A defendant's right of appeal against conviction and/or sentence in the magistrates' court to the Crown Court by way of re-hearing should be abolished.
303. It should be replaced by a right of appeal to the Crown Division (Crown Court), with leave from that court, on the same grounds that would support appeal from the Crown Division (Crown Court), sitting in its original capacity, to the Court of Appeal.
304. The constitution of the Crown Division (Crown Court) for this purpose should be a judge sitting alone who, depending on the nature and importance of the appeal, could be a High Court Judge, Circuit Judge or Recorder.

305. There should be no right of appeal from the Magistrates' Division (magistrates' courts) to the High Court by an appeal by way of case stated or by a claim for judicial review.

Appeals from the Crown Court to the Court of Appeal (*paras 36–44*)

306. Where it is sought to challenge the decision of the Crown Division (Crown Court) sitting in its appellate capacity:
   306.1 there should be no right of challenge to the High Court by appeal by way of case stated or by claim for judicial review;
   306.2 instead, appeal should lie to the Court of Appeal under its general appellate jurisdiction enlarged, if and as necessary, to cover matters presently provided by the remedies of appeal by way of case stated or claim of judicial review - and for which the Court should be suitably constituted; and
   306.3 all such appeals should be subject to the permission of the Court of Appeal, which it should only give in a case involving an important point of principle or practice or where there is some other compelling reason for the Court to hear it.
307. Where it is sought to challenge the decision of the Crown Division (Crown Court) as a court of first instance or of the District Division:
   307.1 there should be no right of challenge to the High Court by appeal by way of case stated or by claim for judicial review; and
   307.2 instead, appeal should lie only to the Court of Appeal under its general appellate jurisdiction enlarged, if and as necessary, to cover matters presently provided by the remedies of appeal by way of case stated or of claim for judicial review - and for which the Court should be suitably constituted.

Prosecution rights of appeal (*paras 47–65*)

308. Whilst I support the general thrust of the Law Commission's recommendation for the introduction of statutory exceptions to the double jeopardy rule, I recommend that:

308.1 the exceptions should not be limited to murder and allied offences, but should extend to other grave offences punishable with life and/or long terms of imprisonment as Parliament might specify; and

308.2 there should be no reopening of an investigation of a case following an acquittal without the Director of Public Prosecution's prior, personal consent and recommendation as to which police force should conduct it.

309. I also support the general thrust of the Law Commission's recommendations for:

309.1 extending the present preparatory bearing regime to include appealable rulings on potentially terminating matters such as severance, joinder, quashing the indictment or staying the prosecution as an abuse of process;

309.2 giving the prosecution a right of appeal against an acquittal in certain cases arising from a terminating ruling during the trial up to the close of the prosecution case; and

309.3 giving the prosecution a right of appeal against an acquittal arising from a ruling of no case to answer under the first limb of the rule in R. v. Galbraith.

Appeals against perverse verdicts (*paras 66–67*)

310. Where any special verdict of a jury reveals on its terms that it is perverse:

310.1 if the verdict is guilty, the defence should have a right of appeal to the Court of Appeal, subject to the usual leave procedure, on the ground that the perversity renders the conviction unsafe; and

310.2 if the verdict is not guilty, the prosecution should have a right of appeal to the Court of Appeal, also subject to leave, on the ground that the perversity indicates that the verdict is probably untrue or unfair and such as to merit a re-trial.

Procedure on appeals to the Court of Appeal (*paras 73–101*)

311. Single judges of the Court of Appeal should be allowed time to consider and determine written applications for leave to appeal

against conviction or sentence in chambers as part of their regular sitting plan.

312. A single judge of the Court of Appeal should be empowered, when considering applications for leave to appeal, to give procedural directions for the hearing of the application or of the appeal that need not trouble the Full Court, subject to a right on the part of the applicant or the prosecution, as the case may be, to renew the application to the Full Court.
313. Consideration should be given to combining, or more closely associating in content and time, appellants' grounds of appeal and skeleton arguments, and to making appropriate adjustments to time limits for their filing and service.

Reorganisation and reconstitution of the Court of Appeal *(paras 87–94)*

314. The Court of Appeal should be variously constituted according to the nature, legal importance and complexity of its work:
    314.1 in cases where there is a point of law of general public importance or of particular complexity or public interest, including sentencing cases calling for guidelines or involving some other point of general principle or very long custodial sentences, the Court should consist of the Lord Chief Justice or the Vice-President or a Lord Justice and two High Court Judges;
    314.2 in straightforward appeals against conviction, or in respect of short sentences where the law and procedures are clear and the only issue is whether the trial judge has correctly followed them, or where the issue turns on his treatment of the facts, the Court should consist of two High Court Judges or one High Court Judge and one Circuit Judge; and
    314.3 consideration should be given to introducing a system under which, in cases of exceptional legal importance and complexity, a distinguished academic could either be appointed ad hoc to act as a judge of the Court or be invited to submit a written brief to the Court on the point(s) in issue.
315. A single judge of the Court should be responsible for allocation of appeals to the Full Court as variously constituted under these

recommendations, subject to review by the Full Court before or during the hearing of the appeal.

Practice and procedure (*paras 95–101*)

316. The Court, however it is constituted, should 'slow down' - its judges should be allowed more time for preparation and judgment writing as part of their sitting plan, and appeal hearings should be less rushed so as to allow advocates adequate time to deploy their arguments and judges to consider them.
317. The Lord Chief Justice should consider issuing a Practice Direction for the better conduct by the parties of their preparation for hearing, including provision for pre-appeal directions hearings in complex cases, the form and contents of appeal bundles and advance notification to the Court of last minute changes likely to affect the content or duration of the appeal.
318. Criminal practitioners should provide a standard of service to the Court of the same level as is presently required of their counterparts in the Court of Appeal (Civil Division) and they should be paid properly for it.
319. In conviction appeals the Court should support trial judges' robust case management and control of the trial, so long as it has not prejudiced the fairness of the trial over-all and thereby put the safety of the conviction at risk.
320. In sentence appeals the Court should be vigilant not to 'tinker' with the sentence of the court below, but only to intervene where it is wrong in principle, that is, of the wrong sort or far too long in the circumstances.
321. The Crown Prosecution Service should consider on a case by case basis whether to appear on the hearing of an appeal against sentence so as to be able to assist the Court, if required, on matters of fact, including the effect on any victim, or of law.

Criminal Cases Review Commission (*paras 102–107*)

322. Section 23A of the Criminal Appeal Act 1968 should be amended to extend the Court of Appeal's power to direct the Criminal Cases Review Commission to investigate and report on a matter on appeal, to a matter in an application for leave to appeal.

323. On any reference by the Commission to the Court of Appeal or the Crown Court of a conviction or sentence, those courts should apply the law in force at the time of conviction or sentence as the case may be.

Sentencing Advisory Panel (*paras 108–111*)

324. The law should be amended to widen the remit of the Sentencing Advisory Panel to include general principles of sentencing, in particular as to the courts' use of the various sentencing options available to them regardless of the category of offence.
325. The law should be amended, to enable the Court of Appeal to work more closely with and respond more speedily to the Panel's advice, by empowering it to issue guidelines without having to tie them to a specific appeal before it.

Appeals to the House of Lords (*paras 112–117*)

326. Consideration should be given to introducing a system under which, in cases of exceptional legal importance and complexity, a distinguished academic could be invited to assist an Appellate Committee, say, by the submission of a written brief, with copies to the parties, on the point(s) at issue.
327. On points of law of general public importance, where there are conflicting decisions of the Court of Appeal or the law on them is otherwise in such an unsatisfactory state that only the House of Lords can resolve it, consideration should be given to introducing a form of 'leap-frog' appeal from the Crown Division (Crown Court) to the House of Lords, similar to that provided for civil appeals by Part II of the Administration of Justice Act 1969.
328. Section 34(2) of the Criminal Appeal Act 1968 should be amended to empower the House of Lords and Court of Appeal, as the case may be, to extend the time within which a prosecutor may apply for leave to appeal, as it does in the case of a defendant.

INDEX